MY ONLY COMFORT

The CALVIN INSTITUTE OF CHRISTIAN WORSHIP LITURGICAL STUDIES SERIES, edited by John D. Witvliet, is designed to promote reflection on the history, theology, and practice of Christian worship and to stimulate worship renewal in Christian congregations. Contributions include writings by pastoral worship leaders from a wide range of communities and scholars from a wide range of disciplines. The ultimate goal of these contributions is to nurture worship practices that are spiritually vital and theologically rooted.

MY ONLY COMFORT

*Death, Deliverance, and Discipleship
in the Music of Bach*

Calvin R. Stapert

WILLIAM B. EERDMANS PUBLISHING COMPANY
GRAND RAPIDS, MICHIGAN / CAMBRIDGE, U.K.

© 2000 Wm. B. Eerdmans Publishing Co.
255 Jefferson Ave. S.E., Grand Rapids, Michigan 49503 /
P.O. Box 163, Cambridge CB3 9PU U.K.

Printed in the United States of America

05 04 03 02 01 00   7 6 5 4 3 2 1

Library of Congress Cataloging-in-Publication Data

Stapert, Calvin, 1942–
My only comfort : death, deliverance, and discipleship
in the music of Bach / Calvin R. Stapert.
p.   cm.
Includes bibliographical references.
ISBN 0-8028-4472-3 (paper : alk. paper)
1. Bach, Johann Sebastian, 1685-1750. Vocal music.
2. Bach, Johann Sebastian, 1685-1750 — Religion.
3. Church music — Lutheran Church — 18th century.
4. Heidelberger Katechismus. I. Title.

ML410.B13 S73 2000
782.2'2'092 — dc21   99-462207

Dedicated to the memory of my father,

Raymond M. Stapert

Contents

CONTENTS

THE CATECHISM IN
BACH'S WORKS

CONTENTS

Preface

In the history of Western music, J. S. Bach is unsurpassed, perhaps unequaled, in mastery of technique and profundity of thought. He was a devout Lutheran whose knowledge of Scripture and theology was so broad and deep that the eminent historian of theology Jaroslav Pelikan wrote a book entitled *Bach Among the Theologians.* Given Bach's combination of musical prowess, personal devotion, and theological understanding, it is not surprising that his music stands unexcelled among artistic expressions of the Christian faith. At the center of his musical output stand some two hundred cantatas along with four monumental works — the *Christmas Oratorio,* the two Passions according to St. Matthew and St. John, and the *Mass in B Minor.* The four large works have long been heard fairly regularly in concert and have also been quite readily available in recorded form. The same cannot be said for the cantatas. But at least with regard to recordings, the situation is changing. Although Bach's cantatas are still not as easily found in recorded form as, say, Beethoven's symphonies or Mozart's operas, they are not difficult to obtain. The complete cantatas have been recorded twice, once on the Hänssler label with Helmut Rilling conducting, and once on Teldec with the conducting duties divided between Nikolaus Harnoncourt and Gustav Leonhardt. Two more projects to record them all are in progress — Ton Koopman's performances are being issued by Erato and Masaaki Suzuki's by BIS. In addition, fine recordings of individual cantatas have been made, and continue to be made, by conductors such as John Eliot Gardiner, Philippe Herreweghe, Monica Huggett, Joshua Rifkin, Jeffrey Thomas, and others.

I mention the increased availability of the cantatas on recordings because I think that, given current options, they can best be listened to that way. Normally the best way to listen to music is in live performance. The best way to listen to Bach's cantatas, Passions, and oratorios would be in the kind of liturgical setting for which they were written. But it is a rare church today that has both the musical resources and the desire to perform these works. Those few that do seldom provide the liturgical and theological context within which their full meaning can come through. Concert performances are, of course, much further removed from the proper context. Their trappings — tickets, performers on display on stage, applause, and the like — are obstacles that can mightily hinder an understanding of these works. Which is not to say that I frown on such performances. Far from it. I would like to see more of Bach's vocal works programmed more regularly because, whatever the obstacles, something is gained in live performance. But even though I admit that something is gained when we listen to any music performed on the spot by live musicians, I still think that the best substitute today for hearing Bach's vocal works in their proper liturgical surroundings is listening to them on recordings as aids to personal devotions, provided the listener takes the time to read the relevant Scripture passages and to obtain some guidance in understanding the texts and the way the music illumines and interprets them. The goal of this book is to provide some background and guidance for the thoughtful listener who wants to use these works devotionally.

After an introduction that supplies some background about Bach, his theological knowledge, his musical language, and the various genres of sacred music in his output, the main part of the book provides guidance through specific works that express, interpret, and vivify some of the principal doctrines of the Christian faith. The principal doctrine expressed by a given work is made clear by quotations from that simple, yet rich, exposition of the Christian faith, the Heidelberg Catechism.

Anyone who is familiar with the Heidelberg Catechism will already have caught my reference to it in both the title and subtitle of this book. The title comes from the Catechism's first question: "What is your only comfort in life and in death?" The subtitle comes from the answer to the second question: "What must I know to live and die in the joy of this comfort?" The answer outlines the threefold division of the Catechism.

Three things:
  first, how great my sins and misery are;

second, how I am set free from all my sins and misery;
third, how I am to thank God for such deliverance.

When I was learning the Catechism as a boy, we were given two alliterative sets of words to help us remember the three main divisions — sin,
salvation, and service; guilt, grace, and gratitude. My subtitle provides a
third alliterative trio — death, deliverance, and discipleship — which says
pretty much the same thing as the other two but whose third word, *discipleship,* fits particularly well with a pervasive theme in Bach's works.

I do not know whether Bach knew the Heidelberg Catechism, the
most widely used catechism to come out of the Calvinist tradition. I
know of no evidence that points to his acquaintance with it. His staunch
adherence to orthodox Lutheran teaching is well known, and given the
time and place in which he lived, he probably harbored some strong
anti-Calvinist feelings. Indeed, one of the books he owned had the title
Anti-Calvinismus, which ends by saying, "We have shown that the 'reformed' doctrine overthrows the foundation of belief and therefore de-
serves to be condemned" (quoted from Herz, "Bach's Religion," 131). It
was written by August Pfeiffer (1640-1698), who served as an archdea-
con at the St. Thomas Kirche in Leipzig from 1681 to 1689, a generation
before Bach went to work there. Bach also owned two other volumes by
Pfeiffer, *Evangelische Christen-Schule* and *Antimelancholicus,* and he combined the titles of his three books by Pfeiffer into a cryptic inscription
for the title page of the little clavier book he put together in 1722 for his
second wife, Anna Magdalena: "Ante (sic) Calvinismus und Christen-
schule item Anti Melancholicus von D. Pfeifern."

So why use the Heidelberg Catechism as the framework for a book
on Bach? I wanted to write a small book that would serve as an introductory guide to Bach's text-related works, especially for listeners who would
like to use them devotionally. I wanted to discuss specific works rather
than make generalizations about the works as a whole, and I wanted to se-
lect and organize those works according to some theological basis. The
Heidelberg Catechism is the theological compendium I know best. It was
the basis for my theological instruction as a boy, and I have heard it
preached all my life. But over the years I have also spent a good amount of
time listening to Bach's musical "sermons." And, far from experiencing
dissonance between Calvinist preaching based on the Heidelberg Catechism and the Lutheran preaching of Bach, I found them very much in accord. The preaching I heard in the Calvinist churches I attended and the

music of Bach I listened to at home still seem to me to be very much in harmony.

I am not suggesting that the reason for the harmony I perceive is that there are no important differences between Lutherans and Calvinists, nor am I suggesting that behind a Lutheran facade there lurked a Calvinist Bach. I do not intend my approach to Bach via the Heidelberg Catechism to make any particular historical or theological point; but if the harmony I hear between the two is real, I think it can be explained in two ways.

First, although the Heidelberg Catechism is a thoroughly Calvinist document, it is not narrowly so. From its inception there was a certain ecumenicity about it. To be sure, it arose because Frederick III of the Palatinate felt "the need for a new catechism to replace those of Luther and Brenz" (Klooster, 822). But it was mainly differences concerning the Lord's Supper that gave rise to that need. So while the Heidelberg Catechism is clearly a Calvinist document in "distancing itself from the ubiquity doctrine of Lutheranism and from other Protestant and Roman Catholic views of the sacraments," in every other way it "reflects the rich, ripe fruit of the entire Reformation."

> The Heidelberg Catechism expresses much that was common to all branches of the Reformation. Members of the team project had first-hand acquaintance with Luther, Melanchthon, Heinrich Bullinger, John Calvin, and Théodore de Bèze, as well as numerous earlier catechisms. Its authors have been likened to bees flitting from flower to flower to gather honey. (Klooster, 823)

Second, I am convinced that what C. S. Lewis called "mere Christianity" is a reality, and it is not as negligible and watered-down as the adjective "mere" might suggest. What unites the various branches of the Christian faith is far more extensive and runs far more deeply than the history of our divisions, quarrels, and animosities would indicate. Furthermore, that unity cuts across the boundaries of time and place. Eric Chafe, for example, found that Father Raymond Brown's commentary on the Gospel of John could illuminate Bach's *St. John Passion*. If a Bible commentary by a twentieth-century Catholic can illuminate the work of an eighteenth-century Lutheran, why not as well a catechism by two sixteenth-century Calvinists? Lewis made the point that it "is at [the Church's] centre, where her truest children dwell, that each communion is really closest to every other in spirit, if not in doctrine" (*Mere Christianity,* viii). Therefore, throughout the many years that I have been listening to Bach, I have not been surprised to find that his music, so deeply imbued with Lutheran theology and spirit, resonates so harmoniously with the Calvinist theology and spirit of the Heidelberg Catechism that has instructed and nourished me from my youth.

For each work discussed, I have provided relevant quotations from the Heidelberg Catechism. When the work in question is a cantata, I have also provided the Epistle and Gospel lessons (in translation from the New International Version) that were read in the service for which the cantata was written. This gives the reader immediate access to the Scripture lessons on which both the sermon and the cantata for the day were based. Then follows the complete text of the work in its original German along with a very literal line-by-line translation. Finally there is commentary, both textual and musical, that I hope will contribute to a more perceptive and devotional listening to the work.

A word should be said about the translations, because language is the biggest gulf non–German-speaking people are likely to have to cross in order to enter the world of Bach's vocal works. Recording companies, of course, provide translations with their recordings. However, they are often loose and misleading. At times they are blatantly inaccurate. Even when they are reasonably accurate, it is often hard for a non-German listener to know what word is being sung at a given time. That is a distinct handicap when listening to a composer like Bach, whose music is closely wedded not merely to the general mood of the text but also to the meaning of specific words and phrases. So the translations provided here are not only as accurate as I could make them; they are as close to the German word order as could be done while still remaining within the boundaries of intelligibility. This means, of course, that English style suffers considerably, but I think that is a small price to pay for being able to know exactly what word is being sung at any given time.

The most frequent word order problem arises from the placement of verbs at the end of sentences. Sometimes that leaves an awkward, but intelligible, English word order. For example,

Ich will den Kreuzstab gerne tragen.   I will the cross-staff gladly carry.

In such cases I have kept the German word order. In other cases the problem is more acute. For instance,

Ich bin dein, weil du dein Leben | I am yours because you your life
Und dein Blut, mir zugut | and your blood for my benefit
In den Tod gegeben. | in death gave.

In such cases I have changed the word order and underlined the word that has been moved.

Ich bin dein, weil du dein Leben | I am yours because you <u>gave</u> your life
Und dein Blut, mir zugut | and your blood for my benefit
In den Tod <u>gegeben</u>. | in death.

I should add that there are two books available that give translations of all the cantatas. One is by Z. Philip Ambrose. It contains the translations that accompany the recordings by Rilling. They were done so that the English texts fit the German texts in number of syllables and accentuation. Although Ambrose's translations are masterfully done, the constraints of syllabification and accentuation frequently force precise meaning and word placement to give way. The other book of translations is by Melvin P. Unger. It provides word-for-word translations. Where those make little or no sense in English, it also provides translations in a reordered form that make intelligible English. Both books give the Epistle and Gospel lessons for the day for which the cantata was written. Within the cantata texts Ambrose identifies all chorale texts and direct quotations from the Bible. I have followed his lead by printing chorale texts in boldface print and Bible quotations in italics. Unger goes beyond Ambrose by providing Scripture passages that allude to or are related to the cantata texts. Another book that is especially useful for identifying scriptural content in the cantata texts is Ulrich Meyer, *Biblical Quotation and Allusion in the Cantata Libretti of Johann Sebastian Bach*. I owe much to all three books.

Since the Passions are too large for me to deal with in their entirety in this book, I provide text and translations only for the numbers that are discussed. A superb literal translation of the *St. John Passion* can be found in *Lutheranism, Anti-Judaism, and Bach's St. John Passion* by Michael Marissen. The best complete translation of the *St. Matthew Passion* I have encountered is the one that accompanies Nikolaus Harnoncourt's recording (Teldec 6.35047).

A second gulf that needs to be bridged is the gulf of what we might call musical "language." <u>Some general aspects of musical language</u> might be universal, but it is a mistaken Romantic notion that music is a "universal tongue." Although it is not unusual to hear talk about "the universality of Bach," the fact is that his music speaks a specific language, even a specific dialect of that language. In other words, none of us has some sort of inborn understanding of Bach's (or anyone else's) music. And since we are removed from it by two and a half to three centuries during which major cultural shifts took place, few if any of us can assume we understand his music directly through cultural assimilation. To be sure, there are aspects of his musical language that are immediately understandable. It would be a rare person who does not immediately understand that the opening movement of the *Christmas Oratorio,* for example, is an expression of joyous festivity. But understanding deeper and subtler aspects of the music requires knowledge of specific Baroque musical conventions and rhetorical devices. Keys to unlocking Bach's musical language are provided in a general way in a section in the introduction and in more specific ways in the commentary on the individual works.

I hope that by providing key doctrinal statements from the Catechism, relevant Scripture passages, literal translations, and commentary on the texts and music, this book will make Bach's theologically astute, artistically masterful, and religiously devout works more understandable for many listeners and hence make them more available as means for instruction, edification, and devotion.

I owe thanks to many — to many more than I can mention. Although I can name only a few here, I know that the graciousness of all the others will keep them from feeling slighted. Dr. John Hamersma, by his rigorous, thorough, no-nonsense teaching at Calvin College, laid the foundation that enabled me to pursue music study in graduate school and beyond. Later, during the more than three decades that he and I have been colleagues and friends, through our frequent conversations, both on and off duty, whether about Bach, other music, theology, or what-have-you, he has continued to be a most valued teacher. Dr. Michael Marissen was my student and has become my teacher both through his publications and, even more, through our long but far-too-infrequent conversations (mostly, but by no means exclusively, about Bach). He made many specific suggestions to improve this book. Two other former students who continue to teach me, Drs. Ruth Van Baak Griffioen and John Witvliet, read the entire book and made perceptive and helpful comments.

A different kind of thanks must go to Jon Pott, editor-in-chief at Eerdmans, who for fifteen years has been encouraging me and gently prodding me to write. In 1985 when Bach and Handel had the tricentennial of their births and Heinrich Schütz had the quadricentennial of his, I submitted an article to the *Reformed Journal* on Schütz, hoping to call attention to the greatness of the least-known composer in that triumvirate. Jon not only accepted the article but also said he did not want the anniversary year to pass without a *Reformed Journal* article on Bach. He encouraged me to write one and thus began a small series of articles on Bach that appeared over the next several years in the *Reformed Journal* and, after a merger, in *Perspectives*. Much of what appeared in those articles also appears here, though in varying degrees of revision so as to make it cohere with its new surroundings. What started as an article commemorating the 300th anniversary of Bach's birth has grown into a book commemorating the 250th anniversary of his death.

Thanks of yet a different kind goes to my father, to whose memory I dedicate this book. He loved Bach's music above any other and frequently listened to recordings of it on the hi-fi system in our living room. In that way he provided my introduction to Bach's music. But more importantly, he, with my mother, brought me up by precept and example in the faith that inspired Bach's music and introduced me to Jesus Christ, to whom Bach's music bears such eloquent witness. For that eternal thanks are due.

INTRODUCTION

"Essential" and "Canonical" Bach

The earliest ancestor of J. S. Bach that we know of is a certain Viet Bach, a baker from Hungary who, in the late sixteenth century, fled to the Thuringian region of Germany because of his Lutheran religion. This we learn from a genealogy that Bach compiled in 1735. The genealogy adds that Viet "found his greatest pleasure in a little cittern, which he took with him even into the mill and played upon while the grinding was going on" (*The New Bach Reader,* 283). From this humble, pious baker who loved to play the cittern sprang a line of musicians so numerous that, by the time his greatest descendant, Johann Sebastian, was born in 1685, the name Bach was synonymous with "musician" in Thuringia.

Viet, of course, could have had no idea of the magnitude of the influence his descendants would have on the musical life of Thuringians for the next two centuries. Much less could he have had any idea that one of them would be revered during the nineteenth and twentieth centuries as one of the greatest musicians of all time, perhaps even as the greatest of them all. In his wildest dreams he could not have imagined that at the beginning of the twenty-first century millions of people around the whole world would be paying tribute to that descendant on the 250th anniversary of his death. Even Johann Sebastian himself, though he was very much aware of his musical ability, would no doubt be surprised to see how much fuss the world — not just Thuringia — is making over his anniversary.

Though the whole world is celebrating Bach's anniversary, it is fair to say that few people truly understand his music because an understanding of his music begins with the cantatas. The cantatas are central to what musicologist Richard Taruskin calls the "essential Bach," but they are peripheral to the Bach most people are familiar with — the "canonical Bach" of the Brandenburg Concertos, the suites and sonatas, the *Well-Tempered Clavier*, the *Mass in B Minor*, and, to a certain extent, the Passions. I do not mean to say that these "canonical" works are not in some sense "truly" Bach. That, of course, would be absurd. But I do mean to say that these "canonical" works are best understood in the light of the cantatas, not vice versa.

The great nineteenth-century composer Johannes Brahms understood something of the importance of the cantatas. His friend Siegfried Ochs told a story in his autobiography that reveals the high esteem in which Brahms held the cantatas. One evening Brahms and three friends — Ochs, Hans von Bülow, and Hermann Wolff — were discussing music. According to Ochs, Brahms

> fell upon Hans von Bülow with the reproach that he played much too little Bach, moreover was not concerned enough with him and knew next to nothing of, as an example of the best of his creations, the church cantatas. Bülow defended himself and claimed to know at least seven or eight cantatas well. "That proves that you know none of them, for there are more than two hundred," said Brahms. (Trans. in Knapp, "Finale of Brahms' Fourth," 4)

He then went to the piano and played a movement from Bach's Cantata 150.

Whatever the truth may be regarding the details of this charming anecdote, it certainly rings true with what we know about Brahms. As one of the subscribers to the *Bach Gesellschaft* edition of the complete works of Bach, he was well known for his admiration of Bach. And since that edition begins with the cantatas, and therefore would have been the first works the subscribers received, there can be little doubt that Brahms' knowledge of the cantatas was thorough and comprehensive. Furthermore, at least one of the sources for the theme and some of the technical procedures of the last movement of Brahms' Symphony No. 4 was the movement of Cantata 150 mentioned in the story.

Posterity in general has not been as astute as Brahms, so the cantatas became, and remain, a peripheral part of Bach's output. The reason Bach's cantatas, in the eyes of posterity, moved from the center to the periphery is the post-Enlightenment preference for generic religious feeling over an explicit Christian message. Bach's cantatas do not fit that bill; they are nothing if not explicitly Christian. So after his death in 1750, Bach's un-Enlightened music was hardly known until 1829, when Felix Mendelssohn conducted a performance of the *St. Matthew Passion*. This started a revival that gave Bach's music an honored place in the classical music canon, a place it still occupies today more securely than ever. But, as we have already noted, the "canonical Bach" is not the "essential Bach." The emphasis in the canonical Bach is on the instrumental music. The vocal music, of course, is not totally ignored, but the post-Enlightened mind accepts it only after mentally divorcing the music from the explicitly Christian content of its texts. The *Mass in B Minor*, because of a well-ingrained post-Enlightenment habit of mentally filtering out the undesirably specific content of Mass texts, had little problem entering the canon. It could even be trumpeted as "the greatest piece of music ever written." But the Passions, certainly no less great, present a big problem to the post-Enlightenment mind. So do the cantatas. Although the cantatas are of smaller dimensions than the Passions, they are so numerous and maintain Bachian levels of artistry so consistently that they can hardly be ignored. The problem is that the Passion and cantata texts are more explicitly Christian than post-Enlightened minds can tolerate, and they require great mental gymnastics to render them generically religious. Therefore, for most music lovers, they exist uncomfortably at the margins of Bach's repertory.

In his 1991 *New York Times* review of the Teldec recordings of the complete church cantatas of Bach (reprinted in *Text and Act*, pp. 307-15), Richard Taruskin summarizes the post-Enlightenment problem with the "essential Bach" of the cantatas. It stems, he says, from the Enlightenment definition of music, given classic formulation by Charles Burney in the 1770s and still repeated in various guises in most dictionaries today: "Music is the art of pleasing by the succession and combination of agreeable sounds." To this Taruskin exclaims:

> How utterly irrelevant this whole esthetic is to the Bach of the cantatas!
> [For the] essential Bach was an avatar of a pre-Enlightened — and when
> push came to shove, a violent anti-Enlightened — temper. His music was
> a medium of truth, not beauty. . . . [For him] there is no "music itself."
> His concept of music derived from and inevitably contained The Word.
> (309-10)

5

Post-Enlightenment discomfort with the specific message of Bach's vocal music appeared already on the eve of Mendelssohn's performance of the *St. Matthew Passion*. Mendelssohn's teacher, Carl Friedrich Zelter, said that the obstacle "toward appreciation" in Bach's music was "the altogether contemptible German church texts, which suffer from the earnest polemic of the Reformation." Such a "thick fog of belief," he said, "stirs up nothing but disbelief" (quoted in Taruskin, 311).

That post-Enlightened attitude persists to the present. Here is a blurb that appeared in *Encore,* the magazine of BMG Classical Music Service. To reassure its post-Enlightened customers that buying CDs of Bach's cantatas and Passions would not threaten their generic religious sensibilities, BMG makes this outrageous claim:

> From his cantatas to his epic Passions and oratorios, most of Bach's music was written for the Lutheran Church. Interestingly, Bach never used his music to interpret or dramatize the sacred texts he set. Instead, he distilled their message into music of unparalleled purity and profundity.

Perhaps the most flagrant statement along these lines came from Albert Schweitzer. He said that the texts of the cantatas and Passions "are so insignificant that we need all the beauty of the music to make us forget them" (*J. S. Bach, le musicien-poéte,* 241). Bach would have been horrified! His aim was to write music that would vivify the Christian message of the texts and make them memorable. That was the end to which he bent his uncommon energy and unsurpassed musical skill.

Bach the Theologian

To call Bach a theologian may seem a bit of a stretch. He was not a theologian by profession; he never even went to university. But as a composer for the Lutheran church in the eighteenth century, he had to have more than a little theological knowledge. Even leaving aside the evidence of his compositions, there is good reason to believe that Bach had a fair amount of theological knowledge. What evidence there is should be enough to convince all but the most committed skeptic, not only that Bach did know more than enough theology to do his job well, but that his deep faith drove him to study theology beyond the requirements of his job.

Bach's theological knowledge was rooted in what he learned when he was young. He grew up in the Thuringian area of Germany, in the heart of "Luther country."

> Martin Luther was born at Eisleben, in the northern part of Thuringia, in 1483, and died there in 1546. He went to the Lateinschule in Eisenach (the same that Bach was to attend two centuries later) and to the University of Erfurt, and it was at the Wartburg Castle, overlooking Eisenach, that he found refuge after being excommunicated and outlawed by the Diet of Worms. The spiritual presence of [Luther] remained strong throughout Thuringia. (Boyd, 2)

Since he grew up in an environment steeped in Lutheran tradition, it would be surprising if Bach did not receive a good amount of religious instruction at home.

Bach was eight years old when he first registered in the Latin school in Eisenach. He advanced rapidly in a curriculum that was heavily oriented toward religious instruction.

> In Quinta he studied the Catechism, Psalms, and Bible, history, writing, and reading, particularly the Gospels and Epistles in German and Latin. . . . In Quarta Sebastian studied the German Catechism and Psalter, Latin declensions, conjugations, and vocabulary. (Terry, *Bach: A Biography*, 21)

Two years later, after both of his parents died, he went to Ohrdruf to live in the home of his older brother, Johann Christoph. For five years he attended the Klosterschule, a school with a fine reputation, "where the progressive educational reforms of Comenius . . . had been adopted, and which attracted pupils from as far away as Kassel and Jena" (Boyd, *Bach: A Biography*, 8). Here, too, theology was at the heart of the curriculum, and again his progress was rapid.

> It would appear that, coming to Ohrdruf from Eisenach, probably in February 1695, he worked his way out of Quarta in half a year. He was barely ten when he entered the class, the average age of whose pupils was twelve. Its curriculum comprised 'Teutsche Materien' (Catechism, Gospels, Psalms), Comenius's *Vestibulum*, Reyher's minor Dialogues, essays *(exercitia styli)*, and Greek rudiments. Promoted on the examinations held in August 1695, Sebastian passed up to Tertia and faced the unamiable Arnold, who taught more intensively the subjects already studied in Quarta, substituting Reyher's larger Dialogues for Comenius. Again Sebastian's precocity is evident: the youngest Tertian, he was in July 1696 first among the seven 'novitii'. By July 1697 he climbed to the top of the class and was promoted to Secunda. Here, besides studying Cicero's letters in Johannes Rivius's edition, he was introduced to that stout champion of Lutheran orthodoxy, Leonhard Hutter's (1563-1616) *Compendium locorum theologicorum* (1610), hard fare for a young mind. (Terry, *Bach: A Biography*, 27-28)

Bach's school days concluded with three years at the Michaelisschule in Lüneburg from 1700 to 1702. Again "a distinctly theological education formed the center of instruction" (Stiller, 175). Hutter's *Compendium* continued to be part of the curriculum, and through it Bach

became intimately acquainted with the most essential details of orthodox Lutheran theology.

Thus we may say without reservation that Johann Sebastian Bach's
training in school was extensively carried out and determined theologically, predominately in the sense of strict Lutheran orthodoxy, and that
he possessed a finished theological education when he left school.
(Stiller, 175)

"Finished" is surely too strong a term. Though he advanced rapidly
and is reported to have been of "quick comprehension" and "extraordinary understanding" (Stiller, 175), he was still only seventeen when he left
school. But it is clear that his study did not end with his schooling. His
jobs kept him in close contact with pastors and people in academia. Some
of them — for example, Georg Christian Eilmar, who was the pastor of the
Marienkirche in Mühlhausen when Bach worked at the Blasiuskirche in
the same town — became his close friends. Eilmar was godfather to Bach's
first child, and it is hard to imagine that they did not engage in theological discussions that were more than casual and occasional. Part of the requirement for the job at Leipzig was to pass a substantial and thorough
theological test, and once on the job Bach of necessity had to discuss cantata texts with the pastors.

Bach's library indicates that he "did his homework" and that he
would have been able to hold his own in both professional and convivial
theological discussions with colleagues and friends. When he died, an inventory of his belongings, including his books, was made. Fifty-two titles
(over eighty volumes) appear on the inventory, all of them theological
works (see *The New Bach Reader*, 253-54). At the top of the list is "*Calovius*,
Writings, 3 volumes" (about which more presently). Next come two sets of
Luther's complete works. Also included are Martin Chemnitz's four-
volume reply to the Council of Trent, Olearius's three-volume Bible commentary, and Johannes Müller's *Defense of Luther*. Most of the authors were
orthodox Lutherans, but two Pietists, Auguste Hermann Francke and
Philipp Jakob Spener, also appear on the list. There is a volume by Heinrich Bünting entitled *Itinerarium Sacrae Scripturae*, which describes the travels of characters in the Bible. Josephus's *History of the Jews* is there, as is a
volume of sermons by Johann Tauler, a fourteenth-century Dominican
monk and follower of the mystic Meister Eckhart.

The only books from Bach's library known to survive today are those
at the top of the inventory, the three volumes of the Bible commentary of

Abraham Calov. Actually Calov was more the compiler than the author, as the title page makes clear.

> J. N. J. [*In Nomine Jesu.*] The German Bible of Dr. Martin Luther so clearly and thoroughly expounded from the original language, the context, and the parallel passages, with the addition of the exposition to be found in Luther's writings, so that, in addition to proper arrangement, everywhere the real literal understanding, and to a considerable extent also the salutary application, of Holy Scripture, especially together with the inspiring words of that man of God, is presented by Dr. Abraham Calov. (Trans. Leaver, *J. S. Bach and Scripture*, 52)

Bach's copies of these three volumes are now in the possession of the Concordia Seminary library in St. Louis, but their whereabouts was unknown until they were discovered in a farmhouse near Frankenmuth, Michigan, in 1934. In his introduction to *J. S. Bach and Scripture*, Robin Leaver tells the fascinating story of the rediscovery of these volumes by Pastor Christian G. Riedel of Detroit, a delegate to the meetings of the Michigan District of the Lutheran Church–Missouri Synod in Frankenmuth. Riedel was staying with his cousin, a seventy-four-year-old farmer named Leonard Reichle, who showed him the third volume of the Calov Bible commentary. Riedel noticed something on the title page that Reichle had missed — Bach's monogram and the date 1733! Subsequent searching eventually led to the discovery of the remaining two volumes in a chest in Reichle's attic. Bach's monogram was on each volume.

The volumes were given to Concordia Seminary library, where they vanished from public and even scholarly view. Leaver tells the story as follows:

> Then followed the war years, and the volumes were put into a safe place — so safe, in fact, that in November 1950 the musicologist, Walter E. Buszin, who was then professor of liturgics at Concordia Seminary, had no knowledge of its whereabouts. He wrote to Pastor Sauer, who was then living in retirement in Oak Park, Illinois, to find out whether they had been presented to the seminary library or Concordia Historical Institute or whether they had been given at all. Just exactly when and where they were rediscovered again is uncertain, but the fact that they were not shown publicly until November 1961 suggests that the volumes came to light again when the resources of the old library, Pritzlaff

Hall, were being investigated in preparation for removal to the new library building . . . which was opened in September 1962. (20)

The volumes were made public again at the 1969 Heidelberg Bachfest, and only since that time has serious scholarly work been done on the volumes.

The Calov Bible commentaries were not just owned by Bach. The corrections, underlinings, and marginalia in Bach's hand show that he read and studied them carefully. Some of Bach's markings are corrections of printer's errors, some according to the list of typographical errors at the end of volume 3, others apparently caught by Bach himself, like correcting "Dan" to "Gad" in the commentary on Genesis 49:19. Some of Bach's corrections supply omitted words. For example, in the commentary on Genesis 3:6-7, Bach supplied in the margin a phrase omitted from Calov's quotation from Luther's commentary. Such markings reveal not only a careful reader but also a knowledgeable one.

Some of Bach's underlinings or marginal comments show his interest in the biblical foundations for church music. For example, at 1 Chronicles 25, a chapter that describes King David making provision for the music of the tabernacle and for its 288 musicians, Bach wrote in the margin, "NB. Dieses Capital ist das wahre Fundament aller gottfalliger Kirchen Music" ["NB. This chapter is the true foundation of all God-pleasing church music"]. Another marking is perhaps related to growing frustrations with his employers in Leipzig (cf. pp. 26-27). Bach obviously looked to his Bible for guidance in his profession.

Bach may not have gone to university, but that did not prevent him from becoming a knowledgeable theologian. Throughout his life he built on the solid theological foundation laid during his childhood and youth. His library reveals a man with a deep and abiding interest in theology, and the only surviving books from that library reveal a man who read them with care, intelligence, and commitment. His music shows that he applied what he learned toward achieving his goal of "a well-appointed church music," well appointed not only musically but also theologically.

Bach's Musical Language

Music is an art closely related to rhetoric, a fact that has been recognized since Greek and Roman antiquity. In no period of history has this been more consciously recognized than in the Baroque period, when theorists overtly described music as a branch of rhetoric and often borrowed their terminology directly from the rhetoricians.

The most important strand of Baroque music theory is known as *Figurenlehre* (theory of figures). It had its origins in the late Renaissance. During the Baroque period it became full-fledged and had a pervasive influence on composition and performance. This theory described musical "figures," that is, devices that were useful for giving music a stronger rhetorical impact — an unusual melodic leap, an ornament, a sharp dissonance, a pause, and the like. Many of these figures had names borrowed from rhetoric since they referred to pretty much the same thing in both speech and music. For example, *aposiopesis* meant a sudden stop. Other terms had closely related meanings in the two arts. *Noëma* in speech referred to something generally known; in music it referred to chordal style, a simpler and hence more "generally known" style. And, for one more example, *hypotyposis* meant the use of illustrative examples in speech; in music it referred to word painting — for example, a high note on the word "heaven," a downward leap on "fall," fast notes on "run," and the like.

Here some words of warning are in order. First, because word painting is so easy to point out, its rhetorical and expressive role in Renaissance and Baroque music has been exaggerated. In saying that I do not mean to suggest that word painting was unimportant. Quite the contrary. Renaissance and Baroque composers — and, for that matter, those of later periods as well — rarely passed up the opportunity to illustrate a word or a phrase of text with appropriate music. When a madrigal composer encountered the line "came running down amain," he would certainly write rapid descending notes. When Handel set "Glory to God in the highest," he employed high, glittering sounds, but when he got to "peace on earth" he changed to quiet, low sounds. But word painting was only one of a large array of rhetorical/expressive tools available to a composer. And it is a good thing. There are not all that many words that can be illustrated literally by music, and it would be a serious mistake to think that the rhetorical and expressive impact of music in the Renaissance and Baroque periods was limited to word painting.

Second, although word painting might seem to be a rather naive method of expression, the fact that composers since the Renaissance, great and small alike, have made extensive use of it should make us reconsider whether the practice is as naive as it first seems. Perhaps one thing that makes it effective is that it encourages a more convincing performance. After all, it is hard to sing "Thou art gone up on high" with conviction to a descending scale!

Third, rhetorical devices should not be confused with word painting. Although many of the figures can have a literal relationship to a specific word, they do not necessarily "mean" the same thing in all situations. A composer might have used a figure called *quinta deficiens* ("deficient [i.e., diminished] fifth") for its nearly literal relationship to the words "I am poor and needy." But he could also have used it in relation to other words that have no relationship to "deficiency" simply because it is a striking figure that will call attention to any word regardless of its meaning. Early scholars, notably Albert Schweitzer, often made the mistake of associating a rhetorical figure too closely with a specific meaning. For example, Schweitzer associated the rhythm of an eighth note followed by two sixteenth notes specifically with joy (*J. S. Bach,* 2:109-14). But this is simply a rhythmic figure that could be used for rhetorical effect in a variety of situations. It is prominent, for example, in the "Let him be crucified" choruses in the *St. John Passion.* So it is wrong simply to label that figure as the "joy motive." On the other hand, to give Schweitzer his due, it has to be acknowledged that Bach did use that figure very frequently in situations of joy, a fact that, if used with discretion, can be a useful clue to interpretation.

A second strand of Baroque music theory has come to be called

Affektenlehre (theory of affects). This strand does not have the deep roots of *Figurenlehre* and was prevalent mainly in the late Baroque period among German theorists. An affect (pronounced A'fekt) is an emotional state, so *Affektenlehre* dealt with the portrayal of the affects in music. Closely related to this strand of theory is the fact that late Baroque music is "single affect" music. That is, a given piece or movement or large section presents only a single affect or feeling. Unlike music of the Classical period, in which several different affects are presented in dramatic interaction, Baroque music paints a vivid portrait; it captures the affect of a dramatic moment and holds it up for the listener's contemplation.

Much of what the *Affektenlehre* theorists said is rather obvious and commonplace. For example:

> Since . . . joy is an expansion of our soul, thus it follows reasonably and naturally that I could best express this affect by large and expanded intervals. Whereas if one knows that sadness is a contraction of these subtle parts of our body, then it is easy to see that the small and smallest intervals are the most suitable for this passion. (Mattheson, 104-5)

Some of it is more specific, as, for example, when specific dance types are associated with specific affects — the minuet with "moderate cheerfulness," the gavotte with "jubilation," the courante with "sweet hopefulness," and the like (see Mattheson, 451ff.). Needless to say, such associations cannot be mechanically applied across the board to every dance of a particular type, but neither should they be ignored. They can point our interpretation in the right direction.

Certain styles did develop very specific associations. For example, the French overture, with its stately dotted rhythms, had clear associations with ceremonial pomp. But even in clear-cut cases like this it is important to realize that other factors enter the picture. Key, instrumentation, melodic shape, degree of dissonance, and the like all play a role in shaping the affect. Those additional factors help determine, for example, whether the ceremonial pomp of a given French overture is for a king's victorious return from battle or for his funeral.

Instruments often had specific associations. Trumpets, to mention the most obvious example, were associated with glory and majesty. In Bach's music, oboes were often associated with love. Bach also used unusual instrumental combinations that, apart from any specific association or "meaning," simply by virtue of their striking color, helped to underscore a particularly meaningful text. For example, a key text, perhaps *the* key text, of the *St. Matthew Passion* is the aria, "Aus Liebe will mein Heiland sterben" ["For love will my Savior die"], sung between the two cries from the crowd, "Let him be crucified." It is scored for soprano, flute, and two oboes da caccia without the otherwise ubiquitous continuo. It does have the oboe sound (although only in an accompanying role) with its association with love, but even more important is the sheer uniqueness of the sound. Its uniqueness alerts the listener that this aria has something uniquely important to say.

Sometimes even a compositional technique could take on a specific meaning. Canons, for example, offered some intriguing possibilities. The word *canon* means "rule" or "law." Therefore canons were often associated with texts that had to do with law. But since a canon involved one part following another in exact imitation, it could also "mean" follow or chase.

A composer's use of keys often had significance. It is not so much that keys had specific associations, although that was sometimes the case. D major, for example, was often associated with majesty and splendor, and E minor, the central key of the *St. Matthew Passion,* was often associated with suffering. But more important than specific associations was the relationship of keys to each other, or, to put it another way, the direction of the movement of keys. This may sound too complex or esoteric to someone untrained in music theory, but in its essentials it is not hard to understand; and far from being esoteric, it is an element of expression that is directly felt by an attentive listener, even if the listener is not able to identify and explain what is happening.

Very simply, it has to do with whether the progression of keys is in an upward or a downward direction. The more sharps (or the fewer flats) a key has the "higher" it is; the more flats (or the fewer sharps) a key has the "lower" it is. Or, to change the metaphor, it is a matter of "harder" and "softer" keys. The original theoretical terms are *durus* (hard) and *mollis* (soft). Moving in the direction of more flats is movement to a "softer" or "milder" key, whereas moving to more sharps is movement to a "harder" or "harsher" key. But the two different directions should not be equated with positive and negative either way because while a sharp key might at one time be used to depict strength (positive) and a flat key weakness (negative), it is just as possible to use a sharp key for anger (negative) and a flat key for comfort (positive). The following explanation with examples from the *St. Matthew Passion* will, I think, be helpful.

15

Bach aligns the full range of tonalities [keys] in the work to the text . . . so that its *durus* (hard) and *mollis* (soft) states are given expression according to the traditional *proprietates*. The "hard" realm of affections encompasses all that was described of old as *asperitas* [harshness or bitterness]: the crucifixion in all its stages — the trial and the shouts of the mob for Jesus' death, the scourging, and so forth. But it also represents a group of positive emotions which derive from the traditional interpretation of *durus* as masculine and *fortius* [strong]: Christ's prediction of the Kingdom of God, the spread of the gospel, the resurrection, the *parousia*, Peter's repentance, Jesus' resolve at the close of Part I, and so on. Contrariwise, the "soft" affections comprise weakness . . . : Jesus' difficulty accepting the cup at first, His depressed states on the Mount of Olives . . . and on the cross. . . . *Mollis* also represents the comforting, gentle and sympathetic associations of "feminine": the Christian reactions to Jesus' sufferings . . . , the reaction of Pilate's wife, the disciples' sleep in the garden, Jesus' final sleep in the grave, His arms open to the Christian seeking redemption, His finding rest in the believer's heart. (Chafe, "Key Structure," 45-46)

All of the above methods for heightening the rhetorical and expressive impact of the music were available to all Baroque composers. But Bach had other means that were more exclusive. For example, he, like other Lutheran composers, could introduce chorale melodies into their works in unexpected places. Because their listeners knew the words associated with the melody, their incorporation of the melody into the piece added another dimension to the piece's meaning.

Even forms could sometimes have meaning. Particularly important in Bach are forms that are symmetrical around a central axis, for example, ABCACBA. Such forms are called "chiastic." The name comes from the Greek letter *chi,* which is X-shaped, itself a chiastic shape. Since *chi* is the first letter of Christ (hence our abbreviation Xmas) and its shape is suggestive of the cross, chiastic forms could symbolize Christ and the cross.

German composers of the Baroque also had a melodic symbol for the cross. It consists of four notes (although it could be made more elaborate with additional notes) that go in a zigzag pattern — up, down, up, down (or the reverse). If one imagines a line drawn between the first and fourth notes and another between the second and third notes, a cross appears:

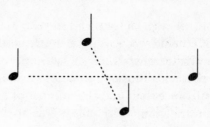

Notation furnished another cross symbol. The sharp sign (♯) has an obvious resemblance to the cross, so much so that the German word for "sharp" is *Kreuz* ("cross").

Numbers could also be symbols. Number symbolism is an age-old phenomenon common to many cultures. Several numbers have obvious and long-standing significance in Christian art — 3 as a symbol of the Trinity, 10 representing the Law, and 12 representing the disciples and, by extension, the church. The numbers 2, 33, and 5 are symbols of Christ — 2 because he is the second person of the Trinity and has two natures, human and divine; 33 because that is the traditional number of years he lived on earth; and 5 because of the five wounds (two nail-pierced hands, two nail-pierced feet, and one sword-pierced side) and the five "mysteries" (incarnation, death, resurrection, ascension, and second coming).

Another possible type of number symbolism derives from equating the letters of the alphabet with numbers — A = 1, B = 2, etc. Applying this to Bach's name results in B + A + C + H = 14 and J + S + B + A + C + H (when I and J are the same letter) = 41. Although there is concrete evidence for the existence of several more complicated "number alphabets" in Bach's time, there is none for this simplest and most obvious of them. Therefore doubt has been cast upon the equation of 14 with Bach and 41 with J. S. Bach. However, since the equations come as the result of such a direct method, they cannot be ruled out simply because the method is not mentioned in esoteric treatises.

There is a wide range of opinion about the extent to which Bach employed number symbolism. Some scholars dismiss it out of hand; others seem bent on finding it everywhere by the most arcane of methods. Of course, there can be no proof one way or the other. So I will not engage in the argument here other than to say that, if Bach did not use number symbolism, there are a remarkable number of remarkably apt coincidences in his music, including several involving the simple number alphabet. And since I find it hard to believe in the existence of so many apt coincidences, I will call attention to some number symbolism in the discussion of some of the pieces, but always with the realization that, as Malcolm Boyd puts it, "the workings of coincidence can never be discounted in a particular case." But he also mischievously adds: "The number of bars or notes in any given passage of Bach's music is therefore no more certain to be of numerological significance than, say, the number of chapters or music examples in a book on the composer" (223). This at the end of a book on Bach with fourteen chapters and fourteen musical examples!

If we cannot be sure that Bach used numbers to place his name into compositions, we can be fairly certain that he occasionally did it with notes. In German notation b stands for B flat and h stands for B natural. So Bach's name can be represented by the notes:

B = B flat
A = A
C = C
H = B natural.

I have strayed from discussing the elements of Bach's musical language that he shared with his contemporaries to elements that are more esoteric and even private. Although we should not ignore the more esoteric elements, they should not dominate our attention. So I end by recalling the common elements to our attention, for they are what made Baroque music understandable to the general populace. Baroque composers, unlike those who came under the sway of Romanticism, did not feel a compulsion to be "original." This freed them to "speak" in the commonly understood musical parlance; they could compose with a fair amount of assurance that they would be understood by most of their audience. They were like orators, making use of whatever rhetorical tools they had available to capture the attention of their listeners and then to persuade them of the truth and move them to virtue. Johann Mattheson, one of the most important music theorists of the early eighteenth century, said that it was incumbent upon a musician "to present the virtues and vices in his music well, and to arouse skillfully in the feeling of the listener a love for the former and disgust for the latter" (104).

Bach was no doubt in agreement with those goals. More specifically he was concerned to persuade his listeners of the truth of the gospel and to move them to the virtues of discipleship, of being Christlike. But perhaps *persuade* and *move* are not precisely the right terms for what Bach's music does. I agree with Richard Jeske that there is an "invitational character . . . that is . . . compellingly present in his church cantatas." For Bach it did not suffice

> simply to bring musical interpretation to the biblical text, no matter how magnificent, colorful, or dramatic. The music must lay open the invitation of the text, the gospel invitation to the reader and the hearer to confront the claim of the text and to understand him- or herself anew in view of the grace of God. (87)

Cantatas

C antatas easily make up the largest part of Bach's output. According to the obituary written by his son Carl Philipp Emanuel and his student Johann Friedrich Agricola, Bach wrote "five full annual cycles of church pieces [cantatas], for all the Sundays and holidays" (*The New Bach Reader*, 304). Figuring approximately sixty-five per year, that would amount to well over three hundred works. Of that number about two hundred have survived. They are works for voices and instruments written to be performed in the Lutheran liturgy after the reading of the Gospel lesson for the day. Their texts usually have direct connections to the Gospel lesson; indeed, they functioned something like musical sermons.

"Cantata" comes from the Latin *cantare*, "to sing." In its most generic usage, the term simply designates a vocal piece as opposed to an instrumental piece or "sonata" (from *sonare*, "to sound"). During the seventeenth century, "cantata" came to be used in a more specific sense. It was used to designate secular Italian works for solo voice(s) and continuo. In content and in style these works are closely related to opera. They consist mainly of a series of recitatives and arias. Although not staged, they have all the other earmarks of operatic scenes.

It was not until much later that "cantata" came to be used in a generic sense to designate fairly large-scale sacred compositions for voice(s) and instruments. The "church pieces" referred to in the obituary were very rarely called cantatas by Bach. He sometimes used terms like "ode," "dialogue," "motet," or "concerto." Mostly he did not use any term at all to designate them. He simply identified them by the day in the liturgical year for which they were written. Nevertheless, "cantata" has become the standard designation for his "church pieces," and I will stick with it here.

Bach's cantatas belong to a lineage of Lutheran liturgical and devotional music employing both voices and instruments. This line began early in the Baroque period, when the use of continuo became standard and the use of obbligato instruments became quite frequent. Works in this line were extremely various. Their texts came from a variety of sources — the Bible, chorales, and newly composed sacred poetry often called odes. Another type of text commonly used was the dialogue. These texts told stories, usually from the Bible, in dialogue form, with different singers representing the different characters — for example, Abraham and Isaac, or the angels and the shepherds. During the seventeenth century, the texts of Lutheran "cantatas" typically came from one or more of these sources and were often mixed in various combinations and proportions.

The musical ingredients were equally various. Composers employed various styles, both old and new, both solo and choral. Prominent among those styles were the new styles of solo vocal writing, recitative and aria, that had originated in opera. Also prominent was the incorporation, in a variety of ways, of the old chorale tunes.

Around the year 1700, the situation changed. Variety gave way to standardization, largely due to the popularity of a new style of religious poetry developed by Erdmann Neumeister. Beginning in 1700, while he was a clergyman in Eckartsberga, he provided

> the court chapel at Weissenfels with sacred poetry for every Sunday and feast day. This was all then set to music by the Hofkapellmeister in charge, Johann Philipp Krieger (1649-1725). Four years later, having meanwhile been appointed minister of the church at Weissenfels, he was able to arrange for a reprint of his librettos under the title *Geistliche Cantaten statt einer Kirchen-Music* (Sacred cantatas instead of church music). A preface added to this new edition tells us the reason for these poems and their appearance: Neumeister wanted the essential contents of his private meditation after each of his Sunday sermons to appear in the shape of rhymed verse. (Schulze, 101)

The title of Neumeister's collection of librettos is interesting because it seems to indicate that he intended them for devotional rather than liturgical use. He seems to have intended a sacred counterpart to the secular Italian cantata. In any case, the "rhymed verse" he wrote based on "his private meditation after each of his Sunday sermons" took the form of a series of alternating recitatives and arias; and whatever his intent, and despite some initial resistance to using texts so obviously indebted to secular models, Neumeister's texts and similar ones by others who followed his lead became standard fare in many Lutheran churches during the early eighteenth century.

Bach seems to have had a great deal of respect for Neumeister. That Neumeister was pastor at the Jakobikirche in Hamburg may have been one of the reasons for Bach's interest in a job there. He was offered the job but refused to accept it because of "his unwillingness to acquiesce in the simony that apparently accompanied such appointments in Hamburg" (Boyd, 68). Johann Mattheson referred to the incident a few years later and reported how Neumeister, not so subtly, denounced the simony (i.e., the buying and selling of ecclesiastical office) in a Christmas sermon.

> [T]he eloquent chief preacher [Neumeister], who had not concurred in the Simoniacal deliberations, expounded in the most splendid fashion the gospel of the music of the angels at the birth of Christ, in which connection the recent incident of the rejected artist [Bach] gave him quite naturally the opportunity to reveal his thoughts, and to close his sermon with something like the following pronouncement: he was firmly convinced that even if one of the angels of Bethlehem should come down from Heaven, one who played divinely and wished to become organist of St. Jacobi, but had no money, he might just as well fly away again. (*The New Bach Reader*, 91)

Despite the apparent respect Bach and Neumeister had for each other, Bach used Neumeister texts in only five or six of his two hundred surviving sacred cantatas, and then usually with other texts as well. But that does not mean that Bach avoided the new-style texts of Neumeister and his followers. Far from it. He used them frequently but selectively while retaining many of the older types of texts — chorales, Bible verses, and dialogues. In this respect he showed his conservatism, a conservatism he shared with other municipal cantors and organists. As Peter Wollny points out:

> It could hardly be a coincidence that the musical protagonists of this new form were Kapellmeisters at the Saxon and Thuringian courts, such as Johann Philipp Krieger in Weissenfels and Philipp Heinrich Erlebach

in Rudolstadt, who were both very much at home with the operatic music of their time. Only at a later stage was the new type of cantata taken up by municipal cantors and organists, more often than not only after Neumeister and other librettists in his wake had found a compromise: although the real novelty of Neumeister's reform — alternating recitative and aria in free poetry — continued, biblical dicta and the chorale made their reappearance in the cantatas, mostly as the introduction and closing movements. (26)

Most of Bach's cantatas date from his years of service in Leipzig (1723-1750), but a not insignificant number date from earlier places of employment. The oldest of his cantatas were written during his short term of employment as organist at the Church of St. Blasius in Mühlhausen (1707-1708), including one of his most popular cantatas, *Christ lag in Todes Banden* (Cantata 4, cf. pp. 151-64).

When Bach received an appointment to the court at Weimar in 1708, he wrote a request for dismissal from his Mühlhausen post in which he gave the following reasons for wanting to leave: "Now, God has brought it to pass that an unexpected change should offer itself to me, in which I see the possibility of a more adequate living and the achievement of my goal of a well-regulated church music without further vexation . . ." (*The New Bach Reader*, 57). Although Bach apparently saw in the Weimar position a greater opportunity for the composition of cantatas, at first cantata composition was not a regular part of his duties. But in 1714 he was promoted to concertmaster, with the specific assignment "to be obliged to perform new works monthly" (*The New Bach Reader*, 70). These "new works" were cantatas, and so the promotion occasioned a steady output. In all, twenty-two cantatas survive from Bach's Weimar period, including nos. 61 (cf. pp. 78-87), the first version of 147 (cf. pp. 182-83), and 199 (cf. pp. 67-73).

After Weimar, Bach's next career move took him to Cöthen, a Calvinist court where no "concerted" church music was permitted. Therefore Bach had no occasion to write liturgical cantatas. He did, however, write two liturgical cantatas, nos. 22 and 23, to be performed as part of his application for the post of cantor in Leipzig. He received the position only after the Leipzig officials failed to land their first two choices, Georg Philipp Telemann and Christoph Graupner.

It has long been known that most of Bach's cantatas date from his Leipzig years. But before the 1950s it was thought that they were composed over the entire span of his employment at Leipzig. Bach's great biographer, Philipp Spitta, had established a chronology by 1880 in which the cantatas were spread more or less evenly over his Leipzig years, culminating in some thirty chorale cantatas thought to have been written between 1735 and 1744. The chorale cantatas are based on chorale texts and tunes familiar to the worshiping Lutherans of Bach's day. Typically they begin with a monumental chorale fantasy and end with one of Bach's incomparable four-part harmonizations. They are generally regarded as Bach's greatest cantatas and among his greatest works in any genre. Spitta's chronology, however, was based on some errors regarding the watermarks of the manuscripts and on a mistaken assumption about Bach's stylistic development. Spitta assumed a kind of "organic" growth that required some time for maturation before culminating in the great chorale cantatas.

But during the 1950s, startling discoveries were made that forced a radically changed chronology for the Leipzig cantatas and resulted in a re-examination of the traditional view of Bach as a devout and diligent church musician. Two German scholars, Alfred Dürr and Georg von Dadelsen, working simultaneously but independently and employing different methods, came up with essentially the same chronology for the cantatas, a chronology radically different from Spitta's. Their careful, scientific examination of the paper (Dürr) and the handwriting (Dadelsen) of the cantata manuscripts convincingly established that a great majority of Bach's cantatas were written during an incredibly short time. Rather than being written over a span of more than twenty years, most of Bach's Leipzig cantatas were written at a pace of about *one per week* during his first two years of employment at the St. Thomas School. Prominent among the cantatas that Bach turned out during that remarkable creative outburst are the chorale cantatas, the very works that Spitta saw as the pinnacle of Bach's "organic" development, works he thought were written over a span of about a decade when Bach was at his peak. But as the new chronology shows, the great chorale cantatas were turned out once a week throughout most of Bach's second year at Leipzig beginning in June 1724.

Then suddenly, in March 1725, Bach's composition of chorale cantatas stopped and, after May 1725, his steady, weekly flow of cantatas slowed drastically. 1725 and 1726 saw Bach abandon the chorale cantatas for much less ambitious solo cantatas, and frequently he resorted to performing cantatas written by his cousin, Johann Ludwig Bach. By 1727 he had virtually ceased cantata composition.

The question why Bach so abruptly stopped writing cantatas has elicited much speculation. Obviously that is the kind of question for which we will never have a certain answer. But what concerns us here is whether that sudden cessation of cantata composition says anything about the traditional image of Bach. Dürr's assessment of what the new chronology says, or does not say, about Bach's religious convictions or sense of vocation is very level-headed.

> I do not see why a man should not be regarded as a church musician — and as fully conscious of his bent — just because when he first took office, he devoted superhuman energy to providing himself with a stock of practicable compositions of his own, to be repeated as necessary. Indeed I doubt whether it would have been physically possible for Bach to continue such exertions throughout his life; and in any case I cannot see how the known facts can be used to prove that Bach lost his vocation — any more than I can see the converse would be true; that is to say, that writing church cantatas at regular intervals throughout the Leipzig period would have proved that he was a devout Christian. (484-85)

Not all scholarly reaction to the new chronology was as reasonable as Dürr's. Some scholars thought that it shattered the traditional image of Bach as a devout church musician. Some Lutheran scholars like Friedrich Smend, fearing what the new chronology might say about Bach's dedication to his church, questioned its validity. Scholars from what was then communist East Germany greeted it as evidence that clinched their view of a nonreligious Bach. More disturbing than the predictable response from the former East Germany was the response by Friedrich Blume, longtime president of the International Musicological Society, editor-in-chief of the outstanding German music encyclopedia *Musik in Geschichte und Gegenwart,* and the author of the highly respected *Protestant Church Music: A History.* In a lecture given in June 1962 at the Bachfest in Mainz, Blume claimed that the new chronology destroyed "Spitta's picture of the supreme cantor toiling away for years on end at the task of supplying his Leipzig congregations with cantatas" (217). Obviously, given the new chronology, one cannot quarrel with the literal meaning of that statement; Bach did not "toil away for years on end" composing cantatas. But not all of Blume's statements were that circumspect. For example:

> Did Bach have a special liking for church work? Was it a spiritual necessity for him? Hardly. There is at any rate no evidence that it was. Bach

the supreme cantor, the creative servant of the Word of God, the staunch Lutheran, is a legend. (219)

And this:

> [N]umerous works, oratorios, masses, and cantatas, which we have grown deeply to cherish as professions of Christian faith, works on the basis of which the Classical-Romantic tradition has taught us to revere the great churchman, the mighty Christian herald, have *a limine* nothing in common with such values and sentiments and were not written with the intention of proclaiming the composer's Christian faith, still less from a heartfelt need to do so. (220)

Those were fighting words, and for a while the result was scholarly warfare. Now the new chronology of Dürr and Dadelsen is generally accepted, and the warfare has calmed down as new evidence, in particular the discovery of Bach's copy of the Calov Bible and commentary (cf. pp. 9-11), has given renewed credence to the traditional picture of Bach and his devotion to his vocation in the church. A passage marked by Bach in his Calov Bible perhaps reveals him finding a biblically sanctioned way to handle the strained relationship that had developed between him and his employers at Leipzig. Next to the commentary on Matthew 5:26, Bach wrote "NB" and some emphasis marks. Part of that passage he also underlined. The passage marked and underlined goes as follows:

> Of course, as we have said, anger is sometimes necessary and proper. But be sure that you use it correctly. You are commanded to get angry, not on your own behalf, but on behalf of your office and of God; you must not confuse the two, your person and your office. As far as your person is concerned, you must not get angry with anyone regardless of the injury he may have done to you. But where your office requires it, there you must get angry, even though no injury has been done to you personally.... But if your brother has done something against you and angered you, and then begs your pardon and stops doing wrong, your anger, too, should disappear. Where does the secret spite come from which you continue to keep in your heart? (Leaver, *J. S. Bach and Scripture*, 121-22)

Is it farfetched to see here a frustrated, angry church musician who sees his high ideals thwarted at every turn by his superiors and finds his work unappreciated? I think not. I think Bach's frustration with the authorities at Leipzig is probably the key to his "retirement" from cantata composition after his first few years of employment there. Bach went to Leipzig with high hopes of being able to work toward the goal of "a well-appointed church music." When he got there he launched into his new assignment with a burst of creative energy that has seldom, if ever, been matched. As time went on, troubles with the authorities mounted, appreciation diminished, and even his enormous energy was reaching its limits. Furthermore, he had already written at least three yearly cycles of cantatas. Were not these the achievement of his goal? Why should he continue to put forth nearly superhuman effort in the face of unappreciative opposition? Far from calling Bach's commitment to his church into question, it seems to me that the new chronology actually shows something of the depth of that commitment. If his commitment had not been so deep, if his goals had not been so lofty, his disappointments and frustrations would not have been so great. If writing cantatas were merely a job, he would have neither plunged into it with such vigor nor abandoned it so abruptly.

But it was not merely a job; it was a vocation. Or rather, writing music to the glory of God was his vocation, as he usually proclaimed at the end of his scores with the initials SDG — "Soli Deo Gloria." His primary goal within that vocation was to write music that would be of use to his church in her worship, to write "musical sermons" for the edification of her members. But if that goal had in some sense already been reached and his church was turning a deaf ear to his preaching, it was not a betrayal of his vocation to write a second volume of the *Well-Tempered Clavier* or *A Musical Offering* or *The Art of the Fugue* instead of more cantatas. Bach's attitude toward his work, as Jaroslav Pelikan says,

> bespeaks the conviction of Luther and the Reformers that the performance of any God-pleasing vocation was the service of God, even if it did not lead to the performance of chorales. The Bach of the Peasant Cantata, the partitas, and the concertos was not "too secular." These were, rather, the expression of a unitary (if to modern eyes sometimes inconsistent or even self-contradictory) world view, in which all beauty, including "secular" beauty, was sacred because God was one, both Creator and Redeemer. (139)

Bach's late period, the period following his initial intense activity at Leipzig, is perhaps the most representative of that unitary worldview.

While continuing to direct cantatas and Passions in the Leipzig churches, he also directed the Collegium Musicum performances at Zimmermann's coffeehouse. And side by side with his work on such great secular works as the Goldberg Variations, Book II of the *Well-Tempered Clavier,* and *The Art of the Fugue,* we find him putting the finishing touches on his great Passions and chorale preludes, composing the Catechism Chorales of *Clavier Übung* III, and completing the *B Minor Mass.* Variations and chorales, fugues and Passions, all say "Soli Deo Gloria."

Motets

The cantatas are the biggest part of Bach's output; the motets are the smallest. Traditionally six motets have been ascribed to Bach (BWV 225-30), but the attribution of one of the six, *Lobet den Herrn* (BWV 230), to Bach has long been questioned. Its status remains questionable. In his recent study of the motets, Daniel Melamed concludes that "the problems of its authenticity . . . still loom large" (101). On the other hand, Melamed offers quite convincing reasons to believe that another motet, *Ich lasse dich nicht* (BWV Anh. 159), can be added to Bach's output. Furthermore, a work that is numbered with the cantatas, *O Jesu Christ, meins Lebens Licht* (BWV 118), has little, if anything, in common with cantatas and much in common with motets. It is now quite generally considered a motet rather than a cantata.

In Bach's time motets were compositions for choir typically on biblical and/or chorale texts. Unlike cantatas, motets generally did not call for instruments other than continuo. However, the use of instruments to double the voices was a common practice, and the inclusion of some independent instrumental parts did not necessarily prevent a piece from being classified as a motet. But such instrumental parts did not have the prominence they had in cantatas. Also unlike cantatas, motets did not make use of the solo vocal genres, recitative and aria. They usually featured contrapuntal writing, which showed their lineage back to the motet of the late Renaissance. Often they were written for double chorus, another feature that points back to the late Renaissance.

Finally, again unlike the function of the cantatas, the function of

Bach's motets is little known. The only one for which we know the occasion of a performance is *Der Geist hilft unser Schwachheit auf* (BWV 226). We know the reason for this motet

> because we are in possession of Bach's composing score, on which he noted the work's purpose. There is some debate over the specific event at which the motet was performed, but we can be certain that it was heard in connection with the death of the Thomasschule Rector Johann Heinrich Ernesti, who was buried on 20 October 1729. In addition, a nearly complete set of original parts survives, datable to the same period and clearly documenting a performance. (Melamed, 63)

The others have long been thought to have been written, like *Der Geist hilft*, for funeral or memorial services, and various specific occasions have been put forth, but that is all conjectural.

The small number of motets and the uncertainty about their function might seem to suggest that they are a negligible part of Bach's output. However, the quantity is not as small as first appears because motet-like movements are not uncommon in Bach's larger vocal works. But more importantly, it must be emphasized that the small quantity does not indicate negligible quality. Although few in number, Bach's motets have few, if any, peers among works of their kind and rank with the best work Bach did in any genre. We can take Mozart's response to *Singet dem Herrn ein neues Lied* (BWV 225) as an indicator of their excellence. In 1789, just two years before his death, Mozart visited Leipzig. An eyewitness, Friedrich Rochlitz, reported on his visit to the St. Thomas School.

> On the initiative of the late Doles, then Cantor of the St. Thomas School in Leipzig, the choir surprised Mozart with the performance of the double-chorus motet *Singet dem Herrn ein neues Lied*, by Sebastian Bach. Mozart knew this master more by hearsay than by his works, which had become quite rare; at least his motets, which had never been printed, were completely unknown to him. Hardly had the choir sung a few measures when Mozart sat up, startled; a few measures more and he called out "What is this?" And now his whole soul seemed to be in his ears. When the singing was finished he cried out, full of joy, "Now, there is something one can learn from!" (*The New Bach Reader*, 488)

Chorale Preludes

A chorale prelude is a piece for organ based on a chorale melody. Since the melodies of the chorales and the words that went with them were well known by his fellow Lutherans in the eighteenth century, Bach could assume that the hearing of a familiar tune would bring the words to their minds. So the music in his chorale preludes played a similar role to that of the music in his vocal works. It served to emphasize, illustrate, and interpret a text.

Some 130 chorale preludes by Bach have survived. Given his expertise as an organist and his love for the traditional chorales of the Lutheran church, it is not surprising that he wrote a large number. Most of them are contained in four collections — the *Orgel-Büchlein [Little Organ Book]*, *Clavier Übung* III, the so-called Leipzig Chorales, and the Schübler Chorales. The rest occur in miscellaneous manuscripts, the most important being the one associated with Bach's pupil J. P. Kirnberger, hence the "Kirnberger Collection."

The compositions in the *Orgel-Büchlein* probably date from Bach's Weimar period, mainly the years 1713-1716. They are mostly short, compact works that are particularly remarkable for the musical imagery Bach invented to underscore the meaning of the texts.

The third volume of *Clavier Übung* (lit. "keyboard practice") was published in 1739. It contains mostly large, complex chorale settings. The main contents of the collection are twenty-one chorale preludes. The chorale preludes begin with a series based on chorales for the first two items of the Lutheran Mass. There are two each for the three Kyrie chorales

31

("Kyrie, Gott Vater in Ewigkeit" ["Lord, God the Father in Eternity"], "Christe, aller Welt Trost" ["Christ, Comfort of All the World"], and "Kyrie, Gott heiliger Geist" ["Lord, God the Holy Ghost"]) and three for the Gloria chorale ("Allein Gott in der Höhe sei Ehr" ["Alone to God in the Highest Be Honor"]). This makes a total of nine (3 × 3), a fitting trinitarian symbol to go with the Kyrie and the Gloria chorales, the texts of which are both organized in trinitarian form. What is more, the three "Allein Gott" preludes are all trios. The remaining twelve preludes are based on the six chorales that are specifically related to Luther's catechism. There are two settings of each, a large one with pedals and a small one without. This, too, is symbolic, for Luther wrote both a large and a small version of his catechism.

The symbolism does not end there. Bach added four duets to the collection and then framed it with the famous Prelude and Fugue in E♭ Major (the fugue is sometimes referred to as "St. Anne" because its opening notes happen to be the same as those of the hymn tune "St. Anne"). E♭ major has three flats, and both the Prelude and the Fugue are built out of three subjects. The total number of pieces in the collection — prelude, fugue, duets, and chorale preludes — is 27 (3 × 3 × 3), and it went on sale for three thalers (Boyd, 179)!

Late in his life Bach polished, revised, and made a fair copy of eighteen chorale preludes he had composed in Weimar (one is unfinished). These contrast strongly with those in the *Orgel-Büchlein*. As Boyd puts it, "Length and quality seem to have been the main criteria for inclusion, and if the *Orgel-Büchlein* shows Bach as a poetic miniaturist in chorale writing, the 'Leipzig' collection shows him as a master of chorale settings on the grandest scale" (55).

Finally, also late in his life, Bach arranged six movements from cantatas for organ. They were published in 1748-1749 by Johann Georg Schübler of Zella, hence the collection has become known as the "Schübler Chorales." It contains what is probably the best known of Bach's chorale preludes, the setting of "Wachet auf" that originated as the fourth movement of Cantata 140 (cf. pp. 214-15).

Passions and Oratorios

The Passions have the deepest liturgical roots of all Bach's works. Tangible evidence for this form goes all the way back to the fourth century, when a Spanish nun named Egeria went on a pilgrimage to the Holy Land. She kept a journal for the benefit of the sisters back home in Spain. Prominent in her account are descriptions of the liturgical observances she participated in while in Jerusalem. Her account of the services held during Holy Week includes the earliest surviving reference to the chanting of the Passion story. Not much later, in the late fourth or early fifth century, St. Augustine referred to the same practice, and by the middle of the fifth century Pope Leo the Great had decreed that the Passion story as told by St. Matthew should be chanted during the Masses for Palm Sunday and Wednesday in Holy Week, while the Passion according to St. John should be chanted on Good Friday. Some two hundred years later the St. Luke Passion replaced the St. Matthew Passion during the Wednesday Mass, and during the tenth century it became the custom in the Roman Church to sing the Passion according to St. Mark on the Tuesday of Holy Week.

At different times, in different places, and in different liturgical traditions, specifications varied as to which Passion accounts were to be chanted on which liturgical days during Lent and Holy Week. But the liturgical practice of chanting the entire Passion account as the Gospel reading for the day was common throughout Christendom from very early times, and it continued unabated for centuries. In the eighteenth century, Bach's Passion settings were still part of the tradition we first hear of from Sister Egeria in the fourth century.

Throughout the Middle Ages the Passion was performed in a chant style consisting mainly of simple recitation formulas. During the Renaissance, composers started to set the Passion story in parts, sometimes setting the entire account in parts but more usually leaving the narrative in chant while reserving part-singing for the words spoken by the groups of people and, sometimes, also for the words of individuals, such as Jesus, Pilate, and Peter.

After the Reformation the Lutherans retained the ancient practice. Both monophonic and polyphonic Passions were sung on specified days during Lent and Holy Week. Luther's friend, the composer Johann Walter, provided simple models for singing the Passion. In them the Evangelist and the individual characters chant their words while the groups of people sing their words to a simple recitation formula in four parts.

About the middle of the seventeenth century, musical settings of the Passion became much more elaborate. Under the influence of the new musical styles coming out of opera, Passion settings began taking on both musical and textual accretions. Instruments were added, and the continuity of the Gospel narrative was broken up by the insertion of chorales and musical settings of newly written poetry. During the eighteenth century this development went in two directions, producing two rather distinct types of Passion settings. The key difference between the two lies in what they did with the biblical narrative.

The first type, which can be called the "oratorio Passion," retained the Gospel narrative intact, even though the story was frequently interrupted by the insertion of chorales and newly written meditative poetry. Because the Gospel narrative remained intact, "oratorio Passions" retained their liturgical function as Gospel lesson.

The second type, which can be called the "Passion oratorio," lost its connection to the liturgy because it abandoned the literal Gospel narrative in favor of a new poetic retelling of the story and did not include chorales. "Passion oratorios" became popular in concert settings. Many of the big names of early eighteenth-century music, Bach excluded, set their hand to writing them. Especially popular was a text by B. H. Brockes, which was set to music by Handel, Telemann, Mattheson, and Stölzel among others.

Although the concert-style "Passion oratorio" became the norm during the first half of the eighteenth century, Bach's Passions adhere to the liturgical type by retaining the Gospel narrative without cuts or paraphrases. As if to emphasize his adherence to the liturgical type and to highlight the centrality of the Gospel narrative, in the fair copy he made of the score of the *St. Matthew Passion* Bach wrote the words of the Gospel in red ink.

Despite the popularity of the newer types of Passion settings, the venerable plainsong and polyphonic Passion settings of the Middle Ages and Renaissance still continued in use, especially in theologically and liturgically conservative places like Leipzig. The tradition of Passion singing in Leipzig prior to Bach's tenure there was to use simple, unaccompanied settings like those of Johann Walter. In 1721 Bach's predecessor, Johann Kuhnau, instituted the practice of performing an elaborate musical setting of the Passion on Good Friday. But as Robin Leaver points out, these musically grander settings did not replace the older, simpler settings. He describes the liturgical place and function of the old and new types as follows:

> On Palm Sunday morning, 2 April 1724, five days before the first performance of Bach's first Passion in Leipzig, the *St. John Passion*, the Leipzig congregation heard, as usual, as the Gospel for the day, the simple, unaccompanied *Passion according to St. Matthew*, by Johann Walter, written about 1550. Then on the morning of Good Friday itself, at the principal Communion service, Johann Walter's *Passion according to St. John* . . . was sung as the Gospel for that day. Thus Bach's [Passions were] not composed to replace but rather to complement these simple, austere settings of the Passion story.
>
> There was a difference in function involved. The simple Passion settings were used at the main morning Communion service as the Gospel for the day, and therefore there was the need to present the details of the Passion narrative with clarity and economy in this rather long and liturgically complex service. The sexton's notes and a Leipzig liturgical directory both underline that the singing of the plainsong Passion was the Gospel for the day. On Palm Sunday during the singing of the last verse of the hymn ["All Glory, Laud, and Honor"] which followed the Epistle, the clergy and small choir moved to the lectern in the chancel. At the conclusion of the hymn Walter's *St. Matthew Passion* was sung, with the evangelist's part being taken by the arch deacon, the part of Christ by one of the deacons, and the crowd by the choir of boys from the [St. Thomas School], while the congregation stood throughout in quiet meditation. . . .
>
> But Bach's Passions were [not] written for [the morning communion

service but for] the Good Friday Vespers service, which took place in the early afternoon. The liturgical form of the Vespers service was much simpler, consisting of psalms, hymns, prayers, and Bible readings. . . . But the central element was the Sermon, for Vespers was very much a preaching service. . . . The service was referred to as the *Vesper-Predigt.* (*J. S. Bach as Preacher,* 17-19)

Bach's Passions were written specifically for this preaching service, and their division into two parts is due to the liturgical structure of Vespers, which called for the preaching of a sermon between the two halves of the Passion setting.

To understand Bach's Passions it is important to grasp their liturgical function. Despite all their additional text and music, their core remains the Gospel narrative. The additional text and music — the recitatives, arias, and chorales — are there to highlight the Gospel story, to make it vivid and meaningful to the worshiper.

So in the *St. Matthew Passion* and in the *St. John Passion* the story of Jesus' suffering and death is sung in its entirety directly from chapters 26 and 27 of Matthew and chapters 18 and 19 of John, respectively. With the exception of the words spoken by groups of people, the entire story is sung in a recitative style that in its declamation, melodic shape, and harmonic language closely adheres to the rhythm, punctuation, inflection, tone, and meaning of the words. Most of the words are sung by a tenor soloist, the "Evangelist," while the words spoken by the various characters in the story are assigned to different soloists. In the *St. Matthew Passion,* Jesus is set apart from the rest of the characters by having his words accompanied by the strings, a feature that is often referred to as a musical "halo." The notable exception to this are his words from the cross, "My God, my God, why hast Thou forsaken me?" (no. 61a), during which the halo of string sound is absent.

The words spoken by groups of people — the disciples, the priests, the soldiers, the crowd — are sung by the choir. Most of the *turba* choruses, as these crowd choruses are called, are short, and they capture in vivid musical strokes the tone of the crowd, which, on the whole, is decidedly nasty. Bach wanted to make sure his congregation was repulsed by the cries of the crowds. A notable exception in the *St. Matthew Passion* is his setting of the words of the centurion and those with him, "Truly, this was the Son of God" (no. 63b). For these words Bach wrote some of the most compelling music imaginable. These were words for the congregation to identify with; this was a confession for them to make with the centurion.

Told in this way, with recitative and *turba* choruses, the Gospel narrative is heard clearly, and the story it tells unfolds directly. But after each episode in the story, and sometimes even in the midst of an episode, Bach and his librettists inserted recitatives, arias, and chorales that provide responses to the action and time for contemplative meditation on the significance of the events. The recitatives and arias, sung by soloists, represent the meditative response of the individual believer, whereas the chorales, sung by the choir and known and loved by the entire congregation, represent the response of the believing community. Together, the chorales and solo numbers, as theologian Paul Minear put it, "bridge the distance in space and time between those earlier events and . . . an eighteenth-century German congregation" (p. 43), or, now, a twenty-first–century audience.

In the *St. Matthew Passion* the insertions provide yet another dimension. Following the designation of his librettist, Picander, Bach set six of the insertions as dialogues between participants called "Zion" and the "Faithful." These dialogues occur at strategic places throughout the Passion. Four of them frame Parts I and II. The other two occur at important climaxes, one in the Gethsemane scene, the other in the Golgotha scene. (See figure 1 on p. 38.)

If the arias and chorales function to bring the modern listener into contact with the ancient story, the dialogues, by identifying one of the participants as Zion, give the story "a wider historical frame," for Zion represents the entire Christian church that stretches from the Old Testament to the New Jerusalem. In these dialogues, then, the Faithful — that is, the body of believers gathered in worship — are in conversation with Zion, the "true Israel," "the messianic community in whom and for whom the law and the prophets are fulfilled" (Minear, 53).

All of this — Gospel narrative, chorales, meditative recitatives, arias, and dialogues — is framed by gigantic choral numbers at the beginning and end of the works. (The *St. Matthew Passion* also has a third one in the middle.) The result is two very large works whose monumentality fittingly corresponds to the importance of the cross in Bach's theological thinking.

Bach's obituary tells us that he wrote five Passions. Two — those according to Matthew and John — have survived complete. A *St. Mark Passion* survives in text only, and, if the obituary is correct, two are completely lost. However, we need not be too distraught that three of Bach's

FIGURE 1: The "Zion/Faithful" Dialogues in the *St. Matthew Passion*

Beginning of Part I
    Chorus: "Kommt, ihr Töchter" ["Come, you daughters"] (no. 1)

Climax of the Gethsemane scene
    Solo and Chorus: "O Schmerz" ["O grief"] (no. 19)

End of Part I
    Duet and Chorus: "So ist mein Jesus nun gefangen" ["Behold, my Jesus
       now is taken"] (no. 27a)

Beginning of Part II
    Solo and Chorus: "Ach, nun ist mein Jesus hin" ["Alas! Now is my Jesus
       gone!"] (no. 30)

Climax of the Golgotha scene
    Recitative: "Ach Golgatha!" ["Ah, Golgotha!"] and
    Aria and Chorus: "Sehet, Jesus hat die Hand . . . ausgespannt" ["Look, Je-
       sus has his hand outstretched"] (nos. 59 and 60)

End of Part II
    Recitative and Chorus: "Nun ist der Herr zur Ruh' gebracht" ["Now the
       Lord to rest is laid"] (no. 67)

Passions are unavailable to us, because the two that have survived would seem to be unsurpassable, if not unmatchable, even by Bach himself. Furthermore, the two that survive complement each other beautifully. It has long been noted that the *St. Matthew Passion* is more meditative and contemplative whereas the *St. John Passion* is more dramatic. But beyond being complementary in character, the two Passions complement each other in theological emphasis. The *St. Matthew Passion* emphasizes the satisfaction theory of the atonement, the *St. John Passion* the *Christus Victor* theory (cf. pp. 113-15). Thus Bach's two surviving Passions stand as musical monuments not only to the theology of the cross in general but to the two main ways by which the church has sought to understand the mystery of the atonement.

* * *

Bach's Passions are a specific type of a broader musical/liturgical genre called *historia*. Passions, of course, tell the history of Jesus' suffering and death directly from the biblical account; other *historiae* tell the histories of the other great events in Jesus' life — his birth, his resurrection, and his ascension. Heinrich Schütz, Bach's greatest Lutheran musical predecessor, wrote *historiae* for Christmas and Easter as well as three Passions. These works are often referred to as oratorios, even though as *historiae* they stand in a very different line from the nonliturgical oratorios of, for example, Handel. Like Schütz, Bach wrote other *historiae* besides his Passions. These, too, are often referred to as oratorios — the *Christmas Oratorio* and the *Ascension Oratorio*. In addition, Bach gave the label oratorio to one other work, the *Easter Oratorio*.

The *Easter Oratorio* is essentially a cantata, differing from the typical cantata only in that it presents a self-contained story told by characters in that story — Mary the mother of James, Mary Magdalene, Peter, and John. Unlike the true *historia*, the *Easter Oratorio* has no Evangelist and the words are not directly from the Bible.

The *Ascension Oratorio*, like the *Easter Oratorio*, is on the scale of a cantata; in fact, it is numbered among the cantatas as Cantata 11. But like the Passions, the *Ascension Oratorio* is a true *historia* since it tells the story directly from the Bible in recitative sung by an Evangelist and soloists who represent the characters. The relative brevity of the *Ascension Oratorio*, in comparison to the Passions, is largely the result of the brevity of the story, a mere six verses taken from Luke, Mark, and Acts.

The *Christmas Oratorio* is another matter. It was written in six distinct parts to be performed on six separate occasions — the First Day of Christmas, the Second Day of Christmas, the Third Day of Christmas, the Feast of Circumcision, the First Sunday in the New Year, and the Feast of Epiphany — and each part can stand alone as a separate piece. Because of that it is sometimes viewed not so much as an oratorio but as a cycle of six cantatas. But Bach did call it an oratorio, and he never seems to have performed any part of it apart from the others in any given Christmas season. And he took considerable care to unify and give coherent shape to the six parts together, particularly in the succession of keys and instrumentation. Above all, the continuity of the story holds the six parts together. Parts I-III tell the story of Christ's birth in typical *historia* fashion as it appears in Luke 2:1-20; Part IV tells of the circumcision from Luke 2:21; and Parts V and VI do the same for the account of the visit of the Wise Men in Matthew 2:1-12. As in the Passions, the story is framed by choruses and interspersed with responses in the form of recitatives, arias, and chorales.

The *Christmas Oratorio* contains many movements that are parodies. A parody movement has music that was originally written for another occasion and has been refitted with new words for the occasion at hand. Parody was a common practice during the Baroque period, but it is a practice with which later centuries, influenced by Romantic notions about the importance of originality, have been uncomfortable. A full-scale defense of the practice is not necessary here, but a few comments may help to forestall thoughts that parodies in general, and the *Christmas Oratorio* in particular, are second-class citizens in Bach's output.

First, there is no way to maintain that Bach resorted to parody because of busyness. Most of his parodies come in the last decades of his life, after his incredible feat of composing cantatas nearly weekly during his first three years at Leipzig, so he was not swamped with compositional deadlines when he was doing most of his parodies. Furthermore, for a composer with the facility of a Bach (or of any other competent Baroque composer), a new composition can hardly have been much more work in most cases than a careful parody.

Second, there is no way to maintain that Bach resorted to parody because of waning creative powers. A composer who could still write the *Goldberg Variations* and *The Art of the Fugue* was not experiencing a loss of creativity. Quite the contrary. His creative powers were never higher.

So why parodies? In Bach's case a clue might be found in the fact that his parodies usually go from secular works to liturgical works. Occasionally they go from liturgical works to liturgical works, very rarely from secular works to secular works, and never from liturgical works to secular works. Could it be that Bach saw in parody an opportunity to preserve some of his finer secular works from falling into total disuse because they had a one-time function? Or could it be that Bach saw the opportunity to give some of his finer secular works a higher function, a function more worthy of the consummate craft that went into them? Take, for example, the *Christmas Oratorio*. When he set out to "compose" it, he had already lavished a great deal of his art on secular cantatas to celebrate the birthdays of various dukes and princes. Why not give that music another chance to be heard? Or even many more chances to be heard? Christmas comes around every year; so does a prince's birthday. But even if the prince would tolerate the same cantata for one of his subsequent birthdays, he would eventually die and the occasion for the music with him. Furthermore, why not let this splendid music serve to celebrate the birth of the King of Kings rather than limit it to the birthday of a minor Baroque princeling?

A final point about the *Christmas Oratorio*. Although it has all the celebrative joy one would expect of a "birthday cantata" for the King of Kings, it does not overlook the reason this King was born. Bach's awareness of the centrality of the cross would not let him overlook it. So just as visual artists sometimes placed the manger within a cross, Bach framed the *Christmas Oratorio* with subtle references to the cross. Near the beginning of Part I, after the Evangelist has sung "the time came that she should be delivered," the first pieces of response are a recitative (no. 3) that brings in Bridegroom imagery and an aria (no. 4) urging Zion to prepare herself to meet the Bridegroom. There is an eagerness in the musical expression and perhaps even a bit of bustle as Zion tries to make her cheeks shine lovelier for the Bridegroom. But then, as if it suddenly dawns on her that all this effort to make herself lovely is futile, we hear the chorale "Wie soll ich dich empfangen" ["How shall I receive you?"]. It is sung to the tune of the so-called "Passion Chorale" (now best known in English with the words "O Sacred Head Now Wounded"). The same tune is sung at the end of Part VI, decked out in the festal, triumphal splendor one expects for a Christmas celebration, suggesting that Bach intended to link the incarnation with the atonement.

Some have questioned whether Bach intended this connection because that melody was used with several different texts. But as Robin Leaver points out, "at least in Leipzig hymnals in use in Bach's time, the other hymn texts sung to this melody all had passion connections" ("The Mature Vocal Works," 98). There seems to be little room to doubt that by using a chorale tune with such close connection to the passion as the first and last chorale movements in the *Christmas Oratorio,* Bach was indeed reminding attentive listeners that Christ was born to die to atone for the sins of his people.

Mass in B Minor

While the Passions have the deepest liturgical roots of all of Bach's music, his *Mass in B Minor* belongs to the richest musical tradition. Liturgically, of course, the Mass is very ancient, having its origins in the earliest years of the church. But the tradition of musical settings of the Mass to which the *Mass in B Minor* belongs goes back only to the late Middle Ages. This tradition consists of more or less musically unified polyphonic settings of the five principal texts of the Ordinary of the Mass, that is, the texts that are the same in every Mass regardless of the day in the liturgical year. The opening words of those five texts are "Kyrie eleison" ["Lord have mercy"], "Gloria in excelsis Deo" [Glory to God in the highest"], "Credo in unum Deum" ["I believe in one God"], "Sanctus, sanctus, sanctus" ["Holy, holy, holy"], and "Agnus Dei" ["Lamb of God"]. Guillaume de Machaut (c. 1300-1377) made the first known contribution to this tradition in the mid-fourteenth century, but the tradition was not established until a century later with the cyclic Masses of Guillaume Dufay (1397-1474). After Dufay, during the next century and a half (1450 to 1600), Mass composition reached its apex, with nearly every major composer contributing to the genre. Some have compared the place of the Mass during this period to the place of the symphony during the late eighteenth and nineteenth centuries. The tradition continued strong through the seventeenth century, but then it waned with the increasing secularization of Western civilization after the Enlightenment. However, it never died out. Major composers after Bach such as Mozart, Haydn, Beethoven, Schubert, Bruckner, and Stravinsky all contributed to the tradition, as did many others. Today composers continue the tradition and have broadened it into popular styles. When one hears of jazz or folk or rock Masses, one can be pretty sure that they are settings of the same five texts of the Ordinary.

The *Mass in B Minor* has a strange history. Bach had no occasion for which to write such a work, and he never heard it performed as a whole. Indeed, it was never performed as a whole during his lifetime, although parts of it, as we shall see, were performed and heard by Bach. Its peculiar history has led some to question whether it is even legitimate to speak of a piece called the *Mass in B Minor*. They doubt that what Bach had in mind was a complete Mass setting (a *missa tota*) and suggest that what posterity has called the *Mass in B Minor* is really a collection of separate pieces. We will return to that question, but first let us look at the order in which Bach wrote the various sections of the piece now referred to as the *Mass in B Minor*.

Three parts of the *Mass in B Minor*, the Kyrie, the Gloria, and the Sanctus, had their origins as separate pieces for specific occasions. The Sanctus seems to have been composed in 1724, since we know it was performed on Christmas Day of that year in Leipzig. Nine years later, in 1733, Bach wrote a *Missa brevis* — that is, a "short Mass" consisting of only the first two texts of the Ordinary, the Kyrie and the Gloria. This *Missa brevis* later became the Kyrie and Gloria for the *Mass in B Minor*. It was originally written, however, for the new Elector, Frederick Augustus II, successor to Frederick Augustus the Strong who died on February 1, 1733. Along with the *Missa*, Bach sent the following letter to the Elector, asking to have an honorary title of Court Kapellmeister conferred on him. Apparently Bach wanted the title in order to strengthen his hand in the many disputes he had with his Leipzig colleagues and superiors.

> To Your Royal Highness I submit in deepest devotion the present small work of that science which I have achieved in *musique*, with the most wholly submissive prayer that Your Highness will look upon it with Most Gracious Eyes, according to Your Highness's World-Famous Clemency and not according to the poor *composition;* and thus deign to take me under Your Most Mighty Protection. For some years and up to the present moment, I have had the *Directorium* of the Music in the two principal churches in Leipzig, but have innocently had to suffer one injury or another, and on occasion also a diminution of the fees accruing to me in this office; but these injuries would disappear altogether if

Your Royal Highness would grant me the favor of conferring upon me a title of Your Highness's Court Capelle, and would let Your High Command for the issuing of such a document go forth to the proper place. Such a most gracious fulfillment of my most humble prayer will bind me to unending devotion, and I offer myself in most indebted obedience to show at all times, upon Your Royal Highness's Most Gracious Desire, my untiring zeal in the composition of music for the church as well as for the orchestra, and to devote my entire forces to the service of Your Highness, remaining in unceasing fidelity Your Royal Highness's most humble and most ardent servant. (*The New Bach Reader,* 158)

Not until very late in his life did Bach supply the remainder of the Mass, completing it in 1749, which made it "the last project of his compositional career" (Butt, 14). To complete the project he added the entire Credo and the Osanna/Benedictus/Agnus Dei et/Dona nobis pacem, much of which, like the *Christmas Oratorio,* is parody. All the sections were bound together and paginated consecutively from beginning to end, suggesting that Bach conceived of it as a *missa tota.* However, he also numbered the sections as follows —

1. Missa
2. Symbolum Nicenum (the Nicene Creed)
3. Sanctus
4. Osanna/Benedictus/Agnus Dei et/Dona nobis pacem

— which suggests a collection rather than a single whole. Still, the weight of evidence supports the argument that Bach intended it to be a *missa tota.* To be sure, at least the first three sections could function separately for different liturgical occasions. The *Missa* (i.e., the Kyrie and Gloria) certainly had liturgical use in the Lutheran liturgy. In addition to the 1733 *Missa,* Bach wrote at least four others. With regard to the Credo, Robin Leaver suggests that "during the late 1730s and early 1740s concerted settings of the Nicene Creed were perhaps becoming more frequent in the Leipzig liturgy" ("The Mature Vocal Works," 117). But it is hard to make a case for an independent liturgical use for section 4. Friedrich Smend was probably the most ardent advocate of the theory that the manuscript is a collection. His advocacy, as John Butt points out, was obviously based more on fear "that the work could be interpreted as evidence of a move by Bach towards Roman Catholicism" (21) than on good evidence. Smend's theory that section 4 contains music to be sung during communion is hardly convincing. As Leaver points out, "The Agnus Dei was certainly *musica sub communione,* but to perform the Osanna and Benedictus at this point, isolated from the *Sanctus* to which they liturgically belong, does not make any sense" ("The Mature Vocal Works," 121).

But if the manuscript was intended to be a *missa tota,* the question still arises, Why did Bach do this? He definitely had no occasion for its use in its entirety; indeed, it was too big for liturgical use. Despite its size and lack of occasion, it would be wrong to see in the *Mass in B Minor* what is clearly the case with Beethoven's equally monumental *Missa solemnis,* whose "obvious overstretching of [the liturgical] context coincides historically with the essential division between music for church and the more bourgeois requirement of religious music for the concert hall" (Butt, 3). It would fly in the face of all we know of Bach's pre-Enlightenment mentality to say of his Mass, as Butt correctly says of Beethoven's, that "At last the mass was released from its serfdom as a mere component of established worship; throughout the nineteenth century it could be taken as a cultural symbol of what was purportedly a 'universal' humanity" (3). Throughout the *Mass in B Minor,* and especially in the Credo, Bach explicitly expressed a Christ-centered, cross-centered faith. To write a work that would be a "cultural symbol of . . . a 'universal' humanity" most certainly was not his goal.

So we are still left with the question, Why did he do it? I think the answer becomes clear when we look at Bach's compositional activity during his last two decades. During that time, a tendency that was already apparent early in his career came to a peak. Bach had what could be called a *summa* mentality. *Summa* carries with it the connotation, not only of summing up and of being encyclopedic, but also of bringing something, usually some area of knowledge ("science" in the old sense), to its highest development. If we look at Bach's entire output, several examples of this are immediately apparent. His *Orgel-Büchlein,* though never finished, was conceived as a collection of chorale preludes for the entire liturgical year; his Brandenburg Concertos are a summation of the styles, forms, and subgenres of the Baroque concerto; his sonatas and partitas for solo violin and cello summarize and bring to their highest development the techniques of string playing; and, not to be overlooked, his cycles of cantatas for the entire liturgical year must be viewed as a bringing to completion of his life's goal, a *summa* of "a well-ordered church music."

During the last two decades of his life his *summa* mentality became especially pronounced. Bach revised and polished earlier chorale preludes, which are now referred to in their final form as the "Leipzig" chorale preludes. He also brought his two great Passions to their final form. He wrote a second volume of *The Well-Tempered Clavier*, which, like the first one, contains twenty-four preludes and fugues for harpsichord, one for each major and minor key. Each of the four volumes entitled *Clavier Übung* is a *summa*. Volume 1 consists of six partitas (suites) for harpsichord. If not by itself, then certainly taken with the six French Suites and the six English Suites he had written earlier, this is a *summa* of the suite genre. Volume 2 consists of the *Ouvertüre nach französischer Art* and the *Concerto nach italiänischen Gusto*, Bach's final word on the French and Italian styles, the two most important national styles of his period. Volume 3 is mainly a collection of chorale preludes based on the chorales for the *Missa* (i.e., the Kyrie and the Gloria) and those related to Luther's catechism. (See pp. 31-32.) Finally, volume 4 contains the *Goldberg Variations*. This tour de force of variation technique also presents something of a summary of canonic writing because every third variation is a canon, making nine canons in all at intervals successively from unison to ninth. To cap off his *summae* on the art of contrapuntal technique, Bach wrote the *Musical Offering* (two fugues, ten canons, and a trio sonata, all based on a theme presented to him by King Frederick II) and *The Art of Fugue* (fourteen fugues and four canons, all based on the same subject).

It seems to me that the *Mass in B Minor* does more than fit comfortably into all of Bach's summing up activity; it crowns it all. It brings together music that spans Bach's career, from "Crucifixus," which is a parody of a movement from an early Weimar cantata, to a movement like "Confiteor," which was composed in 1748-1749. In a broader sense it spans the centuries. It not only employs the high Baroque style but also reaches back to the Renaissance in its *stile antico* ("ancient style") movements and forward at times to the lighter, simpler *galant* styles. (See, for example, the three movements of the Kyrie, which are high Baroque, *stile galant*, and *stile antico*, respectively.) Bach even reached back to the Middle Ages in the "Credo" and "Confiteor" movements, where he incorporated Gregorian chant melodies. Besides its chronological inclusiveness, the *Mass in B Minor* exhibits, as might be expected, the whole panoply of compositional techniques. The first movement alone exhibits, among other things, canonic writing and a fusion of fugue and concerto. But in the *Mass in B Minor*, unlike in his instrumental *summae*, Bach was able to do more than summarize and bring to culmination various styles, genres, and compositional techniques. He was also able to put the whole range of his musical/rhetorical skills to work expressing the Christian faith in the words that Christians had used daily over the centuries and to which most of his great predecessors since the time of Machaut had also devoted their utmost skill.

Bach was viewed by his contemporaries as being behind the times. Just as his thought was decidedly pre-Enlightenment, so was his music out of tune with the new styles spawned by the Enlightenment. These new styles spurned the complexities of Bach's art in favor of a simplicity that the Enlightenment took to be "natural." In 1737 Johann Adolph Scheibe expressed typical Enlightenment thought when he wrote the following criticism of Bach's music:

> This great man would be the admiration of whole nations if he had more amenity [*Ahnnehmlichkeit*], if he did not take away the natural element in his pieces by giving them a turgid [*schwulstig*] and confused style, and if he did not darken their beauty by an excess of art. . . . In short, he is in music what Mr. von Lohenstein was in poetry. Turgidity has led them both from the natural to the artificial, and from the lofty to the somber; and in both one admires the onerous labor and uncommon effort — which, however, are vainly employed, since they conflict with Nature. (*The New Bach Reader,* 338)

The push for "naturalness" and simplicity was part and parcel of the Enlightenment view of music as nothing more than an innocent pleasure. Charles Burney (1726-1814) defined music as "the art of pleasing"; it is "an innocent luxury, unnecessary, indeed, to our existence, but a great improvement and gratification of the sense of hearing" (from Burney's *A General History of Music,* quoted in *Music in the Western World,* 303). His contemporary, the great philosopher Immanuel Kant, said something similar in his *Critique of Judgement.* He placed music lowest on the hierarchy of the arts because "it merely plays with sensations" (*Music in the Western World,* 297).

Bach could not have subscribed to such a low view of music. The "*Gemütsvergötzung,* that 'refreshment of spirit', which his title-pages promised, and which his music so richly provides" (Boyd, 221), is certainly something higher than mere "gratification of the sense of hearing" or playing with sensations. But beyond its being a source of refreshment, Bach saw music as a powerful rhetorical art for conveying the truth of the gospel. And beyond that, he saw it as an art that brought glory to God.

Bach could not help but be aware that the times were changing and that he and his art were being left behind. In his later years he labored to erect monuments to the venerable art of which he was a custodian. The *Mass in B Minor* was the last and greatest of these monuments, a monument to keep alive the memory, not only of the art that went into its making, but also the highest purposes for which that art could be used.

THE CATECHISM
IN BACH'S WORKS

Prologue: My Only Comfort

I n a troubled world, ravaged by injustice, hunger, disease, war, corruption, cruelty, hatred, fear, uncertainty, and, finally, the inevitability of death, we naturally look for something secure and comforting. But looking all around, we find little reason not to lament for ourselves as Jeremiah lamented for Jerusalem because "there was none to comfort her" (Lamentations 1:9). Yet into the perennial human situation God does come, as the carol says, with "tidings of comfort and joy." He told Isaiah to "comfort my people" (Isaiah 40:1). All who love Jerusalem "will nurse and be satisfied at her comforting breasts" (66:11).

For this is what the LORD says:

> "I will extend peace to her like a river,
>   and the wealth of nations like a flooding stream;
> you will nurse and be carried on her arm
>   and dandled on her knees.
> As a mother comforts her child,
>   so will I comfort you;
>   and you will be comforted over Jerusalem."
>
> (66:12-13)

I suspect that one of the reasons for the continuing popularity of Handel's *Messiah* is that its theme, set out so compellingly in the opening tenor solo, is comfort. And I have little doubt that the Heidelberg Catechism is so dear to those who know it because it begins immediately with the question about "my only comfort in life and in death."

Our comfort "in this sad world," as the Catechism describes it, is a topic that looms large in the works of Bach. As a rough-and-ready indicator of how large it looms, we can note that more than one-third of the cantatas contain the noun *Trost* ("comfort") or its adjectival or verbal equivalents. In the eight cantatas that we will be studying in this book, we will encounter it three times. In Cantata 199 the penitent sinner sings:

Auf diese Schmerzensreu	Amid these pains of remorse
Fällt mir alsdenn dies Trostwort bei.	comes to me now this word of comfort.

In the cantata that makes up Part II of the *Christmas Oratorio* the shepherds are told

Dass dieses schwache Knäbelein	that this weak little boy
Soll unser Trost und Freude sein.	shall be our comfort and joy.

And in Cantata 147 the disciple testifies, "Jesus bleibet . . . meines Herzens Trost" ["Jesus remains . . . my heart's comfort"].

Heidelberg Catechism, Q. & A. 1

Q. What is your only comfort in life and in death?

A. That I am not my own, but belong — body and soul, in life and in death — to my faithful Savior Jesus Christ. He has fully paid for all my sins with his precious blood, and has set me free from the tyranny of the devil. He also watches over me in such a way that not a hair can fall from my head without the will of my Father in heaven: in fact, all things must work together for my salvation. Because I belong to him, Christ, by his Holy Spirit, assures me of eternal life and makes me wholeheartedly willing and ready from now on to live for him.

* * * * * * * * *

Motet: *Fürchte dich nicht*

Fürchte dich nicht, ich bin bei dir,	*Fear not, I am with you.*
Weiche nicht, denn ich bin dein Gott,	*Do not give way, for I am your God.*
Ich stärke dich, ich helfe dir auch,	*I strengthen you, I help you also,*
Ich erhalte dich durch die rechte Hand	*I uphold you with the right hand*
meiner Gerechtigkeit. (Isaiah 41:10)	*of my righteousness.*

Fürchte dich nicht, denn ich habe dich erlöset.	*Fear not, for I have redeemed you.*
Ich habe dich bei deinem Namen <u>gerufen</u>.	*I have <u>called</u> you by your name.*
(Isaiah 43:1)	

Herr, mein Hirt, Brunn aller Freuden,	**Lord, my shepherd, source of all joys,**
Du bist mein, ich bin dein:	**you are mine, I am yours;**
Niemand kann uns scheiden.	**no one can separate us.**
Ich bin dein, weil du dein Leben	**I am yours because you <u>gave</u> your life**
Und dein Blut, mir zugut	**and your blood for my benefit**
In den Tod <u>gegeben</u>.	**in death.**

Du bist mein, weil ich dich fasse,	**You are mine because I hold you**
Und dich nicht, o mein Licht,	**and <u>let</u> you not, O my light,**
Aus dem Herzen <u>laße</u>.	**out of my heart.**
Laß mich hingelangen	**Let me come**
Wo du mich, und ich dich	**where you me, and I you,**
Ewig werd umfangen.	**Evermore may embrace.**

Fürchte dich nicht, du bist mein.	*Fear not, you are mine.*

The issue in the motet and in the first question and answer of the Catechism is the same: the comfort of the believer. The Catechism raises the issue as directly as possible by asking the question, "What is your only comfort in life and in death?" The motet is framed by God's comforting words, "Fear not." Both the motet and the Catechism place the source of comfort in belonging to God, the God who saves his children and cares for them. These ingredients for comfort are presented in a different order in the motet than they are in the Catechism, and in the motet they are sometimes presented in imagery rather than in direct statement, but none of the main ingredients of the Catechism answer is missing from the motet. The Catechism moves from belonging ("I am not my own") to salvation ("He has fully paid for all my sins") to care ("He also watches over me"). The motet moves in the other direction. In the opening verse, Isaiah 41:10, God assures his children of his care with the words, "I am with you," "I strengthen you," "I help you," and "I uphold you." Then, in Isaiah 43:1, he speaks of his saving work ("I have redeemed you") and of belonging to him ("I have called you by your name").

In quoting from Isaiah 43:1, Bach made what at first might seem to be a strange omission. The first sentence of that verse in Luther's translation reads: "Fürchte dich nicht, du bist mein, denn ich habe dich erlöset" ["Fear not, you are mine, for I have redeemed you"]. Bach, however, left out the phrase of the verse in which God says, "you are mine." As we shall see, it is not an omission but merely a postponement, for it will come in later. But here Bach omitted the phrase and in its place inserted two stanzas of a chorale by Paul Gerhardt. God has been speaking in the words from Isaiah. Now, in response to God's saying "I have called you by name," the believer says, in the words of the chorale, "Lord, my shepherd." This calls to mind some beloved passages that believers associate with belonging to Jesus. Psalm 23, of course, comes immediately to mind. But this phrase refers even more directly to John 10, where Jesus speaks of himself as the good shepherd who "calls his own sheep by name" and who "lays down his life for the sheep."

As the chorale text goes on, it amplifies on belonging to this good shepherd. In the second line the believer says, "You are mine, I am yours." Here we encounter something that is not explicit in the Catechism answer. The Catechism does not reverse the believer's confession, "I am yours," by adding "You are mine." There are, of course, senses in which a believer can, with scriptural warrant, say to God, "You are mine." If "mine" is changed to "my" and followed by a noun such as "savior," "protector," "lord," etc., there is surely no theological problem in believers claiming that God "belongs" to them. At a deeper level, the scriptural imagery of Christ as the bridegroom and the church as the bride supports the idea of mutual belonging between God and his people. The last two lines of the chorale, in speaking of an embrace, perhaps allude to that imagery.

Several of Bach's works give vivid expression to the Bible's marriage imagery, none more so than the sixth movement of Cantata 140 (see pp. 215-16), a duet sung by a soprano (representing the believer) and a bass (representing Jesus).

Believer:	Mein Freund ist mein,	My friend is mine,
Jesus:	Und ich bin sein,	and I am his,
Both:	Die Liebe soll nichts scheiden.	our love shall nothing separate.
Believer:	Ich will mit dir	I will with you
	in Himmels Rosen weiden,	on heaven's roses feed,
Jesus:	Du sollst mit mir	You shall with me
	in Himmels Rosen weiden,	on heaven's roses feed,
Both:	Da Freude die Fülle, da Wonne	there joy in fullness, there rapture
	wird sein.	shall be.

Nevertheless, legitimate though it may be for a believer to say to God, "You are mine," the Catechism is right in placing the emphasis on our belonging to God. In the reciprocal belonging of God to believer and believer to God, our belonging to God is primary. Bach expressed the primacy of our belonging to God by ending the motet with the words he had omitted earlier — those comforting words of God to his children, "You are mine."

After stating the reciprocal belonging of Christ and believer (or Christ and church, since it operates on both the personal and the communal level), the third line of the chorale speaks of the indissolubility of that relationship. The believer says, "No one can separate us," words that resonate with another of the great comforting passages in the Bible, Romans 8:35-39.

Who shall separate us from the love of Christ? Shall trouble or hardship or persecution or famine or nakedness or danger or sword? As it is written:

"For your sake we face death all day long;
we are considered as sheep to be slaughtered."

No, in all these things we are more than conquerors through him who loved us. For I am convinced that neither death nor life, neither angels nor demons, neither the present nor the future, nor any powers, neither height nor depth, nor anything else in all creation, will be able to separate us from the love of God that is in Christ Jesus our Lord.

The last three lines of the first stanza of the chorale elaborate on the believer's belonging to God: "I am yours," says the believer, "because you gave your life and your blood for my benefit in your death." The second stanza then follows with God belonging to the believer: "You are mine," says the believer, "because I hold you and let you not, O my light, out of my heart."

The chorale ends with a reference to eternal life in the imagery of an eternal embrace. The Catechism also ends with an assurance of eternal life: "Because I belong to him, Christ, by his Holy Spirit, assures me of eternal life and makes me wholeheartedly willing and ready from now on to live for him." The idea in the last phrase about living for Christ does not appear in the motet (though it is the topic of several cantatas). Instead, Bach ends by bringing back the key words of assurance — God saying to the believer, "Fear not, you are mine." Those words, omitted earlier, give the conclusion of the motet the same emphasis with which the Catechism begins. "Fear not," says God at the end of the motet, "you are mine." "My only comfort," says the believer at the beginning of the Catechism, is that "I am not my own, but belong to my faithful Savior Jesus Christ."

Musically the motet is beautifully and ingeniously proportioned. One way of construing the structure of its 154 measures is in two equal parts, a prelude and fugue each seventy-seven measures long. The prelude is sung by two four-part (SATB) choirs in antiphonal style and has Isaiah 41:10 as its text. It ends with the words "Fear not," words that at one and the same time return to the opening words of Isaiah 41:10 and begin the next verse, Isaiah 43:1. The fugue presents the rest of Isaiah 43:1, ". . . for I have redeemed you. I have called you by your name." It is sung by the alto, tenor, and bass voices. Above them the sopranos sing the melody and text of Gerhardt's chorale. This imposing chorale/fugue ends by returning to the double-chorus antiphony of the opening for the final repetition of the key words from Isaiah, "Fear not," plus the phrase that had been omitted earlier, "you are mine."

Another way of construing the structure of the motet is in three parts, each clearly separated from the others by rests, and each proportionally larger than the previous one. The first part is twenty-eight measures long and sets the words of Isaiah 41:10. The second part is forty-five measures long and sets Isaiah 43:1. The final section is eighty-one measures long and consists of the chorale sung by the sopranos over the fugue in the lower three voices on the words "for I have redeemed you. . . ." This final section is framed by two short sections in double-chorus antiphony on the key words, "Fear not. . . ." Reduced by their highest common denominator, the proportions of these three sections are 3:5:9 (or at least as close as possible to that, given that there are 154 measures). These numbers, it might be noted, are symbolically significant. Three and nine (3 × 3) are trinitarian symbols, and five is a christological symbol (cf. p. 17).

These two ways of construing the overall structure of the motet can be made clearer by means of the following figure.

FIGURE 2: The Form of *Fürchte dich nicht*

Measures	2-part form	Text	3-part form	Measures
1-77 (77)	*Prelude*		*Part 1*	1-28 (28 [3])
	à8	"Fürchte dich nicht, ich bin bei dir, Weiche nicht, denn ich bin dein Gott."	à8	
			Part 2	29-73 (45 [5])
		"Ich stärke dich, ich helfe dir auch, Ich erhalten dich durch die rechte Hand meiner Gerechtigkeit."	à8	
			Part 3	73-154 (81[9])
		"Fürchte dich nicht . . ."	à8	
78-154 (77)	*Fugue*			
	à4	(ATB): ". . . denn ich habe dich erlöset. Ich habe dich bei deinem Namen gerufen. (S): "Herr, mein Hirt . . . ewig werd umfangen."	à4	
	à8	"Fürchte dich nicht, du bist mein.	à8	

This complex, yet beautifully proportioned structure is filled with musical-rhetorical devices that not only highlight the meaning of the words but also interpret them. The music not only heightens the expression; it also makes the motet say more than the words alone say.

The opening of the motet effectively brings out the contrast between the first and second halves of the first two lines from Isaiah 41:10 — "Fürchte dich nicht, ich bin bei dir" ["Fear not, I am with you"] and "Weiche nicht, denn ich bin dein Gott" ["Do not give way, for I am your

God"]. In the first line the syncopated entrances and dissonances on "Fürchte dich nicht" ["Fear not"] stand in sharp contrast to the even, sturdy rhythms and the simple, uncluttered cadential harmony on "ich bin bei dir" ["I am with you"]. The fearful, uncertain music of the first half of the line gives way to strong, reassuring music for the second half. At the end of the setting of this first phrase of text, which is nine (3 × 3) measures long, there is a threefold repetition of "ich bin bei dir" ["I am with you"], as if Bach wants to stress that it is the triune God who is saying these words.

The kind of contrast found between the two halves of the first line continues in the second line, where, as John Eliot Gardiner points out, the

> dichotomy is even more pronounced . . . : here the injunction "weiche nicht" ["do not give way"] emerges in the lower voices as a fragmented sigh (the word [in the bass] is actually split down the middle to empha-size the element of doubt and hesitation), to which "denn ich bin dein Gott" ["for I am your God"] is the confident riposte. (Liner notes to ECD 88117)

For the remainder of Isaiah 41:10, Bach's setting emphasizes two words, the verbs "stärke" ["strengthen"] and "erhalte" ["uphold"]. This section begins by declaiming "Ich stärke dich" ["I strengthen you"] in strong, eight-part, block chords, which are led into each time by one part singing a sixteenth-note melisma on "stärke" ["strengthen"]. Then Bach presents the whole sentence — "Ich stärke dich, ich helfe dir auch, ich erhalte dich durch die rechte Hand meiner Gerechtigkeit" ["I strengthen you, I help you also, I uphold you with the right hand of my righteous-ness"] — as an unbroken unit. The rhythm that pervades the whole sen-tence is derived from the phrase "ich helfe dir auch" ["I help you also"] —

It is a rhythm that will play a prominent role later in the work. Here it gives the music a march-like forward propulsion that culminates with even greater forward movement as it drives toward the cadence on the fi-nal words, "durch die rechte Hand meiner Gerechtigkeit" ["with the right hand of my righteousness"]. But in the midst of all this forward move-ment, whenever a voice gets to the word "erhalte" ["uphold"], it holds the word on a long, sustained note (sometimes coupled with a melisma at the end), literally depicting the meaning of the word. At one point the basses sing a long, seven-measure phrase just on the words "ich erhalten dich" ["I uphold you"]. Six and a half of these seven measures consist of long, sustained notes and sixteenth-note melismas on "-halt-" of "erhalten" ["uphold"].

This section ends with all eight parts in succession picking up the last of those melismas, building to a thrilling eight-part climax with sixteenth notes running through all the parts and a long, high melisma sung by the sopranos of Choir I, emphasizing the word "Gerechtigkeit" ["righteousness"].

After a short pause, the words "Fürchte dich nicht" ["Fear not"] return with music reminiscent of the opening, so at first it sounds as if this will round off the first part of the motet. The same words, however, are the beginning of the next verse, Isaiah 43:10. So rather than rounding off the first part, these four measures of "Fear not" do not cadence conclusively. Instead, they lead directly into a fugue on the remaining words of Isaiah 43:1, "denn ich habe dich erlöset. Ich habe dich bei deinem Namen gerufen" ["for I have redeemed you. I have called you by your name"].

The fugue, sung by the lower three parts underneath the chorale in the soprano, is made up of a subject and a countersubject. The subject is always set to the words, "denn ich habe dich erlöset" ["for I have redeemed you"], while the countersubject is always set to the words, "Ich habe dich bei deinem Namen gerufen" ["I have called you by your name"]. It is a long fugue that includes thirty-three statements of the subject, a fitting number for a line of text dealing with our redemption because thirty-three is a christological number symbol (cf. p. 17). One reason for the fugue's length is that it is sung under both stanzas of Paul Gerhardt's chorale. In order to do that, Bach simply wrote a fugue with sixteen statements of the subject to go with the first stanza of the chorale and repeated it for the second stanza, thus making thirty-two statements of the subject. The total of thirty-three results from a short link between the two stanzas, a link containing one statement of the subject.

The effect of this long fugue is to give a great amount of emphasis to the fact of redemption. (The key words, "I have redeemed you," are sung thirty-three times to the fugue subject alone, to say nothing of all the times it is sung to other lines of music.) But the emphasis on this theologically crucial fact is not achieved merely by length and frequent repetition. The subject itself is both striking and meaningful. It begins with three descending half-steps, leaps up a fourth, and then descends three more half-steps. Wherever they appear (and they are nearly ubiquitous) these descending half-steps always strike the ear and hence draw attention to the text. But they do more than simply call attention to the text; they also point to the way redemption was accomplished. During the Baroque period, a melodic line descending in half-steps was almost synonymous with lamentation; it has been called the Baroque "emblem of lament." More specifically, for Bach it pointed to the crucifixion. So the reason for a lamenting subject on the joyful words "denn ich habe dich erlösen" ["for I have redeemed you"] is that Bach wanted to point to the cross and remind the listener of the cost of redemption. But Bach did not leave the subject in a lamenting mode; after the descending half-steps, the melodic line turns upward and the rhythm enlivens to the eighth- and two sixteenth-note rhythm that had dominated the earlier phrase, "I also help you." It is a rhythm found so often in Bach with texts of joy that Albert Schweitzer called it Bach's "joy motive" (*J. S. Bach,* 2:65-66). Thus the first half of the fugue subject reminds us what redemption cost — Christ's death by crucifixion — and the second half expresses the joy it brings.

While the lower three voices are singing the fugue, the sopranos are singing the melody and words of Gerhardt's chorale. All of the text from Isaiah has God speaking to the believer; in the chorale the words are the believer's, sung in response to God for his redeeming work. We noted above that in the previous section Bach left out a short phrase of text. In Luther's translation, Isaiah 43:1 begins, "Fürchte dich nicht, du bist mein" ["Fear not, for you are mine"], but Bach left out "du bist mein" and went right on to "denn ich habe dich erlöset" ["for I have redeemed you"]. We also noted that Bach was not simply omitting the phrase but saving it for the conclusion of the whole motet. But there is more to what Bach did with that important but temporarily omitted phrase, "you are mine." To explain what he did requires a close look at the structure of the chorale text.

Each stanza of the chorale has six lines of text with the following pattern of syllables per line: 8 6 6 8 6 6. The second and fifth lines, however, have internal rhyme, which divides them into 3 + 3. The second line, the one that concerns us here, is the key line expressing the mutuality of belonging, believers to Christ and Christ to believers: "Du bist mein, ich bin dein" ["You are mine, I am yours"]. The remainder of these two stanzas of the chorale expands upon the idea of that mutual belonging. The second half of stanza one expands on "I [the believer] am yours [God's]":

". . . because you gave your life and your blood, for my benefit, in death." Stanza two then elaborates on the other side of the mutuality, "You [Christ] are mine": ". . . because I hold you and let you not, O my light, out of my heart." Then the second stanza ends with the mutual, eternal embrace.

Now back to the music again. As soon as the sopranos have finished the short half phrase of the chorale, "ich bin dein" ["I am yours"] (remember the chorale's words come from the believer), the basses twice respond with God's words from Isaiah 43:1 that Bach had previously omitted, "du bist mein" ["you are mine"]. Bach saved those words until the point where he could introduce them as part of a brief dialogue during the chorale/fugue:

sopranos (the voice traditionally representing the believer):   "I am yours."
basses (the voice traditionally representing God/Jesus):   "You are mine."

The same thing happens after the sopranos sing the fourth line of the chorale: "Ich bin dein, weil du dein Leben . . . gegeben" ["I am yours because you gave your life . . ."]. Again the basses respond with God's words, "du bist mein" ["you are mine"]. The basses' "you are mine" then appears again in the analogous places during stanza two of the chorale and at the end of the fugue after the sopranos' line about eternal embrace. With these bits of dialogue in the chorale/fugue, Bach subtly emphasized that we belong to God.

That same emphasis comes through more obviously at the end. The motet ends as it began with antiphonal shouts of "Fürchte dich nicht" ["fear not"] followed by the double choir emphatically singing God's words, "du bist mein" ["you are mine"], in decorated block chords. So first subtly and then obviously, Bach placed the emphasis on the same side of the mutual belonging as the Catechism does — I belong "to my faithful Savior Jesus Christ" — and by means of the big fugue with its meaningful subject on God's words, "I have redeemed you," he made it clear that this Savior "fully paid for all my sins with his precious blood."

Part I: Death

According to the Catechism, in order for me "to live and die in the joy of this comfort," I must first know "how great my sin and misery are." So Part I of the Catechism deals with sin and misery — and that means death. After God created Adam and Eve and placed them in the garden, he commanded them, "You are free to eat from any tree in the garden; but you must not eat from the tree of the knowledge of good and evil, for when you eat of it you will surely die" (Genesis 2:16). But Adam and Eve did not obey; they ate of that tree and their disobedience led to death, theirs and ours. As Paul put it simply and directly, "in Adam all die" (1 Corinthians 15:22).

Heidelberg Catechism, Q. & A. 2, 7, and 8

Q. What must you know to live and die in the joy of this comfort?

A. Three things: first, how great my sin and misery are. . . .

Q. Where does this corrupt human nature come from?

A. From the fall and disobedience of our first parents, Adam and Eve, in Paradise. This fall has so poisoned our nature that we are born sinners — corrupt from conception on.

Q. But are we so corrupt that we are totally unable to do any good and inclined toward all evil?

A. Yes, unless we are born again, by the Spirit of God.

* * * * * * * * * *

Chorale Prelude: "Durch Adams Fall"

Durch Adams Fall <u>ist</u> ganz verderbt	Through Adam's fall entirely ruined <u>is</u>
menschlich Natur und Wesen;	man's nature and essence.
Desselb Gift ist auf uns geerbt,	The same poison is by us inherited,
dass wir nicht könnten g'nesen	so that we cannot recover
Ohn Gottes Trost,	without God's comfort,
Der uns <u>erlöset</u>	which <u>has redeemed</u> us
<u>hat</u> von dem grossen Schaden,	from the great harm
Darein die Schlang	into which the serpent
Evam <u>bezwang</u>,	<u>forced</u> Eve
Gotts Zorn auf sich zu laden.	God's anger upon herself to take.

    The opening lines of the chorale, "Durch Adams Fall," written by Lazarus Spengler at the outset of the Reformation, are as direct and unabashed a statement of the depth of human corruption as is the Catechism answer. Note the close correspondences between chorale and Catechism. The chorale says that human nature is "entirely ruined"; the Catechism says that we are "corrupt from conception on" and "unable to do any good and inclined toward all evil." The chorale says that we inherit the "poison" of Adam's fall; the Catechism says that "this fall has so poisoned our nature that we are born sinners — corrupt from conception on." And both chorale and Catechism make it clear that this corruption stems from Adam's fall.

    In his collection called the *Orgel-Büchlein (Little Organ Book)*, Bach included a chorale prelude based on "Durch Adams Fall." The chorale melody is stated simply in the top part. Below it are two twisting melodic lines and a peculiarly disjointed bass line. Even with a casual listening the work sounds tortured and twisted, as befits the subject. But when one becomes familiar with the musical-rhetorical devices with which Bach filled the work, something of Bach's deep understanding of this doctrine and his desire to convey it as vividly as possible becomes clear.

Many commentators have pointed out that the twisting inner parts depict the snake in the Garden. No doubt. But the real depth of Bach's understanding of the doctrine contained in the opening words of the chorale is revealed in the musical-rhetorical figures found in the disjunct bass line. These figures were first pointed out in a seminal study by Arnold Schmitz. The bass line is made up almost entirely of dissonant, downward leaps. In Baroque musical-rhetorical theory, such a leap is called a "hard fall." Some of those leaps are major sevenths, a type of musical movement referred to as "contrary to natural movement." Furthermore, there are unresolved dissonances — "misuse" — and lots of rests — "cutting off." Putting all these musical-rhetorical devices together, one gets a good idea of what Bach wanted to express. Adam's fall was a "hard fall" that went "contrary to natural movement" and was a "misuse" of free will. As a result he and all the human race with him were "cut off" from God. And since all of this occurs in the bass line, the part that in Baroque music is fundamental, the chorale prelude expresses that this doctrine is fundamental.

Epistle Lesson: 1 Corinthians 15:1-10

Now, brothers, I want to remind you of the gospel I preached to you, which you received and on which you have taken your stand. By this gospel you are saved, if you hold firmly to the word I preached to you. Otherwise, you have believed in vain.

For what I received I passed on to you as of first importance: that Christ died for our sins according to the Scriptures, that he was buried, that he was raised on the third day according to the Scriptures, and that he appeared to Peter, and then to the Twelve. After that, he appeared to more than five hundred of the brothers at the same time, most of whom are still living, though some have fallen asleep. Then he appeared to James, then to all the apostles, and last of all he appeared to me also, as to one abnormally born.

For I am the least of the apostles and do not even deserve to be called an apostle, because I persecuted the church of God. But by the grace of God I am what I am, and his grace to me was not without effect. No, I worked harder than all of them — yet not I, but the grace of God that was with me.

PART I: DEATH

Gospel Lesson: Luke 18:9-14

To some who were confident of their own righteousness and looked down on everybody else, Jesus told this parable: "Two men went up to the temple ro pray, one a Pharisee and the other a tax collector. The Pharisee stood up and prayed about himself: 'God, I thank you that I am not like all other men — robbers, evildoers, adulterers — or even like this tax collector. I fast twice a week and give a tenth of all I get.'

"But the tax collector stood at a distance. He would not even look up to heaven, but beat his breast and said, 'God, have mercy on me, a sinner.'

"I tell you that this man, rather than the other, went home justified before God. For everyone who exalts himself will be humbled, and he who humbles himself will be exalted."

Cantata 199: *Mein Herze schwimmt im Blut*

1. Recitative

Mein Herze schwimmt im Blut,	My heart swims in blood,
Weil <u>mich</u> der Sünden Brut	because sin's brood,
In Gottes heilgen Augen	in God's holy eyes,
Zum Ungeheuer macht.	a monster makes <u>of me</u>.
Und mein Gewissen fühlet Pein,	And my conscience feels pain,
Weil mir die Sünden nichts	for to me my sins can nothing
als Höllenhenker sein.	but hell's hangmen be.
Verhaßte Lasternacht,	Hated night of wickedness,
Du, du allein	you, you alone
Hast mich in solche Not gebracht!	have me into such need brought!
Und du, du böser Adamssamen,	and you, you evil seed of Adam,
Raubst meiner Seelen alle Ruh	rob my soul of all peace
Und schließest ihr den Himmel zu!	and shut to it heaven!
Ach! unerhörter Schmerz!	Ah! unheard of pain!
Mein ausgedorrtes Herz	My dried up heart
Will ferner mehr kein Trost befeuchten;	will henceforth no comfort moisten;
Und ich muß mich vor dem verstecken,	and I must myself before him hide,
Vor dem die Engel selbst	before whom the angels themselves
ihr Angesicht verdecken.	their faces cover.

2. Aria

Stumme Seufzer, stille Klagen,
Ihr mögt meine Schmerzen sagen,
Weil der Mund geschlossen ist.
   Und ihr nassen Tränenquellen
   Könnt ein sichres Zeugnis stellen,
   Wie mein sündlich Herz gebüßt.
Mein Herz ist itzt ein Tränenbrunn,
Die Augen heiße Quellen.
Ach Gott! Wer wird dich doch
   zufriedenstellen?

Silent sighing, quiet mourning,
you may of my pains tell,
because my mouth is closed.
   And you moist springs of tears
   can a certain witness bear
   how my sinful heart repents.
My heart is now a fount of tears,
my eyes hot springs.
Ah God! Who will you yet satisfy?

3. Recitative

Doch Gott muß mir genädig sein,
Weil ich das Haupt mit Asche,
Das Angesicht mit Tränen <u>wasche</u>,
Mein Herz in Reu und Leid <u>zerschlage</u>

Und voller Wehmut sage:
Gott sei mir Sünder <u>gnädig</u>!
Ach ja! Sein Herze bricht,
Und meine Seele spricht:

Yet God must to me be merciful,
for I <u>am washing</u> my head with ashes,
my countenance with tears;
<u>I am beating</u> my heart in remorse and
grief
and full of sadness I am saying:
God be <u>merciful</u> to me a sinner!
Ah yes! His heart breaks,
and my soul says:

4. Aria

Tief gebückt und voller Reue
Lieg ich, liebster Gott, vor dir.
   Ich bekenne meine Schuld,
   Aber habe doch Geduld,
   Habe doch Geduld mit mir!

Deeply bowed and full of remorse
I lie, dear God, before you.
   I acknowledge my guilt,
   but have yet patience,
   have yet patience with me!

5. Recitative

Auf diese Schmerzensreu
Fällt mir alsdenn dies Trostwort bei:

Amid these pains of remorse
comes to me now this word of comfort:

6. Chorale

Ich, dein betrübtes Kind,	I, your grieving child,
Werf alle meine Sünd',	throw all my sins,
So viel ihr' in mir stecken	as many of them as on me stick
Und mich so heftig schrecken,	and me so sorely frighten,
In deine tiefen Wunden,	into your deep wounds
Da ich stets Heil gefunden.	where I always salvation find.

7. Recitative

Ich lege mich in diese Wunden	I lay myself in these wounds
Als in den rechten Felsenstein;	as in the true rock;
Die sollen meine Ruhstatt sein.	they shall my resting place be.
In diese will ich mich im Glauben schwingen	In them will I myself in faith soar
Und drauf vergnügt und fröhlich singen:	and on them be content and joyfully sing:

8. Aria

Wie freudig ist mein Herz,	How joyful is my heart,
Da Gott versöhnet ist	for God is reconciled
Und mir auf Reu und Leid	and to me after remorse and sorrow
Nicht mehr die Seligkeit	no more the blessedness,
Noch auch sein Herz verschließt.	nor even his heart, is closed.

Cantata 199, a solo cantata for soprano, strings, and oboe, begins unusually with a recitative, and a rather long one at that. Its opening line has the kind of imagery that modern listeners typically find repellent: "Mein Herze schwimmt im Blut" ["My heart swims in blood"]. But if our sin and guilt are as great as the Catechism and the chorale "Durch Adams Fall" say they are, then it has to be admitted that the imagery, repellent though it may be, is not overdrawn.

Other disquieting phrases follow. The soprano sings of "der Sünden Brut" ["sin's brood"], which makes her into an "Ungeheurer" ["monster"] before God's holy eyes. She identifies these sins as "Höllenhenker" ["hell's hangmen"]. She dwells in a "verhaßte Lasternacht" ["hated night of depravity"] and recognizes that the "böser Adamssamen" ["wicked seed of

Adam"] is what robs her of all rest. As Isaiah put it: "The wicked are like the tossing sea, which cannot rest, whose waves cast up mire and mud. 'There is no peace,' says my God, 'for the wicked'" (57:20-21). Later in the cantata, she will come to recognize the same source of comfort spoken of in the first answer of the Catechism, but at this point there is seemingly no way out of the misery. The gates of heaven are shut; there is "kein Trost" ["no comfort"].

Bach's music rhetorically heightens the impact of these words. It highlights the key words with harsh dissonances (both melodic and harmonic) and jagged leaps. A melodic climax is reached by a leap up to an especially harsh dissonance on "Ungeheuer" ["monster"]. An abrupt change of key from G to A♭, which is a very precipitous plunge into the flat key regions, points up the "verhaßte Lasternacht" ["hated night of depravity"]. Then a jagged melodic line gradually ascends to a still higher climax and another harsh, dissonant chord on the words "böser Adamssamen" ["wicked seed of Adam"]. At the same time the tonality reaches its nadir, the key of B♭ minor (5 flats). The phrase then subsides into a tantalizingly peaceful cadence on "Ruh" ["rest"]. But there is no rest, so the melodic line rises once again, this time to reach the highest point of the entire movement on the painful cry that heaven is locked — "und schließest ihr den Himmel zu!"

This is music, as Richard Taruskin puts it, that "cannot be prettified." It is music "to torture the ear" (310). It is music intended to convict the heart of the depth and pervasiveness of sin. It is music that will not let that ugly, painful fact be glossed over.

The three movements that follow — an aria, a recitative, and another aria — all express penitence. Penitence, of course, is the proper response to sin. So these three penitential movements flow naturally from the recognition of the depth of sin shown in the first movement. But it might be wondered why there are three movements, two of them rather long arias. Isn't that a bit much? That question becomes even more pertinent when one notices the disproportion in time between the first four movements and the last four. The first four movements are more than three times longer (about 17 minutes) than the remaining four (about 5 minutes). I think there are three complementary ways to construe this imbalance.

First, one can say that a heavy dose of penitence is needed to counter the depth of the sin portrayed in the opening recitative. Anything less than what Bach provided in movements 2-4 would tend to make the language and rhetoric about sin in the first movement seem excessive.

A second reason for the imbalance, perhaps the most obvious reason, is that the Gospel lesson for the day is about penitence. It is the parable of a Pharisee and a tax collector praying in the temple. The self-righteous Pharisee thanks God that he is not like the tax collector, while the tax collector beats his breast and prays, "God be merciful to me, a sinner." Bach, by virtue of the weight he gave to the three penitential movements, put the emphasis of the cantata where the Gospel lesson put it.

A third reason for the imbalance is subtler, though it is related to the first two. The dramatic progression of the cantata, in both text and music, is in a positive direction. The heart that was swimming in blood in the first movement overflows with joy in the last movement. The tortured rhetoric of the first movement gives way to a lively dance. But the road to the dance is anything but easy. Again one could say that the degree to which Bach and his author might have made it easy is the degree to which the first movement would have been trivialized. An easy journey would have made the first movement seem like much ado about little.

But Bach and his librettist did not make it easy. As Eric Chafe says, the path of Cantata 199 "wavers among the inner states of fear and torment, hope, repentance, entreaty, sorrow, comfort, and, finally, joy" (*Tonal Allegory,* 142). I think that the wavering makes it clear that penitence, though necessary, is not sufficient. Its importance is emphasized in the parable Jesus told in the Gospel lesson for the day, but by itself penitence is not the Gospel. An ingredient is missing. Indeed, it is the fundamental ingredient — Jesus' sacrifice — that is missing. Though a good sermon on this parable would not detail the whole plan of salvation, so as not to dilute the importance of the matter at hand, it would at least point out that salvation is not based on penitence but that penitence can be meaningful only within the context of the saving work of Jesus. There needs to be an answer to the question posed at the end of the middle section of the second movement, a question that Bach highlighted by setting it in a recitative style that halts the flow of the aria: "Ach Gott! Wer wird dich doch zufriedenstellen?" ["Ah God! Who will indeed satisfy you?"]. But in the second movement, the question remains unanswered. The singer simply returns to the beginning of the aria. We hear the same words sung to the same drooping melodic lines and ubiquitous sigh motives in the same C minor key that was the central key of the opening recitative. However sincere, the sighs and tears of the second movement will not satisfy God.

Or will they? The beginning of the following recitative (no. 3) seems to suggest that they will. "Doch Gott muß mir genädig sein" ["Yet God must be merciful to me"], it says, because I anoint my head with ashes and wash my face with tears. So on the surface the cantata seems to be saying that penitence by itself *is* sufficient to merit God's grace. Because of my tears God must be merciful to me — "Gott muß mir genädig sein." That also seems to be what Scripture sometimes says. For example, in 2 Chronicles 7:13-14 God says:

> "When I shut up the heavens so that there is no rain, or command locusts to devour the land or send a plague among my people, if my people, who are called by my name, will humble themselves and pray and seek my face and turn from their wicked ways, then will I hear from heaven and will forgive their sin and will heal their land."

Many other Old Testament passages could be cited. More directly relevant here, though, are two verses from the Gospel lesson for the day, Luke 18:13-14: "But the tax collector stood at a distance. He would not even look up to heaven, but beat his breast and said, 'God, have mercy on me, a sinner.' [Jesus said,] 'I tell you that this man . . . went home justified before God.'"

The cantata quotes the words of the tax collector near the end of the third movement: "Gott sei mir Sünder gnädig!" ["God, be merciful to me, a sinner!"]. Bach highlighted this phrase by starting it on the highest note of the movement and then simply moving down the C minor triad — a musical illustration of the tax collector who "would not even look up to heaven." The downward movement of this phrase contrasts with the prevailing upward movement in the rest of this recitative. Furthermore, this phrase moves mainly in quarter notes rather than eighth notes, a slower, more measured rhythm than the rest of the movement.

But this movement does not end with the tax collector's words. A short, poignant phrase follows, revealing something important about the nature of God. So far the cantata has revealed little about his nature except, perhaps, that he is hard to satisfy. But now the singer tells us something startlingly different. God is a suffering God: "Ach ja! Sein Herze bricht" ["Ah yes! his heart breaks"]. This is a reference to Jeremiah 31:20, where God says:

> "Is not Ephraim my dear son,
>   the child in whom I delight?
> Though I often speak against him,
>   I still remember him.

Therefore my heart yearns for him;
    I have great compassion for him,"
        declares the Lord.

The reference to this text at the end of the movement is not as obvious in this English translation as it is in Luther's German translation. The words that are translated here as "my heart yearns" are rendered by Luther as "bricht mir mein Herz" ("my heart breaks"). These words reveal a suffering God, a God whose mercy runs so deep that his heart breaks!

Again it is the music that highlights the important words. There is an unexpected change of key triggered by a change from a G-major chord at the end of "Gott sei mir Sünder gnädig" ["God be to me, a sinner, merciful"] to a B♭-major chord at the beginning of the phrase that speaks of God's heart breaking. This sudden key change is not only effective in setting off the final phrase; it also sets up a brighter key for the following aria. The ending of a recitative typically sets up the key for the aria to follow. If this recitative had ended with the tax collector's cry for mercy, the following aria would have been set up for another return to the same despairing C minor key that began the cantata. No progress would have been made. But the phrase about God's heart breaking, the phrase that reveals God's deeply merciful nature, turns the music in a positive direction; it sets up the following aria to be in E♭ major. Although E♭ major, like C minor, still has three flats, the progress is clearly audible because the dark minor mode has given way to a brighter major mode.

The following aria (no. 4) continues the penitential theme. Musically it is colored by its pervasive opening musical motive, a falling motive beautifully illustrative of the opening words, "Tief gebückt" ["Deeply bowed"]. But the tone is clearly more positive than that of the second movement. The music has moved to a major key, to a faster tempo (andante instead of adagio), and to a graceful, dance-like triple meter. The sighs have not entirely vanished, but they are infrequent and create little dissonance.

A return to minor keys in the second section of this aria gives it some darker coloring again. That, no doubt, is because one of the key words of the second section is "Schuld" ["guilt"]. Guilt remains, and so the question of the second movement remains, "Ah God, who will satisfy you?" However, there is another key word, the rhyming word "Geduld" ["patience"]. It points again to the merciful nature of God. It is a word that calls to mind another parable, the parable of a servant who owed his king ten thousand talents. Since he could not pay, the king ordered him and his wife and children to be sold. But the servant fell on his knees (cf. "Tief gebückt" ["deeply bowed"]) and said: "Be patient with me [Luther: 'habe Geduld mit mir'], and I will pay back everything." Jesus tells us that "the servant's master took pity on him, canceled the debt [Luther: 'Schuld'] and let him go" (Matthew 18:26-27).

But, of course, the servant could not pay, and neither can we. No one knew that better than Jesus. At times it is necessary to emphasize the importance of penitence and the loving, merciful nature of God. But that is not the whole story. So in the Heidelberg Catechism when the question is asked, "But isn't God merciful?" the answer is, "Yes, but God is also just." In the second part of that answer lies the reason why this cantata does not end with movement 4. A very short recitative (no. 5) leads to the sixth movement, the key movement of the whole cantata. This movement supplies the ultimate "Trostwort" ["word of comfort"] mentioned in the preceding recitative. The ultimate comfort of the sinner is that she can cast all her sins into the deep wounds of Christ — "Ich . . . werf alle meine Sünd' . . . in deine tiefen Wunden. . . ." In Christ's wounds God's justice is satisfied; therefore it is in them that salvation is found — "da ich stets Heil gefunden."

This theologically key movement is musically different from all the other movements of the cantata. It is the only movement that uses a chorale text and tune, and thus it breaks the regular pattern of recitative followed by aria. The simplicity of the chorale melody contrasts with the much more elaborate aria style that a listener expects to hear at this point. But the simplicity does more than set this key movement apart. It also serves as a particularly suitable vehicle for pointing out the humility of the true penitent who is shorn of all delusions that something she might do can purge her sin and remove her misery and who realizes that her only hope is in the wounds of Christ.

Another thing that sets the sixth movement apart from the others is its key. It is in the key of F major, the highest key of the whole cantata (i.e., the key with the fewest flats). Not only is it in the highest key of the cantata, but it also jumps out of the gradual, ascending pattern of keys that had been established in the first five movements. (See figure 3 on p. 73.)

Instrumentation provided yet another way for Bach to set movement 6 apart from the rest of the cantata. The instrumentation of the arias shows a progression from oboe (no. 2) to full string section (no. 4) to full strings and oboe (no. 8). Movement 6 uses only a single low-pitched

FIGURE 3: The Pattern of Key Signatures in Cantata 199

Movements 1-2:		3 flats minor
Movement 3	to	3 flats major
Movement 4		3 flats major
Movement 5	to	2 flats minor
Movement 6		1 flat major (instead of the expected 2 flats major)
Movements 7-8		2 flats major

stringed instrument with the soprano and continuo. (Bach made several different versions of this cantata, but in each case the solo instrument is a low-pitched stringed instrument — a viola, viola da gamba, cello, or piccolo cello.) Just as the key of F major falls outside the overall key scheme, so does the use of a single low-pitched stringed instrument fall outside the overall instrumentation scheme. Its comforting, low-pitched sound is particularly appropriate to the "Trostwort" ["word of comfort"] that the chorale brings.

The final recitative (no. 7) provides a transition to the final aria. Having laid herself in the wounds of Jesus and come to a peaceful cadence on "Ruhstatt" ["resting place"], the soprano soars ["schwingen"] to her highest note of the whole cantata on the word "Glauben" ["faith"] and then reaches it once again as she sings her most elaborate melisma of the cantata on "fröhlich singen" ["joyfully sing"].

Then sing she does in the final aria — along with the full instrumental ensemble of strings and oboe — a song bursting with joy. The question of the second movement — "Ah God! who will satisfy you?" — has been answered. Because of Jesus' sacrifice "Gott versöhnet ist" ["God is reconciled"], his justice has been satisfied. Now after "Reu und Lied" ["remorse and sorrow"] neither "Seligkeit" ["blessedness"] nor God's "Herz" ["heart"] is "verschließt" ["closed"].

Fittingly, this final aria is a dance song; it has the lively rhythm of a jig.

Part II: Deliverance

After considering our being dead in sin in Part I, Part II of the Catechism turns to questions about our deliverance from sin and death,
the deliverance pointed to by the references to Christ's wounds in Cantata
199. The Catechism begins its exposition on deliverance by addressing the
question of what kind of mediator and deliverer is needed. After concluding that the deliverer must be "truly human and truly righteous" and also
"true God," and identifying Christ as the only one who meets those quali-
fications, the Catechism asks, "Are all saved through Christ just as all were
lost through Adam?" The answer is "No. Only those are saved who by true
faith are grafted into Christ and accept all his blessings." There follows a
definition of true faith, an outline of its content in the words of the Apostles' Creed, and an exposition of the meaning of each of the articles of the
Creed.

I will follow but abbreviate the Catechism's order. I will start with
Cantata 61, which deals with the question of what kind of mediator and
deliverer is needed. Then I will discuss Bach's setting of the Nicene Creed
from the *B Minor Mass*. Finally, I will focus on the individual articles of the
Creed, but only the central three that have to do with Christ's saving acts
of birth, death, and resurrection.

What Kind of Deliverer?

Heidelberg Catechism Q. & A. 2 & 12-18

Q. What must you know to live and die in the joy of this comfort?

A. Three things: . . . second, how I am set free from all my sins and misery. . . .

Q. According to God's righteous judgment we deserve punishment both in this world and forever after: how then can we escape this punishment and return to God's favor?

A. God requires that his justice be satisfied. Therefore the claims of his justice must be paid in full, either by ourselves or by another.

Q. Can we pay this debt ourselves?

A. Certainly not. Actually we increase our guilt every day.

Q. Can another creature — any at all — pay this debt for us?

A. No. To begin with, God will not punish another creature for what a human is guilty of. Besides, no mere creature can bear the weight of God's eternal anger against sin and release others from it.

Q. What kind of mediator and deliverer should we look for then?

A. One who is truly human and truly righteous, yet more powerful than all creatures, that is, one who is also true God.

Q. Why must he be truly human and truly righteous?

A. God's justice demands that human nature, which has sinned, must pay for its sin; but a sinner could never pay for others.

Q. Why must he also be true God?

A. So that, by the power of his divinity, he might bear the weight of God's anger in his humanity and earn for us and restore to us righteousness and life.

Q. And who is this mediator — true God and at the same time truly human and truly righteous?

A. Our Lord Jesus Christ, who was given us to set us completely free and to make us right with God.

* * * * * * * * * *

Epistle Lesson: Romans 13:11-14

And do this, understanding the present time. The hour has come for you to wake up from your slumber, because our salvation is nearer now than when we first believed. The night is nearly over; the day is almost here. So let us put aside the deeds of darkness and put on the armor of light. Let us behave decently, as in the daytime, not in orgies and drunkenness, not in sexual immorality and debauchery, not in dissension and jealousy. Rather, clothe yourselves with the Lord Jesus Christ, and do not think about how to gratify the desires of the sinful nature.

Gospel Lesson: Matthew 21:1-9

As they approached Jerusalem and came to Bethphage on the Mount of Olives, Jesus sent two disciples, saying to them, "Go to the village ahead of you, and at once you will find a donkey tied there, with her colt by her. Untie them and bring them to me. If anyone says anything to you, tell him that the Lord needs them, and he will send them right away."

This took place to fulfill what was spoken through the prophet:

> "Say to the Daughter of Zion,
> 'See, your king comes to you,
> gentle and riding on a donkey,
> on a colt, the foal of a donkey.'"

The disciples went and did as Jesus had instructed them. They brought the donkey and the colt, placed their cloaks on them, and Jesus sat on them. A very large crowd spread their cloaks on the road, while others cut branches from the trees and spread them on the road. The crowds that went ahead of him and those that followed shouted,

"Hosanna to the Son of David!"
"Blessed is he who comes in the name of the Lord!"
"Hosanna in the highest!"

Cantata 61: *Nun komm, der Heiden Heiland*

1. Chorus

Nun komm, der Heiden Heiland,	**Now come, the nations' Savior,**
Der Jungfrauen Kind erkannt,	**as the Virgin's child recognized,**
Des sich wundert alle Welt:	**about whom wonders all the world,**
Gott solch Geburt ihm bestellt.	**[that] God such a birth for him**
	ordained.

2. Recitative (tenor)

Der Heiland ist gekommen,	The Savior has come,
Hat unser armes Fleisch und Blut	has our poor flesh and blood
An sich genommen	upon himself taken
Und nimmet uns zu Blutsverwandten an.	and takes us as blood-relatives.
O allerhöchstes Gut!	O highest good!
Was hast du nicht an uns getan?	what have you not for us done?
Was tust du nicht	What do you not
Noch täglich an den Deinen?	still do daily for your own?
Du kommst und läßt dein Licht	You come and let your light
Mit vollen Segen scheinen.	with full blessing appear.

3. Aria (tenor)

Komm, Jesu, komm zu deiner Kirche	Come, Jesus, come to your church
Und gib ein selig neues Jahr!	and grant a blessed new year!
Befördre deines Namens Ehre,	Advance your name's honor,
Erhalte die gesunde Lehre	uphold sound teaching,
Und segne Kanzel und Altar!	and bless pulpit and altar!

4. Recitative (bass)

Siehe, ich stehe vor die Tür und klopfe an. So	*See, I stand at the door and knock. If*
jemand meine Stimme <u>hören</u> wird und die	*anyone <u>hears</u> my voice and <u>opens</u>*
Tür <u>auftun</u>,	*the door,*
zu dem werde ich eingehen und das Abendmahl	*to him will I come in and the evening meal*
mit ihm halten und er mit mir. (Rev. 3:20)	*with him take, and he with me.*

5. Aria (soprano)

Öffne dich, mein ganzes Herze,	Open yourself, my whole heart,
Jesus kommt und ziehet ein.	Jesus comes and enters.
Bin ich gleich nur Staub und Erde,	Although I am only dust and earth,
Will er mich doch nicht verschmähn,	will he me still not disdain,
Seine Lust an mir zu sehn,	[but] his joy [will be] to look on me,
Daß ich seine Wohnung werde.	so that I may his dwelling become.
O wie selig werd' ich sein!	O how blessed shall I be!

6. Chorale

Amen, amen!	**Amen, amen!**
Komm, du schöne Freudenkrone,	**Come, you lovely crown of joy,**
bleib nicht lange!	**delay not long!**
Deiner wart' ich mit Verlangen.	**As yours wait I with longing.**

Cantata 61 and the Scripture lessons on which it is based are for the first Sunday of Advent. One might wonder at first why the Palm Sunday story is the Gospel lesson for the beginning of Advent. The reason, of course, is that this story clearly reveals the humility of Christ. He made his triumphal entry on a donkey, not on a kingly warhorse. His coming into this world was the ultimate act of humility. As Paul wrote to the Philippians:

> Who, being in very nature God,
>   did not consider equality with God something to be grasped,
> but made himself nothing,
>   taking the very nature of a servant,
>   being made in human likeness. (2:6-7)

On its most immediate level, the key word in Cantata 61 is the key word of Advent, *come*. The first movement begins with the emphatic phrase, "Nun komm" ["now come"], and it is repeated three more times. The second movement begins with the announcement that the Savior ["Heiland"] has come ["ist gekommen"] and ends by saying to him, "You come [Du kommst] and let your light . . . appear." The third movement, like the first, begins with a prayer for Jesus to come: "Komm, Jesu, komm."

And in the last movement, "komm" is heard once again. As the cantata unfolds from movement to movement, it proceeds through four different comings: the historical coming of Jesus born of a virgin (nos. 1 and 2), his coming into the church (no. 3), his coming into the believer's heart (nos. 4 and 5), and his coming in glory at the end of time (no. 6).

All of this is most appropriate for the first Sunday of Advent, the season during which believers not only make preparation to celebrate Jesus' coming into this world as a babe in Bethlehem, but also prepare their hearts to receive him daily and to meet him when he comes again at the end of time. All of this also has an analog in Jesus' coming into Jerusalem on Palm Sunday, and so it has a connection with the Gospel lesson for the day. But does the cantata express anything regarding the specific nature of that coming as revealed in the Gospel story? Does it reveal anything about Christ's coming in humility? And does the cantata reveal that this king who came, who comes, and who will come again is qualified to be our mediator and deliverer? Does it tell us that in addition to being true God, this divine king humbled himself to the extent of becoming truly human? It does; but it doesn't reveal that all at once. Rather, the depth to which this divine king humbled himself is revealed gradually through the first five movements.

The cantata begins with a regal movement that proclaims the coming of a king. But already here the point begins to be made that salvation comes from one who is high but who became low. Then throughout the cantata the music, in a variety of ways, points to the descent of the king. The king had to become a servant; God had to become man. Although the cantata deals with several Advent themes, the central theme, that the mediator had to be someone who would be willing to let go of his "equality with God" and descend to be "made in human likeness," is never far from the surface. Whatever else the cantata says additionally, it makes clear what kind of deliverer we have. As the second movement says, he took on "unser armes Fleisch und Blut" ["our poor flesh and blood"] and takes us to be his "Blutsverwandten" ["blood-relatives"].

The first movement is based on a chorale that has ancient roots. Its text is Luther's translation of a Latin hymn from the early Christian era, "Veni redemptor gentium" ("Come, savior of the nations"). Its melody is Luther's adaptation of an old hymn tune that has been commonly associated with "Veni redemptor" at least since the Middle Ages. The chorale is very simple both in its poetic structure and in its melody. Each stanza has four lines; each line is seven syllables long. The melody, correspondingly, has four short phrases. It generally has just one note for each syllable of text and moves smoothly by steps and small skips. The first and fourth phrases are identical, while the third phrase is a close mirror of the second phrase. In the first movement of the cantata, Bach placed this simple chorale tune and the first stanza of its text into an elaborate choral/orchestral setting.

The music of the first movement is in the style and form of a French overture, a type of music that had very familiar connotations for an eighteenth-century listener. As the name suggests, French overtures originated in French opera. During the seventeenth century, French operas typically began with an overture made up of two distinct sections. The first section has a moderately slow pace characterized by pervasive use of dotted rhythms — that is, groups of notes in which the first one is long, taking up three-fourths (or more) of the beat, while the remaining one-fourth (or less) of the beat is taken up by one or more very quick notes. These dotted rhythms give the music a stately, processional kind of movement that was associated with the entrance of the king (in particular, King Louis XIV). The second section is faster and often fugal. The two sections together suggest the kind of pairing of dances that was common in the royal courts — a slow, processional dance followed by a lively one. At the end, the stately, processional style of the first section often makes at least a brief reappearance. The first movement of Cantata 61 has all the earmarks of a French overture. It opens with the orchestra playing in the dotted rhythm style typical of the first section of a French overture. This is followed by a lively second section in fugal style, which concludes with a return to the dotted rhythms of the first section. Into this French overture, Bach inserted the chorale. The first two phrases of the chorale are imbedded in the first section, the third phrase in the second section, and the fourth phrase in the return of the dotted rhythms at the end.

Eighteenth-century listeners would have immediately associated this music with royal splendor. And, of course, that is exactly what Bach intended. This "Heiden Heiland" ["Savior of the nations"] is a king — indeed, he is the divine King of Kings. No music could be too splendid to announce his coming. But this coming was not like the typical coming of a king — all pomp and circumstance that keeps a clear line of division between the king and his people. The difference in the coming of this king is only hinted at in the text. This kingly Savior was a virgin's child ["Jungfrauen Kind"], a bit of information to make one wonder. The music, on the other hand, makes a stronger suggestion that this king is not coming in the typical fashion; he is coming *down*. Bach clearly alluded to the descent of the king by having the choir sing the first line of the chorale four times, once each by the four sections of the choir. The order, significantly, is descending. The sopranos sing the phrase first, followed by the altos, tenors, and basses at successively lower pitch levels. The descent having been made clear, all the voices of the choir join together to sing the second phrase to conclude the first section.

For the second, faster section, Bach constructed a lively, dance-like theme in triple meter out of the opening pitches of the third phrase of the chorale. This creates an affect somewhat different from the one suggested by the verb of the third phrase, "wundert" ["wonders"]. The affect is more of joy and delight than of wonder and amazement. Though the affect of the music is different from what the text suggests, it is not inappropriate. Certainly a response of joy is as appropriate to the coming of a deliverer as is wonder over the nature of that deliverer. Since wonder cannot easily be conveyed by the lively second section of a French overture, Bach chose to keep the conventions of the genre with all its kingly associations rather than disrupt those conventions and associations in order to give a literal rendering of words of phrase three. And since a response of joy is as appropriate as one of wonder, no violence is done to the text. Indeed, it could be argued that by keeping the kingly associations clear throughout the first movement, Bach made the humility that is progressively revealed in later movements all the more telling.

The second movement, a recitative sung by the tenor, begins with an announcement: "Der Heiland ist gekommen" ["The Savior has come"]. By outlining the notes of the C-major triad, the melody suggests a trumpet call and thereby brings in royal connotations again. But then the text goes on and makes a most explicit statement about the degree to which this king lowered himself. This divine king took on himself "unser armes Fleisch und Blut" ["our poor flesh and blood"] and takes us as "Blutverwandten" ["blood-relatives"].

Bach's setting of these lines masterfully brings out the central theological point: this divine king is also truly human; he fulfills both requirements needed to be our mediator. The kingly C major of the first line descends to the darker tonal region of A minor while the melody rises to the highest note sung so far to emphasize the key word, "Fleisch" ["flesh"]. There is also a subtle rhythmic emphasis on "Fleisch." Up until now the tenor has been singing in eighth notes. "Fleisch," however, is lengthened to a quarter note and followed by an eighth rest. This slight lengthening

81

followed by a short rest makes a small but noticeable disruption in the heretofore even flow, highlighting the theologically key word.

The little bit of rhythmic stretching on "Fleisch" has results beyond simply emphasizing that word. Philipp Spitta called attention to what that lengthening does to the declamation. "Bach treats the first period ['Der Heiland ist gekommen'] in the regular manner, but ends the second ['Hat unser armes Fleisch und Blut'] after the word 'Fleisch,' and gives 'Blut' to the following phrase — altogether wrong as regards declamation." Spitta went on to point out how this gives rise "to three *musical* phrases of equal magnitude," thus constituting "a small cycle of beautiful symmetry" (1:508-9). In other words, the three asymmetrical lines of text,

Der Heiland ist gekommen,	[3 stressed syllables]
Hat unser armes Fleisch und Blut	[4 stressed syllables]
An sich genommen	[2 stressed syllables]

were made into three symmetrical lines of three stressed syllables in each:

Der Heiland ist gekommen,
Hat unser armes Fleisch
und Blut an sich genommen.

In addition to producing the "beautiful symmetry" pointed out by Spitta, the regularity of these three lines sets off the fourth line, which extends to five stressed syllables, the third of which is "Blut-" from the key word "Blutsverwandten" ["blood-relatives"], a word that is further emphasized by being approached by an upward leap of an octave to the same high note that was reached on "Fleisch."

The first four lines of the recitative, with their explicit statement that the Savior who has come is fit to be our mediator because he has become our "blood-relative," produce an exclamation, a pair of questions, and an answer:

O allerhöchstes Gut!	O highest good!
Was hast du nicht an uns getan?	What have you not for us done?
Was tust du nicht	What do you not
Noch täglich an den Deinen?	still do daily for your own?
Du kommst und läßt dein Licht	You come and let your light
Mit vollen Segen scheinen.	with full blessing appear.

The exclamation is set at an appropriately high pitch, the highest pitch of the movement, and the questions are asked in an appropriately amazed and thankful tone. The answer, however, receives the most emphasis because the music changes from recitative style to a more aria-like style. The change in style at the end makes this movement what is known as a *recitativo con cavata*. It is a type of recitative "popular in seventeenth-century Italian chamber cantatas. . . . A little aria is drawn *(cavata)* from the last two lines of recitative text. It is usual to call this kind of writing arioso" (Palisca, 325). The change to arioso style at the end serves to highlight the last two lines. More specifically, the music again emphasizes the downward direction of Christ's coming. The melodic motion in both the solo melody and the continuo is pervasively downward. Note, however, that there is always an upward leap to "Licht" ["light"].

Two commentators on the aria that follows (no. 3) characterize it as "warm." Alec Robertson says it is "warmly scored" for unison strings (p. 2), and Claude Palisca says that its beautifully spun-out theme "is the quintessence of warm enticement" (325). That theme, it should be noted — like the continuo part above, which it unfolds — is filled with downward motion. A note of urgency and yearning is added to this warm invitation as Bach rhetorically isolates the word "komm" ["come"] from the rest of the phrase five times (a christological number symbol).

The next two movements (nos. 4 and 5) form a dialogue that represents the final stage in Christ's descent — his entry into the heart of the believer. He came not only so that he might dwell *among* us but also that he might dwell *within* us, making our hearts his home. The dialogue is between Jesus, represented, as was traditional, by the bass voice in the recitative (no. 4), and the believer, represented, again according to tradition, by the soprano voice in the aria (no. 5).

The words of the recitative are Jesus' words of invitation from Revelation 3:20: "Behold, I stand at the door and knock. If anyone hears my voice and opens the door, I will come in to him and eat the evening meal with him, and he with me." Bach's setting of these words is simple yet masterful. Gillies Whittaker calls it not only the "gem" of this cantata but "one of the most priceless treasures of them all." "One can never think of the words," he says, "without their association with the music. No Italian masterpiece of painting brings Jesus so clearly before our eyes as these few bars of simple music" (*Cantatas of J. S. Bach,* 1:148-49).

The accompaniment consists entirely of pizzicato chords, one on each beat, four per measure. This is an obvious musical representation of knocking on the door. Less obvious, but equally important, is the symbolism that Spitta pointed out. The steady, pizzicato strokes symbolize the passing of time by simulating the ticking of the clock or the beating of the heart or both. As Spitta described it, "Anxious waiting breathes out of the *pizzicato* chords which mark the passing of time with steady regularity, like the swings of a pendulum, and measure the hours till the expected One shall come" (1:510).

Although on the surface this accompaniment is simplicity itself, it manages to bring out not only the message of the Gospel lesson for the day but also that of the Epistle lesson. The Gospel lesson, the story of Christ's triumphal entry into Jerusalem on a donkey, showed Christ's coming in humility. Nothing could better represent Christ's humility than the simple, down-to-earth picture in Revelation of him standing at the door knocking and waiting to be let in, and nothing could better represent that humility in music than the childlike simplicity of representing the knocks with steady pizzicato chords. The other image evoked by those pizzicato chords, the passing of time, relates this movement to the Epistle lesson, Romans 13:11-14. In the context of its warning to "put aside the deeds of darkness" because "the night is nearly over," Jesus' invitation, sung to an accompaniment suggesting the ticking of a clock or the beating of a heart, is all the more poignant and compelling.

There is more to the music, of course, than its simple rhythmic plucking of the strings. Harmony and declamation of the text make especially telling contributions to the rich meaning of this movement. Harmonically it begins in E minor on a dissonant chord. Beginning on an unprepared dissonant chord gives the sense that the pizzicato chords did not just begin now but that they have been going on for some time, perhaps since the beginning of time. After several strokes of this dissonant chord in E minor, the music modulates to G major for the phrase "if anyone hears my voice and opens," the modulation being effected, significantly, by the chord on "hören" ["hears"].

Something important also happens in the declamation in the same phrase, again perceptively noticed by Spitta.

> Bars 4 and 5 ... would be a failure in the declamatory ... if the pen of the master had not infused into it an ideal quite apart from the logical distribution of the accent in the words; if it were not treated as a watchman's cry [on the words "If anyone hears my voice"], sounding awfully and mysteriously through the night with a warning to wake up from

sleep, and stand like the five wise virgins ready for the moment of departing. Thus a [foreshadowing] of the Last Judgement is cast over the joyful glory of the festival. (*Johann Sebastian Bach,* 1:510)

This foreshadowing of the last judgment is again related to the Epistle lesson and its warning. It also points ahead to the last movement of the cantata, in which the believers sing with overwhelming joy of their yearning for Christ's return at the end of time, when they will be forever joined with him to eat the "Abendmahl" mentioned in this recitative. Though literally "Abendmahl" means "evening meal," its specific meaning is the Lord's Supper, the Eucharist, Holy Communion.

One final master touch related to the foreshadowing of the last judgment occurs at the end of the recitative. When the words of Jesus are about to come to an end, the music unmistakably approaches a cadence. But the cadence on the last word is deceptive and inconclusive because it avoids the expected tonic chord. This requires another measure in order to end conclusively. Why the deceptive cadence and the resulting extra measure? It seems to me that it suggests Christ delaying his return so that more might be saved, as Peter wrote in his second epistle: "The Lord is not slow in keeping his promise, as some understand slowness. He is patient with you, not wanting anyone to perish, but everyone to come to repentance" (2 Peter 3:9). The deceptive cadence suggests the postponing of the end of time. But the brevity of the cadential tag at the end reinforces the urgency of the Epistle's warning. It also recalls Peter's next words — "But the day of the Lord will come like a thief" (3:10) — and Jesus' familiar words from Revelation: "I am coming soon" (3:11).

In the fifth movement, the soprano soloist, representing the believer, responds to Jesus' invitation by singing "Öffne dich, mein ganzes Herze" ["Open yourself, my whole heart"]. It begins with the simplest of musical motives, a three-note ascending scale. This motive pervades the aria and gives the feeling of opening up. Also pervasive in the movement are the leaping eighth notes in the continuo part, the bottom notes of which are a slightly concealed repetition of the ascending notes of the opening motive. Richard Jeske suggests that these leaping eighth notes depict "an eager anticipation, even a running to meet the Savior" (86).

The second section of this aria changes style to "impassioned arioso" (Palisca, 326). Particularly striking is the ending, where the continuo changes to sixteenth notes as the soprano sings "O wie selig werd' ich sein!" ["O how blessed will I be!"].

As is frequent in Bach's cantatas, Cantata 61 ends with a chorale (no. 6). But in this case Bach did something unique. Instead of using an entire chorale stanza, he used only the last four lines of "Wie schön leuchtet der Morgenstern" ["How Bright Appears the Morning Star"].

Amen,	Amen,
Amen!	Amen!
Komm, du schöne Freudenkrone,	Come, you lovely crown of joy,
bleib nicht lange!	delay not long!
Deiner wart' ich mit Verlangen.	As yours wait I with longing.

By introducing this chorale, Bach brought the subject of the cantata around to the final coming of Christ. The church prays, in poetically decked out language, the words of Revelation 22:20: "Come, Lord Jesus." Even the shape of the chorale text, as it was laid out on the page in early chorale books, calls to mind the eternal feast. As Eric Chafe points out, "This chorale . . . forms a symbolic arrangement of 'Das Himmlische Mahl' ['the heavenly meal'], by means of the visual arrangement of the lines of each strophe in the shape of a goblet" (*Tonal Allegory*, 143). (See below, p. 211, for another example of the same arrangement.) That association, in turn, connects with the words of Jesus in the fourth movement, "werde ich . . . das Abendmahl mit ihm halten" ["I will eat the evening meal (i.e., the Lord's Supper) with him"].

The chorale tune is in the soprano part, while the lower voices supply an especially rich harmonization. The instruments of the orchestra double the voices, as is typical in the final chorales of Bach's cantatas. But this one is further enriched by the addition of a soaring, independent violin part that climbs at the end to a high G, two octaves and a fifth above middle C. Karl Geiringer was no doubt correct when he said that "the indefatigable runs of the violins" and the "dizzy height" they reach at the end, "symbolize the heavenly abode from which the Saviour descended to dwell among [and, we might add, within] mortal beings" (151). But it should be added that this Savior not only descended but also ascended again, and at the end of time he will come down again to bring his followers up with him to his heavenly abode. As the Heidelberg Catechism puts it, "me and all his chosen ones he will take along with him into the joy and the glory of heaven" (Answer 52). Note how the Catechism's words "joy" and "glory" are encapsulated in the chorale's word "Freudenkrone" ["crown of joy"]. The ascending line in the obbligato violin part, then, balances all the descending motion in the earlier movements of the cantata. It points out that Christ descended so that he might ascend and we with him. He came down not only to be with us but also to raise us up from our fallen state and bring us to glory.

Something else has been going on throughout the cantata that also underscores that Christ came down to raise us up. All the while that the text of the cantata is dealing with the *descent* of Christ — first into our history to dwell among us, then into his church, and finally to take up residence in our hearts — the keys of the music progressively *ascend* by thirds from A minor to C major to E minor to G major. This systematic ascent from a minor key with no sharps (A minor) to a major key with one sharp (G major) is a tonal plan in which Eric Chafe hears "anticipation and hope in the events surrounding the coming birth of Christ" (*Tonal Allegory*, 142). Although that interpretation is fitting, it misses a concurrent and even deeper level of meaning. The ascending tonal plan, operating on a less obvious level than the ubiquitous descending melodic lines of earlier movements, represents the lifting up that was the ultimate purpose of Christ's descent, a process that will culminate in the second coming that the church prays for with yearning and eager expectation in the final chorale.

By starting the chorale *in media res* on the word "Amen," Bach achieved two results. First, and most obviously, the "Amen" is a response to the proceeding aria, "Open yourself, my whole heart." It is also a response to the anticipated answer to the prayer of the chorale itself, "Come, you lovely crown of joy!" With amens and with glorious, festive music, this final movement already celebrates the fulfillment of what the words are praying for.

What Must a Christian Believe?

Heidelberg Catechism Q. & A. 20 and 22

Q. Are all saved through Christ just as all were lost through Adam?

A. No. Only those are saved who by true faith are grafted into Christ and accept all his blessings.

Q. What then must a Christian believe?

A. Everything God promises us in the gospel. That gospel is summarized for us in the articles of our Christian faith — a creed beyond doubt, and confessed throughout the world.

* * * * * * * * *

Credo from *Mass in B Minor*

1. *Chorus*

Credo in unum Deum.	I believe in one God.

2. *Chorus*

Patrem omnipotentem,	Father almighty,
factorem coeli et terrae,	maker of heaven and earth,
visibilium omnium et invisibilium.	of all that is visible and invisible.

3. *Duet* (soprano and alto)

Et in unum Dominum Jesum Christum,	And in one Lord, Jesus Christ,
Filium Dei unigenitum	the only-begotten Son of God
et ex Patre natum ante omnia secula.	begotten of the Father before all time,
Deum de Deo,	God of God,
lumen de lumine,	light of light,
Deum verum de Deo vero,	true God of true God,
genitum, non factum	begotten, not made,
consubstantialem Patri,	being of one substance with the Father,
per quem omnia facta sunt.	by whom all things were made.
Qui, propter nos homines	Who for us men
et propter nostram salutem	and for our salvation
descendit de coelis.	came down from heaven.

4. *Chorus*

Et incarnatus est	And was incarnate
de Spiritu sancto ex Maria Virgine,	by the Holy Spirit of the Virgin Mary,
et homo factus est.	and was made man.

PART II: DELIVERANCE

5. *Chorus*

Crucifixus etiam pro nobis sub Pontio Pilato,	He was crucified also for us under Pontius Pilate,
passus et sepultus est.	suffered and was buried.

6. *Chorus*

Et resurrexit tertia die secundum scripturas,	And rose the third day according to the Scriptures,
et ascendit in coelum,	and ascended into heaven,
sedet ad dexteram Dei Patris,	is seated at the right hand of God the Father,
et iterum venturus est cum gloria	and will come again with glory
judicare vivos et mortuos,	to judge the living and the dead,
cujus regni non erit finis.	whose kingdom will never end.

7. *Aria* (bass)

Et in Spiritum Sanctum Dominum et vivificantem,	And in the Holy Spirit, Lord and giver of life,
qui ex Patre Filioque <u>procedit</u>,	who <u>proceeds</u> from the Father and the Son,
qui cum Patre et Filioque	who with the Father and the Son
simul adoratur et conglorificatur;	together is worshiped and glorified,
qui locutus est per Prophetas.	who spoke through the prophets.
Et unam sanctum catholicam	And in one holy catholic
et apostolicam ecclesiam.	and apostolic church.

8. *Chorus*

Confiteor unum baptisma in remissionem peccatorum,	I confess one baptism for the remission of sins,
et expecto resurrectionem mortuorum,	and I look for the resurrection of the dead,

9. *Chorus*

et expecto resurrectionem mortuorum	and I look for the resurrection of the dead
et vitam venturi seculi, amen.	and the life of the world to come. Amen.

The cross is at the center of what Christians believe. So when Bach set the Nicene Creed to music for the *Mass in B Minor*, he placed the

"Crucifixus" chorus (no. 5) in the center. The idea apparently did not occur to him at first, because the words of what is now the "Et incarnatus" chorus (no. 4) were originally part of the duet "Et in unum Dominum." So as first conceived, the *Credo* had eight movements as follows:

1. Chorus: "Credo in unum Deum"
2. Chorus: "Patrem omnipotentem"
3. Duet: "Et in unum Dominum"
4. Chorus: "Crucifixus"
5. Chorus: "Et resurrexit"
6. Aria: "Et in Spiritum Sanctum"
7. Chorus: "Confiteor"
8. Chorus: "Et expecto"

Later Bach took the words "Et incarnatus" and wrote a new choral movement for them. This accomplished two things: (1) it highlighted the incarnation by giving it a movement of its own, and (2) it moved "Crucifixus" to the center of the work, to the fifth of nine movements. Not only was it in the center; it was also surrounded symmetrically by the other movements, making it, most fittingly, the center of a chiastic form (cf. p. 16). Three central choruses are framed by arias, which in turn are framed by pairs of choruses. Each of the pairs of framing choruses has the same structure. The first of each pair (nos. 1 and 8) is in the *stile antico* while the second (nos. 2 and 9) is in the modern, high Baroque style and includes trumpet. In both of the pairs, the two choruses are joined without break. (See figure 4 on p. 91.)

Bach's use of the *stile antico* is especially significant here, but first a word of explanation. The Baroque period began around the year 1600, when Italian composers made a conscious turn away from the contrapuntal style of the late Renaissance. Renaissance counterpoint consisted of vocally conceived parts, all of which were equally important and which typically entered in points of imitation. Melodies and rhythms were smooth. Harmonies were euphonious, with very carefully prepared and resolved dissonance. Although Baroque music grew out of a rejection of this style and developed in quite different directions, the old style never totally died out. In fact, it was consciously kept alive, partly as a respected legacy and partly because it was deemed more suitable for church music than the more theatrical styles of the Baroque. So throughout the Baroque period, side by side with the current styles, the *stile antico* continued to exist. Of

FIGURE 4: **The Chiastic Figure of *Credo* from the**
Mass in B Minor

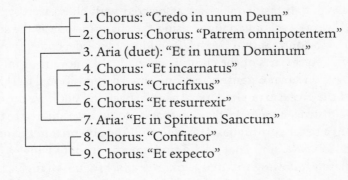

1. Chorus: "Credo in unum Deum"
2. Chorus: Chorus: "Patrem omnipotentem"
3. Aria (duet): "Et in unum Dominum"
4. Chorus: "Et incarnatus"
5. Chorus: "Crucifixus"
6. Chorus: "Et resurrexit"
7. Aria: "Et in Spiritum Sanctum"
8. Chorus: "Confiteor"
9. Chorus: "Et expecto"

course Baroque composers did not slavishly imitate late Renaissance polyphony. Some features of the new styles inevitably rubbed off on the *stile
antico,* but a few features remained quite stable so that the style was easily
distinguishable. Typically *stile antico* pieces are in a duple meter with the
half-note being the unit of beat. The rhythms consist primarily of whole,
half, and quarter notes that move smoothly from longer to shorter notes
and back. There are usually no independent instrumental parts, but the
use of continuo was not uncommon. *Stile antico* pieces usually stay within
a narrow range of keys, avoid striking dissonance, and sometimes retain a
bit of the modal flavor of Renaissance music. The main point, however,
was not to make a perfect imitation of Renaissance music, but to have a
clearly defined style that consciously looked backward and could be
readily associated with the past.

Bach showed a great amount of interest in the *stile antico,* particularly
late in his life. He used it for several movements in the *Mass in B Minor.* Nowhere was it used to greater effect and with deeper significance than in the
"Credo" and "Confiteor" choruses of the *Credo* (nos. 1 and 8). The Creed is
a text that is not only "confessed throughout the world," as the Catechism
says; it has also been confessed throughout the ages. By framing the *Credo*
with choruses in a style that looked back to the past, Bach was pointing to
its timeless truth and expressing his own solidarity with the faith of his
ancestors. It is also significant that the specific words of the two *stile antico*
choruses are "I believe in *one God*" and "I confess *one baptism.*"

Bach was not content simply to write these two choruses in the *stile antico*. He added another ingredient that further expressed unity with the church of all ages. In both the "Credo" and "Confiteor" choruses he used the age-old Gregorian chant melodies associated with those words. For "Credo," Bach wrote a *stile antico* fugue using the chant melody as the subject. The work is a contrapuntal marvel. By adding two independent violin parts to the five voice parts of the choir, Bach made this movement into a seven-part fugue on a preexistent theme — no small compositional feat! Because he used the preexistent Gregorian melody, Bach did not have the opportunity to construct a theme of his own that he could have tailored to the task of writing a seven-part fugue. He had to find the potential in the melody that tradition gave him. That he did find it goes without saying!

Immediately following this marvelous *stile antico* fugue is a fugal chorus in the modern style whose text completes the first sentence of the Creed —

Patrem omnipotentem, factorem
    coeli et terrae,
visibilium omnium et invisibilium.
	Father almighty, maker of
	    heaven and earth,
	of all that is visible and invisible.

This chorus is a parody of the first movement of Cantata 171, or both might be parodies of a lost work.

Bach made some changes in the music from the original, most importantly at the beginning. The cantata is in D major, the key Bach wanted for this movement in the *Credo*. But since this movement completes the sentence begun in the first movement, "Credo," he wanted direct continuity from one to the other. However, "Credo" ends in A major. So he added six new measures at the beginning that provide the required harmonic connection. Instead of starting with the fugue subject in the key of D as the cantata does, Bach started with the subject in the key of A. This A-major statement leads smoothly into the D-major statement, and from there the movement can continue as in the cantata. To the basses' opening statement of the fugue subject on the words "Patrem omnipotentem, factorem coeli et terrae" Bach added the upper three voices singing the words of the opening chorus, "Credo in unum Deum," in strong, declamatory chords. The same declamatory shout occurs in conjunction with the statements of the subject by the tenors and altos, thus making three strong statements of "Credo in unum Deum" as the fugal exposition unfolds.

92

Is there number symbolism in the new opening Bach composed for "Patrem"? It would seem beyond question that the three shouts of "Credo in unum Deum" are symbolic of the triune God. It is also possible that the six additional measures at the beginning are symbolic of the six days of creation, but it must be noted that six measures were added because the fugue subject is six measures long and that the text the subject originally bore has only a tangential relationship to creation. The six additional measures give this movement a total of eighty-four measures, a fact that is intriguing because someone wrote the number 84 at the end, even though there is no practical reason for putting the number of measures at the end of a piece. What makes this intriguing is that 84 is the product of 14 × 6. If 14 is a number symbol for Bach and 6 for creation, the 84 measures could be Bach's cryptic way of affirming his belief in the doctrine being expressed by the text — "I believe in one God, Father Almighty, maker of heaven and earth."

The opening pair of choruses is followed by a duet. It is one of only two movements in the *Credo* that is not choral. The reason for the extraordinary concentration of choral movements at the expense of solo movements is perhaps that Bach wanted to suggest the catholicity of the Creed. The collective voices of the choir better represent the voice of the holy catholic church than do solo voices. But for this much music some solo numbers are needed if for no other reason than for variety. And by their placement, as we have seen, the two arias give the whole a chiastic form. It should be added that they contribute to the form in another way as well. They also serve to articulate the beginning of new portions of the Creed. "Et in unum" marks the beginning of the articles that deal with Jesus Christ, the second person of the Trinity, and "Et in Spiritum Sanctum" marks the beginning of the articles related to the Holy Spirit, the third person of the Trinity. But to think of the two non-choral movements as nothing more than necessary variety and form-giving elements would be a mistake. There is more to them than that.

"Et in unum Dominum" (no. 3) is rich in musical symbolism. It is the third duet in the *Mass in B Minor*. The first two are "Christe eleison" and "Domine Deus." Significantly, all three are texts about Jesus Christ. The duets, with their two voice parts, symbolize the second person of the Trinity and the two natures of Christ, human and divine. Furthermore, all three duets feature canonic writing because canons, consisting of two parts made from one melody, make good symbols of the unity and distinction between the Father and the Son. But in "Et in unum Dominum" Bach went further. As Rilling explains, he expressed

93

this simultaneous unity and difference between the Father and the Son in a single motive, which appears canonically in m. 1 in the two highest orchestral parts and continues to pervade the entire movement. The notes of the motive are identical in both parts, a representation of the common substance of the Father and the Son. But the articulation is different, the last two eighths in the first part being marked staccato, while the same notes in the second part are slurred. The first motive, the stronger of the two, represents the all-powerful Father; the second motive, a gentler musical gesture, represents the Son, begotten of the Father. This perfect musical synonym for the meaning of the text permeates the entire movement. (*B-minor Mass*, 64)

After dealing with the difficult theological questions of Christ's divinity and his relationship to the Father, the next articles of the Creed turn to the work of Christ and the five mysteries involved — his birth, death, resurrection, ascension, and second coming. Bach set these articles in three choruses at the heart of the *Credo*, devoting one chorus each to his birth and death and putting the three events of his exaltation into the third chorus.

Christ's birth, of course, is one of the two events (the other being his resurrection) that trigger the most joyous celebrations of the church. But his birth is also the first step in his humiliation, and that is what Bach emphasized in the chorus "Et incarnatus est" (no. 4). It begins with a heavy and slowly pulsing pedal point above which the violins play a motive that will continue without relief throughout the entire movement. This motive is loaded with meaning, and it all points to Christ's humiliation, his suffering, and, ultimately, his death on the cross. The motive is descending (humiliation), has strong dissonances on nearly every beat (suffering), is filled with sharps (visual symbols of the cross), and, with its alternating up and down movement, forms the traditional melodic shape of the cross in every measure. After three measures the voices come in, one part at a time, one measure apart. The melody they sing is descending, and when they have all entered, they sing together in a solemn, chordal style to the end of the phrase.

The next phrase, "ex Maria virgine," begins with the first and second sopranos, but they are joined after one measure by the lower voices, and the solemn, chordal style continues. The opening notes in the first soprano rise by half-steps. In *Figurenlehre* a line that ascends by half-steps is called a *passus duriusculus,* a "hard way." Here it reinforces the message of the whole movement "that during his whole life on earth," as the Catechism says, "Christ sustained in body and soul the anger of God against the sin of the whole human race" (Answer 37). Additionally, since it occurs on the words "ex Maria virgine," Bach may have wanted to remind us that Mary suffered too. As Simeon said to her when he saw the baby Jesus, "And a sword will pierce your own soul too" (Luke 2:35).

The whole process is repeated in a higher, more intense key (F♯ minor) and then returns to the home key (B minor) for the final words, "et homo factus est." But instead of releasing the tension, this concluding section increases it with a rising sequence that includes the ascending half-step line, the "hard way," in the alto part. Then, following the rising sequence, Bach intensified the cross motives by putting them into the continuo part and writing three canonic imitations a quarter note apart. The canons come to an end in the penultimate measure on a sharp, dissonant chord that resolves into a B-major chord. The B-major chord, however, should not be heard as a "happy ending." B major, with all its sharps, should be heard here as "harsh" rather than "bright." (See pp. 15-16.)

The B-major chord also provides the harmonic set up for the next chorus, "Crucifixus," which is in E minor. This chorus is a parody whose music Bach borrowed from the opening chorus of Cantata 12. The opening words of the cantata are "Weinen, Klagen, Sorgen, Zagen, Angst und Not" ["Weeping, lamenting, sorrow, fear, anxiety and need"]. These anguished words inspired Bach to write one of his most deeply sorrowful movements, and it is not surprising that he returned to it to express the pain and sorrow of the crucifixion.

The movement is built entirely on the chromatically descending bass line so frequently used in Baroque music for laments. In the cantata this bass line moves in half and whole notes. In the "Crucifixus" chorus, Bach kept the same basic rhythm but divided the half notes into two repeated quarter notes and the whole notes into four repeated quarter notes. This is a small change, but the constant throbbing of the quarter notes adds to the intensity of the movement. Bach also increased the intensity by adding two flutes to the obbligato instruments. The flutes and strings play a two-note motive in overlapping antiphony. In the flutes the motives frequently come in pairs that form the traditional cross motive.

The instruments play their motives above the descending bass line once before they are joined by the choir. Then, as in the cantata, the choir sings eleven variations over the repeated bass line. Their descending lines, sighing motives, and very high concentration of dissonance add to the anguished affect. On their eleventh variation they sink down to a cadence on the tonic chord, E minor, low in the range of all the voices. The words at the cadence are "sepultus est" ["was buried"]. The instruments drop out, but the continuo and choir continue for one more variation, repeating the words "sepultus est." Just as the basses are about to reach the bottom of their descending half-step line they turn around, and, in one of the most poignant harmonic progressions in all of music, there is a quiet modulation to G major followed by a moment of pregnant silence before the outburst of joy of "Et resurrexit."

The music that Bach wrote for "Et resurrexit" (no. 6) would be exciting in any context. Coming out of the deep silence following "Crucifixus," it is overwhelming. The silence is broken as the choir and the full orchestra with its three trumpets and tympani burst in all together with a brilliant ascending motive in D major, exclaiming, "Et resurrexit!" From beginning to end the joyful exuberance continues unabated. No doubts intrude upon the vitality of the rhythms or the upward surge of the melodies or the clarity and brightness of the harmonies. "Beyond doubt," as the Catechism says, we believe the unbelievable — "Et resurrexit!"

The movement is divided into four main sections corresponding to the content. (See figure 5 on p. 97.) Each section and most phrases within the sections begin with the upward motive heard at the beginning of the movement. Each section — except section 3, which is given over to a bass soloist — and the concluding orchestral ritornello end with a powerfully rising sequence over a bass line that ascends in half-steps, the "hard way." But with an irrepressible sixteenth-note melisma rising above it, the "hard way" is transformed into a triumphal celebration! The hardest of ways, death, has been defeated! Life is the victor!

After the incredible drama that the three central choral movements present, what can a composer do next? Obviously not more of the same. Contrast is needed, and that is what Bach provided in the second non-choral movement of the *Credo*, the bass aria "Et in Spiritum Sanctum" (no. 7). Probably because it comes in such an unenviable position, "Et in Spiritum Sanctum" has given commentators more problems than any other movement in the *Mass*. They often give the impression that in composing this movement Bach, like Homer, nodded. But they have to admit that even if he nodded, he still wrote beautiful music. As Rilling puts it, "Bach has intentionally created a movement that renounces interest in the text in favor of purely musical values" (*B-minor Mass*, 92).

But are Rilling and the others too hasty in their judgment? It has to

FIGURE 5: The Structure of "Et resurrexit"

Section 1: Resurrection

Et resurrexit tertia die secundum   And rose the third day according to
   scripturas,   the Scriptures,

Section 2: Ascension and Session at the Right Hand of the Father

et ascendit in coelum,   and ascended into heaven,
sedet ad dexteram patris,   is seated at the right hand of the Father,

Section 3: Second Coming

et iterum venturus est cum gloria   and will come again with glory
judicare vivos et mortuos,   to judge the living and the dead

Section 4: Eternal Reign

cujus regni non erit finis.   whose kingdom will never end.

---

be admitted that in this movement neither the quantity of text nor the nature of the text is conducive to the kind of vivid musical interpretation that Bach accomplished in the three preceding choruses. It must have been especially this stretch of text that led Schweitzer to say, "If ever there was a text put together without any idea of its being set to music it is this" (*J. S. Bach,* 2:317). Nevertheless, both Rilling and Schweitzer did make observations about this movement that suggest that Bach's success went beyond simply writing beautiful music for a dry set of doctrines.

Schweitzer looked for and found a key word that may have provided Bach with the overall affect for the movement. "In the dewy-fresh and flowing music of the *Et in unum spiritum sanctum* Bach's imagination had been fired by the word 'vivificantem' ['giver of life']" (*J. S. Bach,* 2:319). Schweitzer's instincts were sound. The flowing and dance-like triplet rhythms are apt for suggesting the life-giving work of the Spirit. His adjective "dewy-fresh" is a fitting characterization of the specific dance-type of this movement. It is a "Gigue-related form . . . tempered by the rather gentle mood of the Pastorale." George B. Stauffer suggests that the reason for Bach's use of pastoral music for the Holy Spirit

> can be found in Luther's gloss of the "et in Spiritum Sanctum" in the Small Catechism, in which he portrays the Holy Ghost as a shepherd who gathers and guides Christians into Christ's fold:
>
>> What does this mean? [The Third Article of the Creed, beginning with "Et in Spiritum"]
>>
>> I believe that neither from my own reason or strength can I believe in Jesus Christ or come to him,
>>
>> Rather the Holy Ghost has called me through the Gospel, illuminating it with his gifts, and has sanctified and preserved me,
>>
>> Just as he has called, gathered, enlightened, and sanctified Christendom throughout the earth, and held it to Jesus Christ in the true and united faith. (130-31)

In addition to having flowing triplet rhythms, this kind of pastorale-gigue has a "simple folksong-like melodic character with euphonious writing in thirds" (Butt, 71-72). The sweet, mellifluous sound of parallel thirds also suggests the affect of love, as their frequent use in love duets attests. They are first heard in the two obbligato instruments, which are oboes, the instrument Bach so often associated with love. In this case they are the type of oboe known as the oboe d'amore (oboe of love). Most likely Bach chose this particular type of oboe because it fit the range he wanted, but if he wanted love to be an ingredient in the affect of this movement, he was no doubt pleased that even the name of the instrument was fitting.

Love certainly makes sense as an ingredient of the affect of a movement dealing with the Holy Spirit. Romans 5:5 says that "God has poured out his love into our hearts by the Holy Spirit," and the first fruit of the Spirit listed in Galatians 5:22 is love. The ancient and widely used Pentecost hymns, "Veni Creator Spiritus" and "Veni Sancte Spiritus," were certainly known to Bach, at least in Luther's translation of them. Each has a line identifying the Holy Spirit with love. Bach's Pentecost cantata *Erschallet, ihr Lieder* [*Resound, You Songs*] (BWV 172) has a dialogue in which the Soul sings to the Holy Spirit, "Höchste Liebe, komm herein" ["Highest love, come in"]. While the dialogue is going on, an instrument plays the chorale melody for "Komm Heiliger Geist" ["Come Holy Ghost"], Luther's translation of "Veni Sancte Spiritus," which contains the prayer, "Kindle your ardent love in them." Another of Bach's Pentecost cantatas, Cantata 34, provides yet another example of how closely love and the Holy Spirit were connected in Bach's mind. Its first line addresses the Holy Spirit as "O ewiges Feuer, O Ursprung der Liebe" ["O eternal fire, O origin of love"]. Significantly, this cantata is a parody that borrows its music from a wedding cantata.

The Spirit's life-giving and love-giving work, then, is behind the overall affect of the entire aria. Within that general affect, various other important details of its long text are highlighted by the music. The text has two main parts. It deals first with the Holy Spirit and then with the church, which was born when the Spirit descended upon the apostles on Pentecost. Bach articulated the beginning of two parts of the text and ensured that they would be clearly understood by having the bass sing the words in syllabic style without the obbligato instruments. Then, within each part he highlighted key words by giving them melismas. In the first part the two words given sizeable melismas are "procedit" and "adoratur," emphasizing the equality of the Holy Spirit with the Father and the Son. The Holy Spirit "proceeds" from the Father and the Son and with the Father and the Son is worshiped and "adored." In the second part three words have sizeable melismas — "catholicam," "ecclesiam," and "apostolicam." These melismas emphasize the church ("ecclesiam") and two of its chief characteristics — it is "catholic" (i.e., universal) and "apostolic." Bach especially emphasized "apostolic" by giving it a melisma *and* having it sung without interference from the obbligato instruments.

Donald Tovey, although he said as little about "Et in Spiritum Sanctum" as most commentators, was right on target with what he did say. "If doctrine is beyond musical illustration, let us illuminate it with musical decoration" (43). With his carefully placed melismatic decorations, Bach illuminated the key doctrines in this text that Schweitzer called a "hard nut for a composer to crack" (*J. S. Bach,* 2:317). But he not only cracked the hard nut; he also gave us lively and lovely music that fittingly represents the Holy Spirit's life-giving and love-giving work.

Bach ended *Credo* the way he began it — with two choruses. The first, "Confiteor," is in the *stile antico,* and the second, "Et expecto," is in the modern, high Baroque style. In "Confiteor," Bach set himself contrapuntal problems of a different sort than in "Credo." This time he did write his own themes, two of them. One was for the first phrase of text ("Confiteor unum baptisma" ["I believe in one baptism"]) and the other for the second phrase ("in remissionem peccatorum" ["for the forgiveness of sins"]). In yet another exhibition of contrapuntal skill, he presented the two themes in a variety of points-of-imitation, both separately and in combination with each other. But he did more. As we noted earlier, Bach used a Gregorian chant in this chorus as well as in the "Credo" in order to emphasize the unity of the church through all ages, and so far none of this music involved the chant melody. But Bach had ideas for how to incorporate the chant melody into this already complex web of counterpoint. Exactly halfway through the movement (measure 73 of 146), he gave the chant melody in half notes to the basses and one measure later to the altos. So while the other three voices continue to work with the two themes, the bass and alto sing the strictest kind of counterpoint — a canon — on a preexistent tune! When the canon was finished, Bach's imagination and skill were still not exhausted. He introduced the chant melody once again. This time he put it into the tenor part in whole notes while the other four parts continued with still more combinations of the two themes. With the two *stile antico* choruses in *Credo,* Bach not only declared his oneness with the church of all ages; he also declared his oneness with her long lineage of skillful composers and with the contrapuntal art with which they had adorned her liturgy through the centuries.

At the end of "Confiteor," the music suddenly slows to adagio, turns sharply in the flat direction, and comes to a half cadence in G minor. Then to a series of slowly unfolding chords we hear the words "Et expecto resurrectionem mortuorum" ["and I look for the resurrection of the dead"]. In the course of this passage Bach did not avoid the obvious word painting of ascending on "resurrectionem" and descending for "mortuorum," but nothing else in it is obvious. Every progression from one chord to the next takes an unexpected turn. The mystery of the harmonies expresses awe and wonder about the final words of the Creed: "I look for the resurrection of the dead." This text will soon be heard again, set to completely different music. It is the only phrase of text in the *Mass* that Bach gave two different musical settings. Obviously, both for musical and textual reasons, the *Credo* needs to end with another celebratory D-major chorus with trumpets and tympani similar to "Et resurrexit." And Bach will not disappoint. In the final movement, "Et expecto," he will give us yet another brilliant chorus in that genre. But before doing so he makes us pause to contemplate the incredible mystery we confess when we say, "I look for the resurrection of the dead and the life of the world to come."

Paul said, "Listen, I tell you a mystery . . ." (1 Corinthians 15:51). Bach, in this remarkable passage at the end of "Confiteor," is saying, "Listen, we confess a mystery: 'We will not all sleep, but we will all be changed. . . . For the trumpet will sound, the dead will be raised imperishable. . . .' Stop. Ponder. Wonder at a marvel beyond our comprehension."

After the contemplation comes the celebration. The harmonies finally do take focus. A half cadence in D major and a direct descent in the continuo to the tonic note lead without break into the final chorus, replete with festive trumpets and marked Vivace e Allegro. It begins with rising, fanfare-like arpeggios in the orchestra and continues with rising motives and ascending sequences throughout as it joyfully repeats and completes the sentence begun at the end of "Confiteor" — "I look for the resurrection of the dead and the life of the world to come. Amen."

*   *   *

These, says the Catechism, are "the articles of our Christian faith — a creed beyond doubt, and confessed throughout the world" — and, Bach would want to add, "throughout the ages." Each of the articles is worthy of further contemplation. But to study a work of Bach on each article would unduly lengthen this introductory guide. So I will limit our further study to three works that go back to the center of the Creed, for the triumphant conclusion hinges on the work of Christ — his birth, death, and resurrection.

Birth of Jesus

Heidelberg Catechism, Q. & A. 35 and 36

Q. What does it mean that he "was conceived by the Holy Spirit and born of the virgin Mary"?

A. That the eternal Son of God, who is and remains true and eternal God, took to himself, through the working of the Holy Spirit, from the flesh and blood of the virgin Mary, a truly human nature so that he might become David's true descendant, like his brothers in every way except for sin.

101

Q. How does the holy conception and birth of Christ benefit you?

A. He is our mediator, and with his innocence and perfect holiness he removes
from God's sight my sin — mine since I was conceived.

* * * * * * * * * *

Christmas Oratorio, Part II

10. Sinfonia

11. Recitative (Evangelist)

Und es waren Hirten in derselben Gegend	*And there were shepherds in the same region*
auf dem Felde bei den Hürden,	*out in the field by the wattled fences,*
die hüteten des Nachts ihre Herde.	*who were tending by night their flocks.*
Und siehe,	*And behold,*
des Herren Engel trat zu ihnen,	*the angel of the Lord appeared to them,*
und die Klarheit des Herren leuchtet um sie,	*and the glory of the Lord shone around them,*
und sie furchten sich sehr. (Luke 2:8-9)	*and they feared greatly.*

12. Chorale

Brich an, o schönes	**Break through, O beautiful**
Morgenlicht,	**morning light,**
Und laß den Himmel tagen!	**and let the heavens dawn!**
Du Hirtenvolk, erschrecke nicht,	**You shepherd folk, fear not,**
Weil dir die Engel sagen,	**because to you the angel says**
Daß dieses schwache Knäbelein	**that this weak little boy**
Soll unser Trost und Freude <u>sein</u>,	**shall <u>be</u> our comfort and joy,**
Dazu den Satan zwingen	**thereby Satan overcoming**
Und letzlich Friede bringen!	**and at last peace bringing!**

13. Recitative

Evangelist: *Und der Engel sprach zu ihnen:*	*And the angel said to them:*
Angel: *Fürchtet euch nicht, siehe,*	*Fear not; behold,*
ich verkündige euch große Freude,	*I announce to you great joy,*
die allem Volke widerfahren wird.	*which to all people will go forth.*
Denn euch ist heute der Heiland geboren,	*For to you is this day the Savior born,*
welcher ist Christus, der Herr, in der	*who is Christ the Lord, in the*
Stadt David. (Luke 2:10-11)	*city of David.*

PART II: DELIVERANCE

14. *Recitative* (bass)
Was Gott dem Abraham verheißen,
Das läßt er nun dem
    Hirtenchor
Erfüllt <u>erweisen</u>.
Ein Hirt hat alles das zuvor
Von Gott <u>erfahren müssen</u>.
Und nun muß auch ein Hirt die Tat,
Was er damals versprochen hat,
Zuerst erfüllet <u>wissen</u>.

What God to Abraham promised,
that he <u>lets be shown</u> now to the
    shepherd choir
fulfilled.
A shepherd had <u>to learn</u> all this before
from God.
And now must also a shepherd the act,
which he at that time had promised,
first <u>know</u> its fulfillment.

15. *Aria* (tenor)
Frohen Hirten, eilt, ach eilet,
Eh ihr euch zu lang verweilet,
Eilt, das holde Kind zu sehn!
Geht, die Freude heißt zu schön,
Sucht die Anmut zu gewinnen,
Geht und labet Herz und Sinnen!

Joyful shepherds, hurry, ah hurry,
lest you too long tarry.
Hurry, the lovely child to see!
Go, the joy is all too fair,
seek grace to gain.
Go and refresh heart and mind!

16. *Recitative* (Evangelist)
Und das habt zum Zeichen: Ihr werdet finden
das Kind in Windeln gewickelt
und in einer Krippe liegen. (Luke 2:12)

And this shall be a sign: you shall find
the child in swaddling clothes wrapped
and in a manger lying.

17. *Chorale*
Schauet hin! dort liegt im finstern Stall,
Des Herrschaft gehet überall!
Da Speise vormals sucht ein Rind,
Da ruhet itzt der Jungfrau'n Kind.

Behold here! there lies in a dark stable,
the one whose majesty surpasses all.
Where food before was sought by an ox,
there rests now the virgin's child.

18. *Recitative* (bass)
So geht denn hin, ihr Hirten, geht,
Daß ihr das Wunder seht:
Und findet ihr des Höchsten Sohn
In einer harten Krippe liegen,
So singet ihm bei seiner Wiegen
Aus einem süßen Ton
Und mit gesamtem Chor
Dies Lied zur Ruhe vor!

So go then hence, you shepherds, go,
that you the wonder may see:
and if you find the Highest's Son
in a hard manger lying,
then sing to him by his cradle
in a sweet tone
and with full choir
this song of rest!

19. Aria (alto)

Schlafe, mein Liebster, genieße der Ruh,	Sleep, my beloved, enjoy your rest,
Wache nach diesem vor aller Gedeihen!	wake after this for everyone's good!
Labe die Brust,	Refresh the breast,
Empfinde die Lust,	experience the joy,
Wo wir unser Herz erfreuen!	where we our hearts gladden!

20. Recitative (Evangelist)

Und alsobald war da bei dem Engel	*And suddenly was there with the angel*
die Menge der himmlischen Heerscharen,	*a multitude of the heavenly host,*
die lobten Gott und sprachen: (Luke 2:13)	*praising God and saying:*

21. Chorus

Ehre sei Gott in der Höhe	*Glory be to God in the highest,*
und Friede auf Erden	*and peace on earth*
und den Menschen ein Wohlgefallen.	*and to men a delight.*
(Luke 2:14)	

22. Recitative (bass)

So recht, ihr Engel, jauchzt und singet,	Then fittingly, you angels, shout and sing,
Daß es uns heut so schön	that it for us today so beautifully
gelinget!	turns out!
Auf denn! wir stimmen mit euch ein,	Up then! we will join in with you,
Uns kann es so wie euch erfreun.	for we can, as well as you, rejoice.

23. Chorale

Wir singen dir in deinem Heer	**We sing to you in your host**
Aus aller Kraft Lob, Preis	**with all our might — praise, honor**
und Ehr,	**and glory —**
Daß du, o lang gewünschter Gast,	**that you, O long-desired guest,**
Dich nunmehr eingestellet hast.	**yourself now have appeared.**

Sin separated the human race from God; it created a humanly un-bridgeable gulf between earth and heaven. A mediator was needed to reconcile God to humankind, to bring heaven and earth together. I know of no more beautiful depiction of that mediation than Part II of the *Christ-*

mas Oratorio, which begins with an instrumental pastorale whose function is to set the scene for the narrative to come — "Und es waren Hirten . . . auf den Felde . . ." ["And there were shepherds . . . in the field . . ."] — but whose deeper purpose is to depict the coming together of heaven and earth.

Pastorale movements abound in Baroque music. Most operas have a pastoral scene. Handel's *Messiah* has a pastoral scene, which, like Part II of the *Christmas Oratorio,* is introduced by an instrumental pastorale (the "Pastorale Symphony" or, as Handel called it, "Pifa"). Later in *Messiah,* for the text "He shall feed his flock like a shepherd," Handel again employed the pastorale style. In the repertory of Baroque instrumental music, there are many concertos known as "Christmas" concertos. They are so called because they contain a movement in pastorale style. Corelli's "Christmas Concerto" is probably the best-known example.

By the time of Corelli and Handel and Bach, certain features unmistakably identified a piece as a pastorale. Pastorales are typically in a compound meter (e.g., 6/8, 12/8, etc.) in a moderately slow tempo. This gives the rhythmic movement a relaxed, lilting feel. They are often in the key of F major (the first key on the flat, i.e., "lower," side of C major), or, if they are in larger, multi-movement works, they are in a key that is on the flat side of the immediate tonal surroundings. This, too, contributes to a quiet, relaxed feel to the music. Harmonies are simple, as befits unsophisticated shepherds. The simple harmonies are often supported by drones suggesting bagpipes. If wind instruments are used, they are typically oboes, suggestive of the reed pipes of shepherds.

As the sinfonia of Part II of the *Christmas Oratorio* begins, we notice telltale characteristics of the typical late-Baroque pastorale — gentle, lilting 12/8 rhythms and the key of G major, the first key on the flat side of the D-major key of Part I. The orchestration is for strings with the violins doubled by flutes, which provide an added sheen without obscuring the basic string sound. Elements not typical of the pastorale are also present in the opening measures: the lack of a drone and the richness of the harmony. Instead of droning, the bass is constantly moving, and above it, instead of a few simple, consonant chords, the upper parts form a rich variety of chords. Dissonances occur in these chords on nearly every strong beat. These, however, are never harsh; rather, they make the harmonies rich and full. So although the music is unmistakably pastoral in affect, its harmonic richness and sophistication make listeners who are familiar with the conventions wonder what this is all about.

In the ninth measure something different happens. A choir of reed instruments (two oboes d'amore and two oboes da caccia) enter, and the strings with doubling flutes drop out. The oboe choir plays the same kind of rhythms as the strings have been playing. But the richness of the strings' harmony has vanished, and in its place we hear the simple harmonies and drone bass of the typical pastorale. The entrance of the oboes initiates three brief exchanges between the oboe and string choirs, making it clear that the main structural feature of this sinfonia is antiphony between the two different instrumental choirs. The oboe choir bears all the earmarks of the pastorale (including its reed-pipe association), while the string choir, although clearly a pastorale in affect, far exceeds the typical pastorale in harmonic sophistication.

As the movement goes on, the exchange between the two ensembles becomes more intricate, and they eventually join together as the simple harmonies and drones of the oboes get drawn into the rich harmonies of the strings. It is all most beautiful, a supreme achievement even for Bach. But does it have anything to do with the story that is about to be told beyond simply conjuring up images of shepherds on a hillside? I think it does, and the key to understanding its deeper meaning is provided by the iconography of musical instruments.

Medieval and Renaissance painters typically depicted angels playing stringed instruments. Wind instruments were reserved for earthly music-making scenes. Of course there were exceptions — the archangel Gabriel playing the trumpet, for example — but the overall association was of stringed instruments with angels. Given that iconographical tradition (a tradition that composers generally followed) and the association of shepherds with reed pipes, it is no great stretch to hear the harmonically rich strings and the harmonically simple oboes as antiphony between angels and shepherd, between heaven and earth. And, of course, that is exactly what the story is about — "Hodie in terra canunt angeli" ("Today angels sang on earth"), as an old Gregorian chant puts it. But this movement suggests something even more marvelous. The shepherds sing with the angels first in alternation, but eventually they are drawn into the angels' harmonies and they sing together, a beautiful musical depiction of heaven and earth brought together, of the reconciliation of God and humankind brought about by the mediator, "the eternal Son of God [who] took to himself . . . a truly human nature."

The rest of Part II unfolds the message of the sinfonia in greater detail and makes it more explicit. Immediately following the sinfonia, the Evangelist, in typical *historia* fashion, begins the story directly from the Bible:

Und es waren Hirten in der selben Gegend	And there were shepherds in the same region
auf dem Felde bei den Hürden,	out in the field by the wattled fences,
die hüteten des Nachts ihre Herde. Und siehe,	who were tending by night their flocks. And behold,
des Herren Engel trat zu ihnen,	the angel of the Lord appeared to them,
und die Klarheit des Herren leuchtet um sie,	and the glory of the Lord shone around them,
und sie furchten sich sehr.	and they feared greatly.

As soon as he sings that the shepherds "feared greatly," the choir bursts in with the chorale "Brich an, o schönes Morgenlicht" ["Break through, O beautiful morning light"]. This familiar chorale speaks directly to the dramatic situation and serves to bring the contemporary worshiper (whether of the eighteenth or the twenty-first century) into the drama. Time barriers are broken as we, the contemporary worshipers, say to the ancient shepherds:

Du Hirtenvolk, erschrecke nicht,	You shepherd folk, fear not,
Weil dir die Engel sagen,	because to you the angel says
Daß dieses schwache Knäbelein	that this weak little boy
Soll unser Trost und Freude sein. . . .	shall be our comfort and joy. . . .

Then the story continues from Luke, with the words of the angel appropriately accompanied by the stringed instruments.

Und der Engel sprach zu ihnen:	And the angel said to them:
Fürchtet euch nicht, siehe, ich verkundige euch	Fear not; behold, I announce to you
große Freude, die allem Volke widerfahren wird.	great joy, which to all people will go forth.
Denn euch ist heute der Heiland geboren,	For to you is this day the Savior born,
welcher ist Christus, der Herr, in der Stadt David.	who is Christ the Lord, in the city of David.

At this point the story is interrupted again, this time for the bass soloist to reflect on the beautiful symmetry between the prophecy and the fulfillment:

Ein Hirt [Abraham] hat alles das zuvor	A shepherd [Abraham] had
Von Gott <u>erfahren müssen</u>.	<u>to learn</u> all this before from God.
Und nun muß auch ein Hirt die Tat,	And now must also a shepherd the act,
Was er damals versprochen hat,	which he at that time had promised,
Zuerst erfüllet <u>wissen</u>.	first <u>know</u> its fulfillment.

The accompaniment to this recitative dealing with shepherds is appropriately given to the oboes, as will be the accompaniment for the bass's other recitative (no. 18), which tells the shepherds to go to the manger. Throughout Part II, Bach was faithful to the iconographical/musical tradition that associated angels with strings and shepherds with reeds.

Following the bass's reflective recitative, the tenor sings an aria (no. 15) urging the shepherds to hasten to see the babe. Two things about this aria might cause a listener to wonder. First, one might expect a very rapidly paced aria to express haste. However, the pace of this aria, though hardly leisurely, is less than hasty, perhaps because Bach wanted something left for two words that appear later in the aria — "Freude" ("joy") and "labet" ("refresh") — both of which he emphasized with very rapid melismas. Since the solo flute also joins in these rapid runs, the last part of the aria expresses haste and joy and refreshment all together.

A second thing a listener might wonder about is the use of a minor key for an aria that urges joyful shepherds to hasten to see the child who brings joy and refreshment. To understand why Bach turned to E minor here, one needs to see what is going on overall in regard to the progression of keys. Eric Chafe points out that Part II "descends from G through E minor (aria, 'Frohen Hirten') to its subdominant, C, for the chorale 'Schauet hin! dort liegt im finstern Stall.'" After the chorale the keys move back up so that Part II "as a whole can be called another of the descent/ascent type" (*Tonal Allegory*, 270). The descent/ascent of keys that Chafe describes takes place in the middle movements (nos. 14-19) and goes from G down to C and back up — or, to express it in key signatures, from one sharp to no sharps back to one sharp. Actually the descent/ascent pattern starts earlier and continues longer, and each step along the way is closely coordinated with the text.

The point from which the descent begins is no. 13, a recitative in which the angel tells the shepherds not to fear, for the Savior has been born in the city of David. It begins in D major and ends in B minor; in other words, it is in two sharps. So the full descending pattern of keys is in descending thirds alternating major and minor keys, except at the end where A minor and C major are reversed. (See figure 6 on p. 109.)

FIGURE 6: **The Descent/Ascent Pattern of Keys in the**
Christmas Oratoria, Part II

no. 13	D major	2 sharps
	B minor	
no. 14	G major	1 sharp
	E minor	
no. 15	E minor	1 sharp
no. 16	A minor	no sharps
no. 17	C major	no sharps

No. 13, being the words of the angel, is appropriately in the highest key, with two sharps. The descent to one sharp occurs in no. 14, where the bass sings of Abraham and the shepherds. No. 15, the aria in question, stays at the level of one sharp in the E minor key that has been associated with the shepherds since the opening recitative of the Evangelist (no. 11). The final step of the descent occurs in no. 16, the recitative that tells the shepherds the lowly state in which they will find the babe — wrapped in swaddling clothes and lying in a manger. The chorale, no. 17, has the contemporary listener contemplating the marvel that

. . . dort liegt im finstern Stall,	. . . there lies in a dark stable,
Des Herrschaft gehet überall!	the one whose majesty surpasses all!

C major is the perfect key for this chorale. In the context of Part II it is the lowest key, fitting for the one who lies in a manger wrapped in swaddling clothes. But in the broader context of key associations in general, C major, the center of the tonal "universe," is appropriate for expressing his "Herrschaft" ["majesty"].

The ascent begins in no. 18, a recitative in which the bass tells the shepherds where to see this wonder. (There is a bit of irony in this. The shepherds were told earlier [no. 15] to hasten to see this babe, but that was before the angel had told them how to find him.) This recitative begins in A minor, rises to C major when the shepherds are told to sing to him ("So

109

singet ihm") in a sweet tone ("süßen Ton" — note the "sweet" chord change here), and in the end modulates to G major, the home key, to prepare for the lullaby aria to follow. G major, however, is not just the home key. The sinfonia established it as the key in which heaven and earth jointly make music. So the key is G major for this lullaby in which the shepherds sing "mit gesamtem Chor" ["with full choir"], implying the angel choir, as it will be in the last chorale (no. 23), in which we all sing with the angels.

But here another question arises. If the lullaby (no. 19), "Schlafe, mein Liebster" ["Sleep, my beloved"], is to be sung by the shepherds and angels together as the preceding recitative states, why is it a solo aria? First, there is simply a matter of balance. There has just been a chorale (no. 17), there will be another at the end (no. 23), and in between there has to be a chorus for the words the host of angels sing (no. 21). If no. 19 also employed the choir, there would be four choral numbers in a row (separated, of course, by recitatives). Overall there would be five choral numbers and only one aria. So it probably barely entered Bach's mind to make this into a choral number. Second, in Cantata 213, a secular cantata from which Bach borrowed heavily for the *Christmas Oratorio,* there was an aria perfectly suited for these words. But Bach did not simply take the aria as it was in Cantata 213. He made some simple but subtly meaningful changes that take into account the suggestion of the preceding recitative — that the shepherds and angels sing this lullaby together at the manger. In fact, with the changes, Bach subtly brought this aria into relationship with the sinfonia, making it another expression of the principal theological theme — that the incarnation brought heaven and earth together.

The changes Bach made were in the instrumentation. It will be recalled that in the sinfonia the strings, doubled by flutes, represent the music of the angelic choir and the oboes represent the music of the shepherds. In the aria from Cantata 213 from which "Schlafe, mein Liebster" was parodied, the vocal soloist was simply accompanied by strings. But here Bach was able to make use of available wind instruments. A flute doubles the alto soloist an octave higher, and the oboes double the strings. Since the alto soloist, according to standard Baroque practice, represents a shepherd, and the flute had been part of the angel choir in the sinfonia, the melody of this aria is performed by a representative from both the heavenly and earthly choirs. Likewise, in the obbligato instrumental accompaniment the heavenly strings and the earthy oboes double each other.

The music of this lullaby to the baby Jesus has many of the characteristics of the pastorale — drone bass, simple harmony, and gently flowing rhythm. The rhythm, however, is not the lilting rhythm typical of the compound meters usually employed in pastorales. Rather, it has an appropriately rocking movement, thanks in large part to the "rocking" octaves in the bass that underlie the main theme in the first eight measures. The melody of the alto and flute features long sustained notes on "schlafe" ["sleep"] and restful descending lines. Gillies Whittaker called it "the most beautiful slumber-song ever written" (2:629). Few, I expect, would quarrel with him.

One more point about this aria. Sleep is a standard poetic metaphor for death. The first line speaks of sleep and rest. The second line speaks of waking, indeed of waking "vor aller Gedeihen" ["for everyone's good"]. Is it too farfetched to read these lines as an allusion to Christ's death and resurrection? Is it reading too much into these lines to hear them as lines that might serve as the "burial lullaby" of a Passion? That Bach seems to have intended such an association is suggested by the remarkable musical resemblance between the opening theme of this aria and the opening theme of the last chorus of the *St. Matthew Passion*. The opening melody of each starts on the third of the scale, has the same shape, and has, with the exception of one note, the same rhythm. Both are in a trio texture with a drone in the bass above which the two upper parts move in parallel sixths. I think Bach, in this aria, was again pointing to the crux of the Christian faith, the cross of Jesus. This aria is a lullaby for the baby in the manger; both its poetry and its musical affect suggest that it is also a lullaby that foreshadows Jesus in the tomb.

Nos. 20 and 21 finish the story. The Evangelist tells that a multitude of angels joined the single angel, and together they sang praise to God. The choir, with the orchestra, sings the song of the angels in high Baroque splendor. The opening phrase of text is sung in a complex contrapuntal texture above a continuo that moves confidently in continuous eighth notes while the oboes and strings toss eighth-note chords back and forth. At "Friede auf Erden" ["peace on earth"], this brilliant, complex texture comes to a halt and gives way to a wonderful hush. Then the irrepressible continuo resumes at "und den Menschen ein Wohlgefallen" ["and to men a delight"], and the voices, now doubled by the strings while the oboes play sustained chords, sing in imitation a new theme that breaks into jubilant sixteenth-note melismas on "Wohlgefallen."

In response (no. 22) the bass soloist not only tells the angels to shout and sing ("jauchzt und singet") but also informs them that we will join them ("wir stimmen mit euch ein"). So the final chorale of praise is sung in an extraordinarily high range — after all, mortals are joining the angels. And along with the singing, the bass instruments provide a rhythmic underpinning reminiscent of the pastorale rhythms of the sinfonia, and in the interludes between the phrases we can hear the shepherds playing their reed pipes. Heaven and earth are united, "God and sinners reconciled" (as a familiar carol has it), thanks to "the eternal Son of God [who] took to himself . . . a truly human nature. . . . He is our mediator [who] removes from God's sight" the cause of separation, "my sin — mine since I was conceived."

Death of Jesus

Heidelberg Catechism, Q. & A. 37, 40, 43, and 44

Q. What do you understand by the word "suffered"?

A. That during his whole life on earth, but especially at the end, Christ sustained in body and soul the anger of God against the sin of the whole human race. This he did in order that, by his suffering as the only atoning sacrifice, he might set us free, body and soul, from eternal condemnation, and gain for us God's grace, righteousness, and eternal life.

Q. Why did Christ have to go all the way to death?

A. Because God's justice and truth demand it: only the death of God's Son could pay for our sin.

Q. What . . . advantage do we receive from Christ's sacrifice and death on the cross?

A. Through Christ's death our old selves are crucified, put to death, and buried with him, so that the evil desires of the flesh may no longer rule us, but that instead we may dedicate ourselves as an offering of gratitude to him.

Q. Why does the creed add, "He descended to hell"?

A. To assure me in times of personal crisis and temptation that Christ my
   Lord, by suffering unspeakable anguish, pain, and terror of soul, especially
   on the cross but also earlier, has delivered me from the anguish and torment
   of hell.

In the course of the church's history, three theories of the atonement
have come to the fore — the *Christus Victor* theory, the satisfaction theory,
and the example theory.

The example theory need not detain us here. Orthodox Christian
theology has never accepted the idea that we can atone for our sins by following Christ's example. To be sure, the theme of imitating Christ is a biblical one, but it belongs to our response for our atonement, not to the
means by which our atonement is accomplished.

The *Christus Victor* theory was developed primarily by the Greek fathers of the church. It pictures the atonement

> as an action directed by God through Christ against the enemies of hu-
> manity: sin, death, the fallen world, and the devil. These enemies hold
> mankind in thrall, illegitimately but effectively, until their hold is bro-
> ken by the cross of Christ. . . . There are infinite permutations of the
> theme, as the Greek fathers rang the changes of metaphor and imagery
> to celebrate the triumph of the heroic Christ and his *nikopoios stauros,*
> the victorious cross. (Pelikan, 106-7)

The *Christus Victor* theory has its origins in biblical passages like
1 John 3:8: "He who does what is sinful is of the devil, because the devil
has been sinning from the beginning. The reason the Son of God appeared was to destroy the devil's work"; and Colossians 2:15: "And having disarmed the powers and authorities, he made a public spectacle of
them, triumphing over them by the cross." Ultimately the roots of this
theory go back to the words of God to the serpent in the Garden of
Eden: "And I will put enmity between you and the woman, between your
offspring and hers; he will crush your head, and you will strike his heel"
(Genesis 3:15).

The satisfaction theory sees the atonement as a sacrifice of the guiltless for the guilty. Like the *Christus Victor* theory, it also has biblical origins.
Paul's letter to the Romans is the central source for this theory.

But now a righteousness from God, apart from law, has been made known, to which the Law and the Prophets testify. This righteousness from God comes through faith in Jesus Christ to all who believe. There is no difference, for all have sinned and fall short of the glory of God, and are justified freely by his grace through the redemption that came by Christ Jesus. God presented him as a sacrifice of atonement, through faith in his blood. He did this to demonstrate his justice, because in his forbearance he had left the sins committed beforehand unpunished — he did it to demonstrate his justice at the present time, so as to be just and the one who justifies those who have faith in Jesus. (3:21-26)

Like the *Christus Victor* theory, the satisfaction theory has roots deep in the Old Testament, for example in the sacrifices the people of Israel were directed to perform and in the famous "suffering servant" chapter in Isaiah.

But he was pierced for our transgressions,
    he was crushed for our iniquities;
the punishment that brought us peace was upon him,
    and by his wounds we are healed.
We all, like sheep, have gone astray,
    each of us has turned to his own way;
and the Lord has laid on him
    the iniquity of us all. (53:5-6)

However, the satisfaction theory did not receive doctrinal formulation until rather late. It was the medieval theologian Anselm (1033-1109) who first formulated it in his treatise entitled *Cur Deus Homo?* [*Why Did God Become Man?*].

Man, said Anselm, has infinitely offended God's honor by his sin, and thus owes an infinite satisfaction. He has to pay back with interest the honor he has stolen. In fact, his debt keeps mounting. . . . So, in Christ, God Himself becomes man. Because He is man, He is able to satisfy in the same human nature in which the disobedience was first committed. . . . And, because He is wholly divine, the offering of His sinless life has infinite worth. Thus Christ earns surplus merits which may be credited or "imputed" to our account. In this way, God's honor and justice are satisfied "vicariously" (i.e., by another). (Plantinga, 81-82)

The satisfaction theory became the consensus explanation of the atonement during the Reformation. It became "more firmly entrenched in Protestant theology than in Roman Catholic theology. By Bach's time it was the touchstone of authentic [Protestant] orthodoxy" (Pelikan, 94). It is interesting to note that Erdmann Neumeister, the influential author of cantata texts in the early eighteenth century (cf. pp. 21-23), wrote a treatise entitled *Solid Proof that Christ Jesus Has Rendered Satisfaction for Us and Our Sins*. In its preface he wrote that this "most precious doctrine of the satisfaction and merit of our Lord and Savior Jesus Christ" is so fundamental that "without knowledge of it and faith in it we cannot be saved" (quoted in Pelikan, 94).

Given this historical development, it is not surprising that the language of the Heidelberg Catechism resonates more with the satisfaction theory. Christ's suffering was "the only atoning sacrifice." In his suffering, he sustained "the anger of God against the sin of the whole human race." He had to suffer all the way to death because "only the death of God's Son could pay for our sins." *Christus Victor,* however, is not entirely absent. When the Catechism speaks of Christ setting us free and delivering us, it is using language that resonates with the *Christus Victor* theory.

Bach was able to depict both theories by writing two Passions, one emphasizing *Christus Victor,* the other emphasizing satisfaction. Furthermore, in writing these two very large works, Bach was not only able to give each theory of atonement more or less equal emphasis, but he was also able to bring out several important themes that arise out of Christ's suffering and death. One of these, the theme of discipleship, is emphasized in both Passions. The Catechism also emphasizes it when it answers the question, "What advantage do we receive from Christ's sacrifice and death on the cross?" Its answer points ahead to the theme of the third main section of the Catechism — living a life of gratitude — and to the discipleship theme that is prominent not only in Bach's Passions but throughout his cantatas as well. "Through Christ's death our old selves are crucified . . . so that . . . we may dedicate ourselves as an offering of gratitude to him."

Since Bach's Passions are so rich in theological themes, it would be impossible to deal with them all in one chapter of this book. Nevertheless, I want to reveal at least some of the theological and devotional wealth in these unmatched works. So I will steer a middle course between dealing only with the two main theories of the atonement and trying to be exhaustive. I will discuss three important theological themes in each of the Passions. For each I will discuss the theory of atonement they emphasize; and

115

for each I will also discuss discipleship. The third theme for the *St. John Passion* will be the freedom of the Christian; for the *St. Matthew Passion,* it will be Luther's three stages in the contemplation of Christ's passion.

*   *   *

There is a prayer in book X of St. Augustine's *Confessions* that strikes me as containing the sum and substance of the *St. John Passion.* What Augustine said so eloquently in the *Confessions,* Bach, with equal eloquence, magnified in the *St. John Passion.*

> How have you loved us, good Father: you did not "spare your only Son but delivered him up for us sinners." How you have loved us, for whose sake "he did not think it a usurpation to be equal to you and was made subject to the death of the cross." He was the only one to be "free among the dead." He had the power to lay down his soul and power to take it back again. For us he was victorious before you and victor because he was victim. For us before you he is priest and sacrifice, and priest because he is sacrifice. Before you he makes us sons instead of servants by being born of you and being servant to us. (X.43)

In particular, the central part of Augustine's prayer articulates the main theme of the *St. John Passion.* The sentence "He had the power to lay down his soul and power to take it back again" is almost a direct quotation of John 10:18, and the next sentence succinctly expresses the *Christus Victor* theory of the atonement: "For us he was victorious before you and victor because he was victim."

The *St. John Passion,* as Jaroslav Pelikan says, is "a celebration of the theme of 'Christus Victor.'" He sees the key to understanding the *St. John Passion* in Bach's treatment of Christ's words, "It is finished."

> There was . . . something of a consensus, at least among Calvinists and Lutherans, that "It is finished" meant the completion of the perfect sacrifice of the cross, by which the justice of God was satisfied and full propitiation obtained.
>
> "It is finished" becomes something quite different from that consensus in Bach's commentary on it [in the *St. John Passion*]. As the alto ponders this word from the cross, the first reaction reflects the interpreta-

tion set forth by Samuel Werenfels [a Lutheran contemporary of Bach's] and John Calvin:

> Es ist vollbracht, es ist vollbracht,
> O Trost für die gekrankten Seelen.
> Die Trauernacht, die Trauernacht
> Lässt mich die letzte Stunde zählen.

> [It is fulfilled, it is fulfilled,
> O rest for all afflicted spirits.
> This night of woe, this night of woe,
> The final hour is passing slow before me.]

Then there is a rest and a change of tempo. . . . Excitement in the orchestra prepares the audience, but does not quite prepare it, for the second half of the aria:

> Der Held aus Juda siegt mit Macht,
> Und schliesst den Kampf.
> Est ist vollbracht!

> [Victorious Judah's hero fights
> And ends the strife.
> It is finished!]

The mood has altered, the scene has shifted: from the altar of sacrifice to the arena of conflict, from propitiation to victory. (105-6)

Just as Bach would look back to the Middle Ages and Anselm's satisfaction theory of the atonement when he later wrote the *St. Matthew Passion,* so too in the *St. John Passion* he looked back, this time to the early Christian era, to the Greek fathers like Gregory of Nyssa. "Bach's *Saint John Passion* is the vindication . . . of . . . the theory of 'Christus Victor,' for which Bach had to reach over Protestant Orthodoxy to Luther, and over the Middle Ages to the Greek church fathers of the early Christian centuries" (Pelikan, 106).

But the ultimate source for the *Christus Victor* emphasis in the *St. John Passion* was John himself. Bach needed to look no further than John's Gospel, for it consistently portrays the power and glory of Jesus the King. Already the first chapter rings with that theme: "We have seen his glory, the glory of the one and only Son, who came from the Father, full of grace and truth" (1:14). Later in the chapter we hear Nathanael declaring, "Rabbi, you are the Son of God; you are the King of Israel" (1:49).

In John's Passion narrative there are several details that again serve to emphasize Jesus' power and glory. Jesus did not hide from his betrayer. Rather, he went where he could be found easily. Jesus was in control. As he said in John 10:18, "No one takes it [my life] from me, but I lay it down of my own accord. I have authority [power] to lay it down and authority to take it up again."

A bit later John, again uniquely, relates two more details that reveal Jesus' power. When his assailants were coming, Jesus did not wait for them to arrive; instead he went out to meet them, and when he identified himself to them "they drew back and fell to the ground" (18:6).

> [T]he reaction of falling back in confusion at Jesus' answer is not simply spontaneous astonishment. The adversaries of Jesus are prostrate on their feet before his majesty, and so there can be little doubt that John intends "I AM" as a divine name. . . . The Johannine scene illustrates that Jesus has God's power over the forces of darkness. (Brown, 818)

The chorus that opens the *St. John Passion* picks up John's emphasis on the power and majesty of Christ with all its "Herr" ["Lord"] words and with its reference to the first verse of Psalm 8.

Herr, unser *Herr*scher, dessen Ruhm	Lord, our master, whose fame
In allen Landen *herr*lich ist!	in all lands is glorious!
Zeig' uns durch deine Passion,	Show us through your Passion
Daß du, der wahre Gottessohn,	that you, the true Son of God,
Zu aller Zeit,	at all times,
Auch in der größten Niedrigkeit,	even in the deepest lowliness,
Ver*herr*lich worden bist!	have been glorified!

The choral shouts proclaiming Jesus as "Herr" ["Lord"], however, are not what we hear first. The orchestra begins without the choir. A heavy pedal point in the bass instruments, an incessant, repetitious sixteenth-note figure in the strings, and long, sustained melodic lines full of piercing dissonances in the oboes all contribute to a picture of turmoil and anguish, of suffering and grief. The orchestral opening reveals to us the human misery that reaches its nadir in Jesus' passion, in his "größten Niedrigkeit" ["deepest lowliness"].

In the midst of this anguish the choir enters with three powerful, chordal acclamations of "Lord" and then continues by transforming the strings' restless sixteenth-note figures into a grand, rising sequence. The choir makes it clear that the Lord about whom this work is sung is not merely a suffering man; he is the Son of God, a member of the Trinity, who is worthy of being addressed three times in this movement with shouts of "Lord."

Although the choir clearly portrays *Christus Victor,* Bach avoided glossing over the suffering that Christ had to endure in order to accomplish the victory by putting the choir's victorious notes in the context of the orchestra's anguish. This was no empty victory over an inconsequential foe. The music, like the text it sets, has it right: Christ's lordship, power, and glory come through his passion and are seen in his "deepest lowliness."

Throughout the *St. John Passion,* Bach's setting of the words of Jesus keeps before us the power and majesty of *Christus Victor.* In contrast to the confused, frightened, or cynical voices of the other characters around him, Jesus' voice is always strong and controlled. A particularly good example is the "solemn and poetic diction" (Brown, 868) of Jesus at the end of the trial before Pilate.

Mein Reich ist nicht von dieser Welt;	My kingdom is not of this world;
wäre mein Reich von dieser Welt,	were my kingdom of this world,
meine Diener würden darob kämpfen,	my attendants would for that reason fight,
daß ich den Jüden nicht überantwortet würde;	so that I to the Jews would not be handed over;
aber nun ist mein Reich nicht von dannen.	but now is my kingdom not from here.

Bach's music beautifully supports both the diction and the structure of this response to Pilate's questions. The strong upward leap of a fourth on the words "mein Reich" ["my kingdom"] to the highest note of the section gives the first phrase a note of power and authority. In contrast to this, the fanfare-like melisma on "kämpfen" ["fight"] sounds pompous but empty and ineffectual, a contrast that is reinforced by a return to the range and melodic shape of the opening phrase as Jesus rounds out his response by repeating "aber nun ist mein Reich nicht von dannen" ["but now is my kingdom not from here"].

Another way in which the *St. John Passion* emphasizes the *Christus Victor* theme is by means of the role it gives to Jesus' enemies. The *Christus Vic-*

tor theory of the atonement requires that the enemies of Jesus play a prominent role. The danger is that this theory could turn into a full-fledged dualism. But even the New Testament, in order to stress the power of evil, uses

> such phrases as "the prince of this world" (John 16:11) or even "the god of this world" (2 Corinthians 4:4) as titles for the devil. These titles press the power of evil to the very outer limit of faith in the unity of God; and repeatedly, in moments of personal tragedy or social crisis, Christian language and thought have crossed that outer limit and have come up with a full-blown dualism. So it was with Luther, who described the human condition as one of being poised delicately between the two, with the question of which would win always in the balance — in the balance existentially, in the concrete struggles of existence, but not in the balance ultimately, because God was still God and because the power of God in Christ had conquered the powers of evil. That made "Christus Victor" indispensable to Luther's faith. . . . Like Luther, Bach took the devil seriously, and therefore, in his cantatas and above all in the *Saint John Passion,* he found in "Christus Victor" a way of acknowledging the power of evil and the tyranny of death and yet of affirming the sovereignty and the ultimate triumph of Christ in God. (Pelikan, 108, 110)

From the outset of his Gospel, John vividly set forth the confrontation of *Christus Victor* with his enemies as a confrontation of light with darkness. "In him was life, and that life was the light of men. The light shines in the darkness, but the darkness has not understood it. . . . The true light that gives light to every man was coming into the world" (1:4, 5, 9). When he got to the passion, John brought out the

> confrontation of Jesus and the forces of darkness . . . with dramatic instinct. Jesus knows what is going to happen and goes to meet his opponents. We have heard him say: "No one has taken it [my life] away from me; rather, I lay it down of my own accord" (x 18). Jesus had given Judas permission to leave the Last Supper to betray him (xiii 27); now he will permit Judas and his forces to arrest him. For John the passion is not an inevitable fate that overtakes Jesus; he is master of his own fate. . . . In John there is to be no physical contact between Judas and Jesus, no kiss as in the Synoptic account. . . . The two sides are divided in warfare. (Brown, pp. 817-18)

The first confrontation between Jesus and his enemies in the *St. John Passion* occurs when "a detachment of soldiers and some officials from the chief priests" come bearing torches, lanterns, and weapons. John is the only evangelist to mention lanterns and torches; the others mention only the weapons. In the recitative telling of this confrontation (no. 2a), Bach took care to emphasize the words "mit Fackeln, Lampen, und mit Waffen" ["with torches, lanterns, and with weapons"] by setting them off with rests, by setting them to high notes, and by appoaching them with upward leaps. By emphasizing these particular words, Bach caught John's theological point.

> In xiii 27, 30, when we last saw Judas, he had become the tool of Satan and had gone off into the night. This was the evil night of which Jesus had warned in xi 10 and xii 35, the night in which men stumble because they have no light. Perhaps this is why Judas and his companions come bearing lanterns and torches. They have not accepted the light of the world, and so they must have artificial light. (Brown, 817)

Bach's principal means of emphasizing the role of Christ's enemies was through the *turba* choruses (i.e., the choral pieces that contain the words spoken by groups of people in the story). The *turba* choruses loom larger in the overall scheme of the *St. John Passion* than they do in the *St. Matthew Passion,* which gives a much bigger role to the meditative ariosos, arias, and chorales. But it is not only by playing a quantitatively larger role that the *turba* choruses stand out in the *St. John Passion*. Their striking character also gives them prominence. Wilfrid Mellers characterizes them as "spiritually 'low' and a bit inane" (97). And Karl Geiringer points to their "strongly wild, passionate, and disturbing character" (196). In quantity and quality the *turba* choruses of the *St. John Passion* give emphasis to Jesus' enemies, an emphasis appropriate to the *Christus Victor* theme.

The culmination of Bach's emphasis on *Christus Victor* comes with Jesus' words, "Es ist vollbracht" ["It is finished"] (no. 29). Bach set these words to a descending line that fittingly depicts the expiration of a dying man. But where, then, is *Christus Victor* in this? Why not set these words as a shout of victory? I think Bach wanted to confront us with the reality of the final enemy, death. There will be time for victory shouts, but those shouts will be empty unless we first realize the power of the enemy.

Jesus' death was real, so it is appropriate that a sorrowful, meditative aria ("Es ist vollbracht") follows his last words (no. 30). The musical theme of this meditation is spun out of the descending line to which Jesus sang "It is finished" in the preceding recitative. But there is more than sorrow in the aria; there are also notes of hope and of peace. The solo obbligato instrument is the viola da gamba, an instrument that by Bach's time was fast approaching obsolescence. This is the only place in the work that Bach called for its unique sound, probably because it was an instrument that symbolized joy in death. Mellers' analysis gets to the essence of the aria.

> The [bass] gamba was the last survivor of the viol family, and even in Bach's day composers — including Bach himself — still wrote for it music of noble spirituality. With its top string tuned a fourth higher than the cello, it had wider range if slighter volume; it sang-spoke with infinite subtlety of nuance, at once humane and ethereal. Its tone is heroic yet melancholy, rich yet purged; nothing could be more appropriate to the drooping phrases of this aria. . . . The ritornello theme starts from the simple falling scale, drooping under its own weight, to which Christ had expired. In the aria, however, the rhythm is dotted and this, at the immensely slow *adagio molto* prescribed by Bach, makes the music limp, almost halt, as the pulse falters and blood drains from the limbs. The effect is the more poignant because the dotted rhythm is a heroic convention of the Baroque age. . . . (137-38)

So the first part of the aria ends with the death of a hero.

Es ist vollbracht!	It is finished!
O Trost vor die gekrankten Seelen!	O comfort for the afflicted souls!
Die Trauernacht	The night of mourning
Läßt nun die letzte Stunde zählen.	now the final hour counts.

But Bach knew that this was not the death of just *a* hero; it was the death of *the* Hero, the Lion of the tribe of Judah. His death was not a defeat; it was a victory. Bach knew Luther's interpretation of the words, "It is finished." According to Luther,

> Christ's suffering is the fulfillment of Scripture and the accomplishment of the redemption of the human race. [The foregoing words were underlined by Bach in his copy of the Calov Bible Commentary.] It is finished;

God's Lamb has been slaughtered and offered for the world's sin. The real High Priest has completed the sacrifice. God's Son has given and sacrificed His body and life as the ransom for sin. Sin is cancelled, God's wrath assuaged, death conquered, the kingdom of heaven purchased, and heaven is unbarred. (in Leaver, *J. S. Bach and Scripture*, 130)

So the second part of the aria, in startling contrast to the first part, bursts in with a shout of triumph. B minor adagio turns to D major allegro, and the descending motif of the solo gamba gives way to battle-like fanfares of the *stile concitato* (the warlike style) in the full orchestra as the alto soloist sings:

Der Held aus Juda siegt mit Macht	The hero of Judah triumphs with power
Und schließt den Kampf.	and closes the battle.

Following this outburst the aria's opening music returns and the alto sings once more, "It is finished." But now, after the victorious assurance of the second section, we can more clearly hear its notes of hope and comfort; we can even, with the symbolic gamba, look at death in joy and rest in the peace won by *Christus Victor*.

The aria, "Es ist vollbracht," then, is the climax of Bach's emphasis on the *Christus Victor* theme. The overwhelming, triumphal outburst in the middle of the aria insures that all who have ears will hear that "the hero of Judah triumphs with power." But Bach was not content to underscore *Christus Victor* only in this obvious way. He organized the music so that the aria, "Es ist vollbracht," occupies the central place in three different chiastic structures in Part II.

The first of these is small, involving only the pieces immediately surrounding "Es ist vollbracht," and therefore can be grasped quite readily by the listener. "Es ist vollbracht" is immediately preceded by a chorale and a recitative and followed by a recitative and chorale. The second chorale is joined with an aria but its connection to the previous chorale is clear because they both employ the same tune. (See figure 7 on p. 124.)

If the joining of the second chorale to an aria slightly obscures this chiasm, it in turn makes two larger chiasms possible, both with "Es ist vollbracht" at the center. The first of these chiasms involves all the solo numbers (arias and ariosos) of Part II, the second all the solo numbers and chorales of Part II.

FIGURE 7: **Chiasm I Centered on "Es ist vollbracht"**

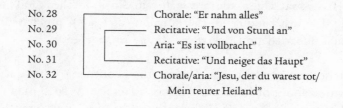

No. 28	Chorale: "Er nahm alles"
No. 29	Recitative: "Und von Stund an"
No. 30	Aria: "Es ist vollbracht"
No. 31	Recitative: "Und neiget das Haupt"
No. 32	Chorale/aria: "Jesu, der du warest tot/ Mein teurer Heiland"

If we look at all the solo numbers of Part II, we find that "Es ist vollbracht" is the only aria that stands by itself. Twice arias are linked to preceding ariosos and twice they are joined by the choir. (See figure 8 below.)

FIGURE 8: **Chiasm II Centered on "Es ist vollbracht"**

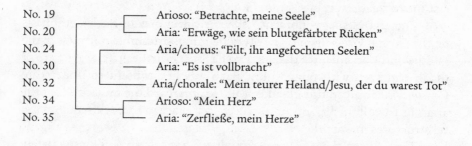

No. 19	Arioso: "Betrachte, meine Seele"
No. 20	Aria: "Erwäge, wie sein blutgefärbter Rücken"
No. 24	Aria/chorus: "Eilt, ihr angefochtnen Seelen"
No. 30	Aria: "Es ist vollbracht"
No. 32	Aria/chorale: "Mein teurer Heiland/Jesu, der du warest Tot"
No. 34	Arioso: "Mein Herz"
No. 35	Aria: "Zerfließe, mein Herze"

Then, if we look at all the solo numbers and chorales of Part II, we find "Es ist vollbracht" in the center of two similarly structured sections. Each section is framed by chorales, two at the beginning and end of the first section, one at the beginning and end of the second; each section has a chorale in the middle; and in each section the central chorale is framed by an arioso-aria pair in front of it and a chorus following it. (See figure 9 on p. 125.)

FIGURE 9: Chiasm III Centered on "Es ist vollbracht"

No. 15	Chorale			
No. 17	Chorale		No. 32	Chorale/aria
No. 19	Arioso		No. 34	Arioso
No. 20	Aria		No. 35	Aria

No. 30 Aria: "Es ist vollbracht"

No. 22	Chorale		No. 37	Chorale
No. 24	Chorus/aria		No. 39	Chorus
No. 26	Chorale		No. 40	Chorale
No. 28	Chorale			

The opening chorus introduced the *Christus Victor* theme, and throughout the work Bach brought it out in a variety of ways, both obvious and subtle, climaxing in "Es ist vollbracht." It would be fitting, then, for Bach to round off the work by calling attention to its main theme again at the end. And so he did, but he did so in an unexpected way that etches the theme all the more indelibly on the mind of the listener. After the burial has been narrated, the choir sings a burial chorus, "Ruht wohl" ["Rest well"] (no. 39), the type of chorus that normally concluded a Passion. But instead of stopping here, Bach added a chorale of great strength (no. 40), one he had previously used for a cantata for the Feast of St. Michael, the warrior archangel. Its opening words, "Ach Herr" ["Ah, Lord"], recall the opening chorus, and then it goes on to address the Son of God ("O Gottes Sohn") on the throne of grace ("Genadenthron") whom the believer will praise eternally ("ich will dich preisen ewiglich!").

A second theological theme developed in the *St. John Passion* is the freedom of the Christian. The freedom of the Christian, a favorite theme of Luther (cf. his treatise by that name), is perhaps more obviously a Pauline than a Johannine emphasis. But as Eric Chafe points out, "Luther viewed John through the eyes of Paul" ("Key Structure," 41). In his "Preface to the New Testament," Luther listed John's gospel and Paul's letters as the premier books, containing "the true kernel and marrow of all the books.... For in them you ... find depicted in masterly fashion how faith in Christ overcomes sin, death, and hell, and gives life, righteousness, and salvation" (362).

If Bach found this theme in John through the eyes of Luther and Paul, John at least provided a detail from which to launch the theme. That detail is the report that "the detachment of soldiers with its commander and the Jewish officials arrested Jesus. They bound him and brought him first to Annas . . ." (18:12-13). The binding of Jesus at this time is a detail unique to John's account, and again Bach's music emphasizes the key word. The Evangelist's recitative relating this incident (no. 6) begins with a five-measure pedal point. Nowhere else in this entire Passion is there such a long pedal point in a recitative. And since five is a christological number, number symbolism may be involved here. The more obvious symbolism, though, is that in a pedal point the music is "bound" to one note. Furthermore there is a visual aspect to the symbol — the ties needed in the notation to sustain this long pedal point visually "bind" the notes together. (In German the word for "ties" is *Takt-Überbindungen.*") Then, when the Evangelist sings the words "und bunden ihn" ["and bound him"], the music emphasizes "bunden" with a dissonant leap to a dissonant note and does it in a dotted rhythm that, in this recitative, is unique to that word.

The aria that follows the Evangelist's telling about Christ's binding brings out the theological point of the episode (no. 7). Its reminder to us is exactly what John Calvin, in his commentary on 18:12, calls us to remember: "And let us remember that the body of the Son of God was bound, that our souls might be loosed from the cords of sin and Satan" (158). So the alto sings:

Von den Stricken meiner Sünden	From the shackles of my sins
Mich zu entbinden,	to unbind me,
Wird mein Heil gebunden.	my Savior is bound.
Mich von allen Lasterbeulen	From all boils of vice
Völlig zu heilen,	fully to heal me,
Läßt er sich verwunden.	he lets himself be wounded.

Bach's music for this aria is full of graphic symbols of binding and loosing. The basso continuo part is made up of eighth notes repeated on the same pitch (symbolizing binding) which are broken away from by a pair of sixteenth notes (symbolizing loosing). The two oboes begin with twisting melodic lines (depicting the twisting ropes) in exact imitation (another symbol of binding) that produce many harsh dissonances. But by the end of the instrumental introduction the dissonances have dissolved into parallel thirds that express the sweetness of freedom. These musical motives run throughout the movement, musically illustrating the contrast in the text and expressing the joy of the free Christian as the loosing motives come to the fore when the text is "mich zu entbinden" ["to unbind me"] and "vollig zu heilen" ["fully to heal me"].

The climax of the theme of the Christian's freedom comes in Part II, in the midst of what Bach scholars refer to as the *Herzstuck* [heart piece] of the *St. John Passion*. This time the piece that brings the theme to its climax is a chorale, "Durch dein Gefängnis" (no. 22).

Durch dein Gefängnis, Gottes Sohn,	Through your capture, Son of God,
Muß uns die Freiheit kommen;	to us freedom must come;
Dein Kerker ist der Gnadenthron,	your dungeon is the throne of grace,
Die Freistatt aller Frommen;	the refuge of all the devout;
Denn gingst du nicht	for had you not gone
die Knechtschaft ein,	into bondage,
Müsst unsre Knechtschaft	our bondage would have had
ewig sein.	to be eternal.

This chorale, with its important theological theme, is strategically placed so as to stand out. It is isolated by its distance from other chorales. There are twelve numbers between it and the previous chorale and eleven numbers between it and the next chorale. Nowhere else in the *St. John Passion* are there more than five numbers between chorales. But it is not merely the distance of this chorale from its neighboring chorales that makes it stand out; it is also the nature of the surrounding music. "Durch dein Gefängnis" stands in the midst of the heaviest concentration of *turba* choruses and its contrast to those raucous cries makes its message stand out all the more.

Furthermore, it is worth noting that the words of "Durch dein Gefängnis" are not the words that belong to the chorale tune to which Bach set them. The text is actually an aria from a Passion libretto by C. H. Postel, but Bach, instead of writing an aria, set the text to a familiar chorale melody by one of his predecessors at Leipzig, J. H. Schein. The familiar melody would have called the attention of perceptive worshipers in Leipzig to the central theological message of the unfamiliar text.

As with "Es ist vollbracht" ["It is finished"], so here Bach placed a central theological theme in the midst of a chiastic structure. This chiasm, in which "Durch dein Gefängnis" is the centerpiece, is both textual and musical. The use of similar music for different choruses (shown by the brackets in figure 10 below) brings out the chiastic order of the words of the crowds (shown by the summary of contents in figure 10).

FIGURE 10: The Chiasm Centered on "Durch dein Gefängnis"

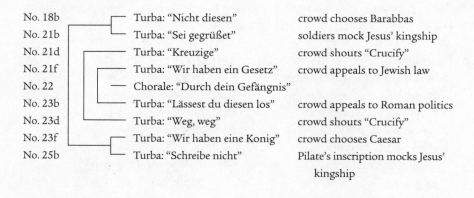

No. 18b	Turba: "Nicht diesen"	crowd chooses Barabbas
No. 21b	Turba: "Sei gegrüßet"	soldiers mock Jesus' kingship
No. 21d	Turba: "Kreuzige"	crowd shouts "Crucify"
No. 21f	Turba: "Wir haben ein Gesetz"	crowd appeals to Jewish law
No. 22	Chorale: "Durch dein Gefängnis"	
No. 23b	Turba: "Lässest du diesen los"	crowd appeals to Roman politics
No. 23d	Turba: "Weg, weg"	crowd shouts "Crucify"
No. 23f	Turba: "Wir haben eine Konig"	crowd chooses Caesar
No. 25b	Turba: "Schreibe nicht"	Pilate's inscription mocks Jesus' kingship

---

A third theological theme developed in the *St. John Passion* is discipleship. John provided the impetus for this theme with his emphasis on Jesus' obedience to the Father.

"My food is to do the will of him who sent me. . . ." (4:34)

"For I have come down from heaven not to do my will but to do the will of him who sent me." (6:38)

"[T]he world must learn that I love the Father and that I do exactly what my Father has commanded me." (14:31)

"If you love my commands, you will remain in my love, just as I have obeyed my Father's commands and remain in his love." (15:10)

There is, of course, a relationship between Jesus' obedience to the Father and the discipleship of the believer. That connection is clear in the last verse quoted: the disciple loves and obeys Jesus' commands just as Jesus loved and obeyed his Father's commands. Therefore the starting point for the discipleship theme in the *St. John Passion* is the episode in which Peter strikes Malchus with a sword. Jesus responds by telling Peter to put away his sword and then asks rhetorically, "Shall I not drink the cup my Father has given me?" (no. 4). Significantly Bach repeated these words, the only time in the recitatives of the *St. John Passion* that words are repeated. Then follows a stanza from the chorale versification of the Lord's Prayer (no. 5):

Dein Will gescheh, Herr Gott, zugleich	Your will be done, Lord God, alike
Auf Erden wie im Himmelreich.	on earth as in the kingdom of heaven.
Gib uns Geduld in Leidenszeit,	Give us patience in time of suffering,
Gehorsam sein in Lieb und Leid;	obedience in love and sorrow;
Wehr und steur allem Fleisch	halt and restrain all flesh
und Blut,	and blood,
Das wider deinen Willen tut!	that against your will act!

The theme of discipleship turns from Jesus to his followers after Jesus is bound and led to Annas and "Simon Peter followed Jesus, and so did another disciple" (18:15). In the brief recitative in which the Evangelist reports this (no. 8), the music subtly suggests what following Jesus really entails. At the climax of the Evangelist's melody is the traditional four-note configuration symbolizing the cross. This musical symbolism tells the perceptive listener that following Jesus means bearing a cross.

This small but important recitative is followed by an aria that expresses joy in following Jesus (no. 9).

Ich folge dir gleichfalls mit	I will follow you likewise with
freudigen Schritten	joyful steps
Und lasse dich nicht,	and let you not [go],
Mein Leben, mein Licht.	my life, my light.

The music of this aria is lighthearted like nothing else in the *Passion*. It is the first piece in a major key; it has a nice, lilting 3/8 rhythm; its theme is simple, its phrasing balanced, and its harmonies uncomplicated. It is sung by a soprano (a boy in Bach's performances in Leipzig), and the obbligato instrument is a flute. All of this not only makes it lighthearted, but it also gives it an air of innocence. Wilfred Mellers calls it an aria "'about' the innocence of acceptance" (p. 104). It depicts the first stage of discipleship — its joy and zeal, but also its naiveté and lack of depth. The new disciple, eager and perhaps even a bit giddy, is not fully aware of what following Jesus is all about. Yet he sings:

Befördre den Lauf	Hasten the way
Und höre nicht auf,	and do not stop,
Selbst an mir zu ziehen,	yourself to me to pull,
zu schieben, zu bitten.	to push, to beseech.

Many commentators on this aria have pointed to the way Bach symbolized following; he wrote canons in which one part, the flute or the voice, imitates the other. But there is more to Bach's musical symbol than that. The imitative writing is of the simplest kind and is always short-lived. Both of these characteristics fittingly portray the immaturity of the new disciple whose understanding is still simple and whose following is often short-lived.

The musical portrayal of the immature disciple is followed by John's account of Peter's denial (nos. 10 and 12). One could say that this episode confirms the immaturity and misguided zeal of Peter, but it also is the next step in Peter's discipleship because he now recognizes his weakness and guilt and weeps bitter tears. John did not report Peter's tears, so at this point Bach inserted the verses from Matthew that tell of Peter's weeping.

Following Peter's denial and weeping is the second aria about discipleship (no. 13). The disciple has reached a new, deeper level of understanding and the music reflects that in every way. B♭ major has become F♯ minor; the solo flute has given way to the full string section; the solo voice deepens from soprano to tenor; the lilting rhythms, graceful melodies, and uncomplicated harmonies have become lashing, jagged, and dissonant. The disciple is in despair and does not know where to turn.

Ach, mein Sinn,	O, my mind,
Wo willt du endlich hin,	where will you finally go,
Wo soll ich mich erquicken?	where shall I myself revive?

The answer to the repeated question, "wo?" ["where?"], is not given until the story brings us to Golgotha. After the Evangelist tells us that "they took Jesus . . . to the place of a skull" (no. 23g), a final discipleship aria follows (no. 24). The voice has now matured to bass as the disciple reaches his deepest understanding of what it means to follow Jesus. He now knows the answer to the desperate question, "wo?" ["where?"]. He must follow Jesus to Golgotha; he knows now that discipleship entails taking up his cross. He can now answer the question posed by the choir of "angefochtnen Seelen" ["anguished souls"].

BASS: Eilt, ihr angefochtnen Seelen,   BASS: Hurry, you anguished souls,
Geht aus euren Marterhöhlen,   leave your dens of torment,
Eilt —   hurry —
CHOIR: Wohin?   CHOIR: Where?
BASS: — nach Golgatha!   — to Golgotha!

    Musically there are some obvious reminiscences of the first discipleship aria. There is the same 3/8 meter and the same key signature although now in the deeper, more serious key of G minor instead of B♭ major. Even the melody is reminiscent of the first aria. In fact its second measure is identical to the first measure of the first aria. The joy of discipleship is not lost because of the cost of discipleship; it is deepened. And the freedom of the Christian is not lost because he goes to Golgotha; there, as the aria says, his "Wohlfahrte blüht" ["prosperity blooms"].

    Christ won the victory over sin and death and hell. By being bound and put to death, he freed the Christian from the sting of death. The Lion of the Tribe of Judah has conquered; we are free! This is the central message of the *St. John Passion*. But Bach knew what Dietrich Bonhoeffer knew (they were, after all, both students of Luther) — that grace, although free, is not cheap. Bach, like Bonhoeffer, knew that "cheap grace is grace without discipleship, grace without the cross . . ." (47).

    Bach, no doubt, deserves the place Pelikan gave him "among the theologians." I began this discussion of the *St. John Passion* by quoting St. Augustine. Let me end it by quoting Bonhoeffer and, by doing so, put Bach squarely between theologians from one end of the church's history to the other. In *The Cost of Discipleship* there is a chapter entitled "Discipleship and the Cross." Both Bach and Bonhoeffer knew and preached the relationship between the two.

    The yoke and the burden of Christ are his cross. To go one's way under the sign of the cross is not misery and desperation, but peace and refreshment for the soul, it is the highest joy. Then we do not walk under the burden of our self-made laws and burdens, but under the yoke of him who knows us and who walks under the yoke with us. Under his

131

yoke we are certain of his nearness and communion. It is he whom the disciple finds as he lifts up his cross. (103)

*   *   *

Bach lived when Western civilization was in the full flush of the Enlightenment. With reason in the vanguard, man, according to Immanuel Kant, was finally emerging from his "self-imposed nonage" (*Music in the Western World,* 384). In many ways Bach's music ran counter to the main currents of its time, none of it more powerfully than the *St. Matthew Passion.* It is not that Bach saw no value in reason. Martin Luther, his chief theological mentor, recognized that reason is a virtue — indeed, that it is a gift of God.

> Luther speaks very forcefully of this gift of God and of its glory. It is the essential and main earthly blessing and it stands far above all other goods of this life as "the best and in a certain sense divine." It is reason that contributes the essential difference between man and other living beings, indeed everything else. Through it, man exercises that lordship over the earth which was given to him in Genesis 1:28. Reason provides the light by which man can see and administer the affairs of this world. Reason is the source and bearer of all culture. It has discovered all arts and sciences, all medicine and law, and it administers them. Reason makes itself felt wherever wisdom, power, industry, and honor are found among men in this life. None of this is to be despised; rather all is to be regarded and praised as the noble gift of God. (Althaus, 64)

But this same Luther also called reason a "whore" because he realized that it is a dangerous gift that can lead to man's ruin if it is allowed to trump faith. The human tendency to rely on reason over faith in God's revealed Word caused Luther to emphasize the negative side of reason.

Several of Bach's cantatas also emphasize the negative side of reason (cf., e.g., Cantatas 2, 152, 178, and 180). That should come as no surprise since they grew out of a context in which faith was seriously threatened by the Enlightenment's emphasis on reason. In an illuminating discussion of the treatment of reason in Bach's cantatas, Eric Chafe summarizes the dominant themes.

> Reason is described as leading man into taking offence at God's designs and as the enemy of faith; it is associated with blindness and deafness

and with the flesh rather than the spirit. . . . [R]eferences to light in several of the cantatas explain that, theologically, reason belongs to the realm of darkness and the flesh rather than of spiritual enlightenment. . . . Other themes associated with reason appear in Bach's cantatas, such as its opposition to the way of the cross and the necessity of placing God's Word above reason. . . . Neglect of the Word gives rise to a characteristic Lutheran notion regarding reason: it is a stumbling block to faith and salvation. (*Tonal Allegory,* 227-28)

The biggest stumbling block for reason is the cross. Reason "is offended at the cross of Christ, the great no to all human endeavor, to all opinions of one's own" (Loewenich, 68).

Our wisdom is offended at God's Word; it is scandalized by the cross of Christ. But Luther knows that it must be so. If the church's proclamation is no longer a rock of offense to the people, this is a sign that it has betrayed the gospel. The cross of Christ vehemently opposes natural understanding. For nothing but lowliness, disgrace and shame are to be seen there, unless we recognize the divine will, yes, God himself under this cloak. It is generally true of divine works that reason does not know what to make of them and tends to despair because of this. Thus the gospel becomes a rock of offense, a scandal. (Loewenich, 76)

One "enlightened" theologian who stumbled over this rock was Bach's contemporary, Herman Samuel Reimarus, author of "a massive book entitled *Apologia for the Rational Worshipers of God,* which was a radical attack on most of those 'principal teachings of the Christian religion' in the name of a thoroughgoing rationalism and deism" (Pelikan, 89). According to Reimarus, Christ's words from the cross, "My God, my God, why hast thou forsaken me?"

can hardly be otherwise interpreted than that God had not helped him to carry out his intention and attain his object as he had hoped he would have done. *It was then clearly not the intention or the object of Jesus to suffer and to die,* but to build up a worldly kingdom, and to deliver the Israelites from bondage. It was in this that God had forsaken him, it was in this that his hopes had been frustrated. (Trans. Pelikan, 90)

Nothing could be more foreign to Bach than this kind of rationalistic approach to Scripture. As an orthodox Lutheran, Bach stood strongly against such "enlightened" thought and in his *St. Matthew Passion* un-flinchingly stood by the "foolishness" of the cross, knowing that "the foolishness of God is wiser than man's wisdom, and the weakness of God is stronger than man's strength" (1 Corinthians 1:25). So in total contrast to Enlightenment thinkers like Reimarus, Bach

> saw precisely that intention [of Jesus to suffer and die] as "clearly" the object of the entire Passion narrative, indeed of the entire Gospel narra-tive; and, as if to emphasize the voluntary character of the death of Christ as ultimately the result of his love rather than of human malice, he divides the two references to the cry "let him be crucified!" in verse 22 and in verse 23 of chapter 27 with the soprano recitative [no. 48], "He has done well for all of us," and the soprano aria [no. 49], "In love my Savior now is dying":
>
> > Aus Liebe will mein Heiland sterben,
> > Von einer Sünde weiß er nichts,
> > Daß das ewige Verderben
> > Und die Strafe des Gerichts
> > Nicht auf meiner Seele bliebe.
> >
> > [It is out of love that my Savior intends to die,
> > Although of sin and guilt He knows nothing,
> > So that my soul should not have to bear
> > Everlasting damnation
> > And the penalty of divine justice.]
>
> With those words Bach states the argument of his *Passion of Our Lord according to Saint Matthew:* that the Savior Jesus Christ suffered and died because of his love for humanity, in order by his innocent death to sat-isfy the justice of God, which had been violated by human sin and guilt, and to make it possible for the mercy of God to forgive sin and guilt without violating divine justice. (Pelikan, 90-91)

Thus the *St. Matthew Passion* stands in the line of theology that began with Anselm's *Cur Deus Homo?* [*Why Did God Become Man?*], a line of theol-ogy that tries to answer the question of Anselm's title. But the *St. Matthew Passion* is not merely a musical treatise on theological dogma; it returned that dogma to its proper setting, the liturgy. We noted earlier that the High Middle Ages was a relatively late time for theologians to start addressing such a fundamental question. Pelikan suggests that the reason for the late start is that

> the proper setting to confess that soteriological concern was not dogma but liturgy, not even the creed in the context of the liturgy but the worship that climaxed, for both East and West, in the dramatic action of the Mass and that was articulated in the hymns of the church. (92)

By bringing that dogma back into a liturgical context, the *St. Matthew Passion* eliminated a serious problem that occurred when the dogma was separated from the liturgy.

> As the history of post-Reformation Protestant orthodoxy had amply demonstrated, the satisfaction theory of the atonement, when it was transposed from devotion to dogmatics, from meditation to systematic theology, created enormous problems: for the doctrine of God, for the portrait of the life of Jesus Christ, for the interpretation of the Bible. With the elimination of its full liturgical and sacramental context, it did not make sense — or, alternately, it made entirely too much sense, transforming the mystery of the cross into the transaction of a celestial Shylock who demanded his pound of flesh. Bach's *Saint Matthew Passion* rescued "satisfaction" from itself by restoring it to a [liturgical] context in which it could give voice to central and fundamental affirmations of the Christian gospel. (Pelikan, 100-101)

The *St. Matthew Passion* begins with what is probably the most monumental of all Bach's choruses. Not surprisingly it is not only an imposing musical structure, it is also rich in theological themes. Its text is a dialogue between Zion and the Faithful set for double choir and double orchestra. Over these a third choir of boys sings the Lutheran chorale version of an ancient Christian chant, the "Agnus Dei" ["Lamb of God"].

Zion: Kommt, ihr Töchter,	Come, you daughters,
helft mir klagen. Sehet —	help me lament. Behold —
Faithful: Wen?	whom?
Zion: — den Bräutigam. Seht ihn —	— the Bridegroom. Behold him —
Faithful: Wie?	how?
Zion: — als wie ein Lamm!	— like a Lamb!
Boy choir: **O Lamm Gottes, unschuldig**	**O Lamb of God, guiltless**

Am Stamm des Kreuzes geschlachtet,	**on the stem of the cross slaughtered,**
Zion: Sehet —	Behold —
Faithful: Was?	what?
Zion: — seht die Geduld.	— behold his patience.
Allzeit erfunden geduldig	**Always found patient,**
Wiewohl du warest verachtet.	**however you were despised.**
Zion: Seht —	Look —
Faithful: Wohin?	where?
Zion: — auf unsre Schuld;	— on our guilt;
All Sünd hast du getragen,	**All sin have you borne**
Sonst müßten wir verzagen.	**else must we have despaired.**
Zion: Sehet ihn aus Lieb und Huld	behold him, out of love and graciousness,
Holz zum Kreuze selber tragen!	the wood of the cross he himself is carrying!
Erbarm dich unser, o Jesu!	Have mercy upon us, O Jesus!

Leonard Bernstein described this opening chorus as follows:

[T]he orchestral introduction . . . sets the mood of suffering and pain, preparing for the entrance of the chorus which will sing the agonized sorrow of the faithful at the moment of crucifixion. And all this is done in imitation, in canon. "Come, ye Daughters, share my anguish," sing the basses, and they are [imitated] by the tenors [while] the female voices are singing a counter-canon of their own. The resulting richness of all the parts, with the orchestra throbbing beneath, is incomparable.

Then suddenly the chorus breaks into two antiphonal choruses. "See Him!" cries the first one. "Whom?" asks the second. And the first answers: "The Bridegroom see. See Him!" "How?" "So like a Lamb." And then over against all this questioning and answering and throbbing, the voices of a boys' choir sing out the chorale tune, "O Lamb of God Most Holy," piercing through the worldly pain with the icy-clear truth of redemption. (244-246)

All this is good drama; it is also good theology. It vividly brings out the essential contrast and mutual exchange involved in the satisfaction theory — the just one suffering for the unjust, the guiltless one dying for the guilty. The first part of that contrast and exchange comes out clearly in the beginning of the chorus, for the Lamb that Zion is urging the Faithful to look upon is the "most holy" Lamb. Although that is fairly clear in most translations, the original German word is unmistakable in its import. It is the word "unschuldig" ["guiltless"]. And in the chorale this word is brought out by being set to the highest and longest notes of the phrase above the "wailing" of the double chorus.

A little further into the opening chorus the other side of the exchange, our guilt, is presented. When Bach got to the fifth phrase, "Seht . . . Wohin? . . . auf unsre Schuld" ["Look . . . Where? . . . upon our guilt"], he did several things to bring out this key ingredient in satisfaction theology. First, there is the length of time he dwells on the phrase. It is the longest uninterrupted segment of music in the movement on a single phrase of text. Second, unlike the earlier phrases in which the questions of the Faithful are asked just once before the answers are given, here there are several repetitions of the question that build to the answer, "upon our guilt." Third, and most obvious to the ear, there is the much thinner texture in the orchestra that allows this phrase of text to come through with great clarity. Instead of being involved in the dense canonic web of voices and instruments that predominates throughout the movement, the words of this phrase come out clearly through the transparent texture of staccato chords in the orchestra.

The librettist, Picander, also helped bring out this essential exchange by placing the key word in this phrase, "Schuld" ["guilt"], as the rhyming word at the end of the line. It is for "schuldig" ["guilty"] humanity that the "unschuldig" ["guiltless"] Lamb must suffer and die. And while the choirs are emphasizing "unsre Schuld" ["our guilt"], the boy choir is singing the line of the chorale that says, "All' Sünd hast du getragen" ["All sin have you borne"]. As Pelikan sums it up: "The innocent Lamb of God — guilty humanity: this is the contrast, and this . . . the mutual exchange, of the *Passion*" (96).

This is the main theme of the opening chorus, and it runs through the whole work, coming out most clearly in the three appearances of the chorale, "Herzliebster Jesu, was hast du verbrochen?" (familiar in English as "Ah, dearest Jesus, how hast thou offended?"). Its first appearance occurs almost before the story has had a chance to get started. Right at the outset Jesus says (no. 2):

Ihr wisset, daß nach zweien Tagen	You know that after two days
Ostern wird,	the Passover will be,

und des Menschen Sohn wird
    überantwortet werden,
daß er gekreuziget werde.
	and the Son of Man will be
	    handed over,
	so that he will be crucified.

These were familiar words to Bach's congregation, and they are to us also — so familiar, in fact, that they and we might go right past them without realizing their astonishing import. But Bach's insertion of this familiar chorale (no. 3) at this moment does not allow us to hear Jesus' words without reflecting on their import. The Son of Man . . . crucified?

Herzliebster Jesu, was hast du
    verbrochen,
Daß man ein solch scharf Urteil
    hat gesprochen?
Was ist die Schuld, in was für
    Missetaten
Bist du geraten?
	Beloved Jesus, what have you
	    done wrong,
	that one so hard a sentence
	    has pronounced?
	What is the guilt, into what sort of
	    misdeeds
	have you fallen?

The same chorale occurs as part of the "Zion/Faithful" dialogue that stands at the heart of the Gethsemane scene (no. 19). Zion sings —

O Schmerz! Hier zittert das
    gequälte Herz;
Wie sinkt es hin, wie bleicht sein
    Angesicht!
Der Richter führt ihn vor Gericht.
Da ist kein Trost, kein Helfer nicht.
Er leidet alle Höllenqualen,
Er soll vor fremden Raub bezahlen.
	O grief! Here trembles the
	    anxious heart;
	how it sinks, how pales his
	    countenance!
	The judge leads him to judgement.
	There is no comfort, no helper.
	He suffers all the pains of hell,
	he shall for others' robbery pay.

— and while Zion is singing the Faithful insert the phrases of another stanza of "Herzliebster Jesu."

Was ist die Ursach aller solcher Plagen?
Ach! meine Sünden haben dich
    geschlagen;
Ich, ach Herr Jesu, habe dies
    verschuldet,
Was du erduldet!
	What is the cause of all such woes?
	Ah! my sins have
	    struck you down;
	I, ah Lord Jesus, have this
	    deserved,
	that which you have suffered!

During the trial the same chorale appears a third time (no. 46), immediately after the crowd has shouted for Jesus to be crucified, this time using a stanza that in its last two lines puts the satisfaction theory in a nutshell:

Die Schuld bezahlt der Herre,	The debt is paid by the master,
der Gerechte,	the just one,
Für seine Knechte!	for his vassals!

And then, so as to underscore the righteousness and innocence of the suffering One, Bach and Picander almost immediately made another insertion. When Pilate asks, "But what evil deed has He done?" (no. 47), the soprano responds (no. 48):

Er hat uns allen wohlgetan,	He has to us all done good,
Den Blinden gab er das Gesicht,	the blind gave he sight,
Die Lahmen macht' er gehend,	the lame made he to walk,
Er sagt' uns seines Vaters Wort,	he told us his Father's word,
Er trieb die Teufel fort,	he drove the devils out,
Betrübte hat er aufgericht',	the troubled he has consoled,
Er nahm die Sünder auf und an.	he received and accepted sinners.
Sonst hat mein Jesus nichts getan.	Other than this has my Jesus done nothing.

If the *St. Matthew Passion* stands in the line of theology that emphasizes the satisfaction theory of redemption, it stands no less in clear relationship to the main points of Martin Luther's little tract "A Meditation on Christ's Passion," published in 1519. In this tract Luther distinguished three stages in the contemplation of Christ's passion. The first is the recognition of sin.

> They contemplate Christ's passion aright who view it with a terror-stricken heart and a despairing conscience. This terror must be felt as you witness the stern wrath . . . with which God looks upon sin and sinners, so much that he was unwilling to release sinners even for his only and dearest Son without his payment of the severest penalty for them. . . .
>
> You must get this thought through your head . . . that you are the one who is torturing Christ thus, for your sins have surely wrought this. (*Luther's Works*, 42:8-9)

This stage in the contemplation of Christ's passion obviously overlaps with the satisfaction theory.

Luther's second stage of contemplation focuses on comforting the conscience — in other words, on God's love as opposed to his demand for justice and punishment. In this stage "you must no longer contemplate the suffering of Christ (for this has already done its work and terrified you), but pass beyond that and see his friendly heart and how this heart beats with such love for you that it impels him to bear . . . your sin" (13).

I cannot trace this theme through the *St. Matthew Passion* without greatly exceeding the bounds of this chapter, but I can at least point out that it, like the satisfaction theory, is set forth in the first chorus, and that its most obvious statement occurs, again like the satisfaction theory, after the crowd cries, "Let him be crucified!"

In the opening chorus the theme of Christ's love emerges in the last two lines:

Sehet ihn aus Lieb und Huld	Behold him, out of love and graciousness
Holz zum Kreuze selber tragen!	the wood of the cross he himself is carrying!

Bach called attention to these lines by returning to the opening music in the milder key of A minor (no sharps) rather than in the central key of E minor (one sharp).

The climax of Luther's second stage of contemplation, the contemplation of Christ's love, occurs in the soprano aria (no. 49), "Aus Liebe will mein Heiland sterben" ["Out of love wills my Savior to die"]. Bach called attention to Christ's love not only by the significant placement of this aria between the cries of "Let him be crucified," but also by its unique instrumental color — a flute and two oboes da caccia without the otherwise ubiquitous basso continuo. It should also be noted that the oboe da caccia was an instrument often associated with love in Bach's works.

Luther's third stage of contemplation — our imitation of Christ's patient and innocent suffering — also appears in the *St. Matthew Passion* and, as with the others, it is introduced in the opening chorus. Again Picander, Bach's librettist, made the start in highlighting the key word of this theme, "Geduld" ["patience"], by placing it at the end of the line where it rhymes with another key word, "Schuld" ["guilt"]. Bach also helped to bring out the word "Geduld." As with "Schuld," it is treated at some length and presented within a clearer texture. It is also, appropriately, in the relative major key, and is followed by the only statement of the opening theme in a major key. Furthermore, Bach arranged the music so that the phrase of the chorale that occurs on top of the "Geduld" phrase in the choirs is the one which ends with "geduldig" on high, long notes as did "unschuldig" earlier. The message is obvious. Christ's patience in the face of undeserved suffering is the model for his disciples to follow.

As the story unfolds, the theme of following Jesus, of being his disciple, is brought to the fore in four episodes, each highlighted by an aria. The first is in Gethsemane where the bass sings "Gerne will ich mich bequemen" ["Gladly will I myself submit"] (no. 23). Second, at the trial when Jesus is silent, the tenor sings "Geduld, Geduld! wenn mich falsche Zungen stechen" ["Patience, patience! When me false witnesses stab"] (no. 35). Third, in the courtyard, after Peter's denial and bitter tears of remorse, the alto sings "Erbarme dich, mein Gott" ["Have mercy, my God"] (no. 39). Finally, after Simon of Cyrene has been conscripted to carry Jesus' cross, the bass sings "Komm, süsses Kreuz" ["Come, sweet cross"] (no. 57). All four of these arias use only stringed instruments. Two of them, "Gerne" and "Erbarme," use the conventional stringed instruments while the other two, "Geduld" and "Komm," use the unique sound of the near-obsolete viola da gamba. In each case the second of the pair has a richer sound. "Gerne" simply uses violins in unison whereas "Erbarme" has a solo violin with the full string section accompanying. In "Geduld" the viola da gamba is the continuo instrument (there are no obbligato instruments) and in "Komm" it becomes the solo obbligato instrument, playing in highly virtuosic (but not flashy) style. Interestingly, and I suspect significantly, all four arias begin with the opening phrase of the chorale "O Haupt voll Blut und Wunden" (familiar in English as "O Sacred Head Now Wounded") subtly incorporated into the continuo part.

The aria that initiates the discipleship theme (no. 23), "Gerne," has words that speak to the heart of the meaning of discipleship —

Gerne will ich mich bequemen,	Gladly will I myself submit,
Kreuz und Becher anzunehmen,	cross and cup to take up,
Trink ich doch dem Heiland nach.	since I drink as my Savior did.

— and Bach filled it with symbols of discipleship, including, perhaps, some personal ones. It is in a typical da capo form, its opening section (A) being followed by a contrasting section (B) and then a return to the opening section (A).

The A section of "Gerne" is replete with the number twelve, which, of course, is the number symbol for disciples and discipleship. It begins with an instrumental introduction (ritornello), a twelve-measure period consisting of a four-measure and an eight-measure phrase. This is immediately followed by another twelve-measure period in which the solo voice repeats the melody of the ritornello. Having established twelve-measure periods, the A section goes on to present four more for a total of six. Since the phrasing after the first two twelve-measure periods gets more complicated, it must be admitted that the larger units can be construed in different ways. For example, the ritornello, in its second appearance, consists of only the first four measures. It could be logically grouped with the eight measures that follow, making another twelve-measure period. But since at the end of the A section the last eight measures of the ritornello appear, the four- and eight-measure phrases could be heard as belonging together though separated by three other twelve-measure periods. In either case, there are seventy-two measures comprised of six twelve-measure periods, and when the A section is repeated, the total is 144 measures comprised of twelve, twelve-measure periods. (See figure 11 on p. 143.)

Each of the phrases in the ritornello begins with a characteristic motive which is identified with the opening word of the phrase. The four-measure phrase begins with three eighth notes on "gerne" ["gladly"]. The first note leaps up a sixth to the second one, which in turn leaps back down a sixth to the third one. I'll call this the "gerne" motive. With the repeat of the A section, the "gerne" motive is heard twelve times and the word "gerne" is sung twelve times. The eight-measure phrase begins with the traditional four-note "Kreuz" ["cross"] motive. Its association with the cross is strengthened here by dissonance, chromaticism, and syncopation.

But there is more. At measure fifty-three the violins stop playing their melodic lines and simply hold a pedal point for five measures. (Five, you may recall, is a symbol of Christ.) The continuo part also slows down its activity, leaving the voice to sing the key words, "Kreuz und Becher anzunehmen" ["cross and cup to take up"], unobstructed in a rising sequence that will lead to the highest pitch of the aria. Textually that sequence leads back to the first phrase, "Gerne will ich . . ." ["Gladly will I . . ."]. But here Bach made a change in the word order that produces a significant change in emphasis. Instead of "gerne will ich" he wrote "will ich gerne" so that "ich" ["I"] occurs on the highest note that the sequence has been leading to.

FIGURE 11: **The Twelve-Measure Periodic Structure of**
"Gerne will ich mich bequemen"

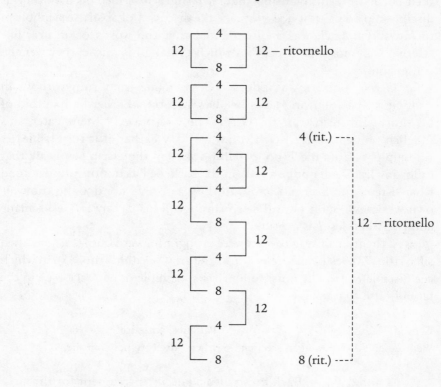

Given what happens soon after this change, we can plausibly inter-pret the emphasized "ich" as referring to Bach himself. This section con-taining the new emphasis on "ich" leads to the final ritornello, which, as will be remembered, includes only its final eight measures that begin with the "Kreuz" motive. But now it is at a new pitch level so that the pitches are B-natural (which in German is designated as H), C, A, and B-flat (which in German is designated simply as B). So in the opening notes of the final ritornello, Bach subtly inscribed his name backwards — HCAB — as a way of identifying himself with those who gladly follow Jesus.

Did he further identify himself as a disciple in the B section of the aria? If one assigns numbers to the letters (A = 1, B = 2, etc.), B + A + C + H equals fourteen. As it happens, in the B part of the aria the bass sings two fourteen-measure periods! Just as painters sometimes painted themselves into their paintings and authors sometimes encrypted their names into their poems, it seems plausible that Bach subtly inscribed his name in this discipleship aria. But it does not take the discovery of abstruse symbolism to know that Bach was a disciple and that the words of an aria like "Gerne" were not merely pegs on which to hang his music; they were *his* confession.

"Gerne," occurring as it does in Gethsemane, is not sung without an awareness that following Jesus involves suffering. Earlier he had told of his death, and just prior to "Gerne," he had prayed, "Mein Vater, ist's möglich, so gehe dieser Kelch von mir" ["My Father, if it is possible, let this cup pass from me"] (no. 21). But although the disciple is aware that following Jesus will not be a walk in the park, he has not fully understood what "Kreuz und Becher" ["cross and cup"] involve, nor does he know his own weakness. Soon he will sleep through Jesus' agony in Gethsemane and flee when Jesus is captured.

At the trial, false witnesses were brought forward but Jesus remained silent (no. 33). Jesus' silence prompts the aria, "Geduld" (no. 35), in which the disciple realizes he must follow Jesus' example of patience even in the face of false charges.

Geduld, Geduld!	Patience, patience!
Wenn <u>mich</u> falsche Zungen stechen.	when false tongues stab <u>me</u>.

As noted above, Bach prescribed a special instrument for this aria, the nearly obsolete viola da gamba whose quiet tone is particularly fitting for the subject of patient, silent suffering. This aria contains two contrasting motives — gently paired eighth notes to represent "Geduld," and vigorous, pointed dotted rhythms to represent the stinging tongues in the face of which patience must be exercised. But the music never seems to achieve what the words counsel. "In fact," as Eric Chafe observes, "although the aria counsels patience, it has a very restless character" (*Tonal Allegory*, 357). The disciple knows what he must do but is not capable of doing it.

It is not surprising that a disciple who has slept through Jesus' agony and fled at his capture would show impatience with the requirement to be patient. But the full depth to which he is capable of sinking has not yet been shown. It soon will be, for while Jesus is in Pilate's court, Peter is outside in the courtyard where, when questioned about his association with

Jesus, he denies with cursing and swearing that he even knows him. "And immediately the cock crew," sings the Evangelist (no. 38c).

Da dachte Petrus an die Worte	Then thought Peter on the words of
Jesu, da er zu ihm <u>sagte</u>:	Jesus, which he <u>said</u> to him:
Ehe der Hahn krähen wird,	Before the cock crows
<u>wirst</u> du mich dreimal <u>verleugnen</u>.	you <u>will deny</u> me three times.
Und ging heraus	And he went out
und weinete bitterlich.	and wept bitterly.

Then follows the aria, "Erbarme dich" ["Have mercy"] (no. 39). Its obvious affect is sorrow. Its characteristic rhythmic movement is that of the siciliano, a dance that Mattheson said expressed "melancholy passions." But as is so often the case with Bach, the affect of "Erbarme dich" is deep and complex. There is more involved than sorrow or melancholy. Paul Steinitz seems to be on track to find that something extra when he points out the identity between the opening of "Erbarme dich" and the opening of the first duet of Cantata 140, a movement "about blissful mystical love" (84). But he immediately dismisses the idea that the affect of love is involved in "Erbarme dich" by commenting that this example "serves to show the folly of pursuing thematic relationships too far."

No doubt his general point is correct — pursuing thematic relationships can go too far. But in this case he may have been too quick to dismiss the relationship. In fact, might not love be the ingredient that helps us account for the unmatched poignancy of the sorrow expressed in "Erbarme dich"? Helen Hoekema Van Wyck catches this by recognizing that the siciliano rhythm, in addition to the melancholy Mattheson associated with it, has pastoral associations, and given the context, it is not a big leap to making associations with the Good Shepherd and the Lamb of God. With those associations "the pastoral setting assures the believer that God is merciful and will respond in love" (49).

Recall the situation. The disciple (he or she is each one of us) has denied his Lord and after having done it in the strongest possible language, the cock crowed and "the Lord turned and looked straight at Peter" (Luke 22:61). Matthew did not report Jesus' look, but Bach, I have no doubt, would have remembered that detail from Luke. In fact, the chorale (no. 14) that Bach used in the *St. John Passion* following Peter's denial and penitence makes significant reference to Jesus' "glance" ["Blick"].

Petrus, der nicht denkt zurück,	Peter, who does not think back,
Seinen Gott verneinet,	denies his God;
Der doch auf ein' ernsten Blick	he, however, at a penetrating glance,
Bitterlichen weinet.	Weeps bitterly.

Michael Marissen points out that "Blick" in this chorale "refers to the *Heyland-Blick* ('gaze of the Savior') from Lutheran sermons on the passion narrative. As explained, e.g., in Heinrich Müller's (1631-75) passion sermons, several of which Bach owned, it is the warmth of Jesus' metaphoric gaze that melts the ice of Peter's heart into tears of repentance" (49).

John Calvin saw the same significance in Jesus' glance. He commented that Peter

> had to meet Christ's eyes to come to himself. This is the experience of each one of us. Which of us does not neglect with deaf ear and uncern . . . the actual voice of God, which in Law and Gospel clearly and distinctly resounds for our learning? And it is not for one day only that our minds are seized with this dumb stupidity, but on and on, until He grants us a sight of Himself. This alone converts the hearts of men. It is well worth noting, that it was no ordinary look . . . , but with the turning of His eyes on Peter, there went the secret power of the Spirit piercing his heart with the radiance of His grace. (*A Harmony,* 173)

The sorrow expressed in "Erbarme dich" is the sorrow of one who knows the radiance of grace received from the one he has denied. The disciple knows that the one he denied is the one who first loved him, who still loves him, and who will always love him with a love that can never be matched in return.

One who writes about Bach has to be careful not to overdo the superlatives lest they become meaningless. However, even superlatives are not enough to give a hint of the achingly beautiful expression of sorrow and love in "Erbarme dich." But nothing less than what Bach has done in "Erbarme dich" could make convincing the tranformation in the disciple between "Geduld" and "Komm, süsses Kreuz" ["Come, sweet cross"] (no. 57). The depth of sorrow and love expressed in "Erbarme dich" finally enables the disciple to sing "Komm, süsses Kreuz" without the duplicity that still existed in "Geduld."

The change from "Geduld" to "Komm" is clearly heard in the music. Both, uniquely, use the viola da gamba, but in "Geduld" that instrument is only used as the basso continuo whereas in "Komm" it is entrusted with an obbligato part that is "the only fully chordal solo gamba piece in Bach's oeuvre" (Chafe, *Tonal Allegory*, 357). Both pieces are pervaded by dotted rhythms, but whereas in "Geduld" these gave the music a restless character, in "Komm" they have been transformed to portray an entirely different affect. To characterize that affect, Chafe uses the words that Bach's contemporary, the theorist Johann Mattheson, used to characterize the allemande: "a broken, serious and well-worked-out harmony, which represents the image of a contented, satisfied spirit that delights in good order and rest" (*Tonal Allegory*, 357). Only after the disciple's heart has been pierced by the radiantly gracious look of Jesus can he sing "Come sweet cross" with a "contented, satisfied spirit."

The *St. Matthew Passion* ends with a tender burial chorus, almost a lullaby, in which descending lines appropriately symbolize laying Christ in the tomb. Although this chorus is well loved for its own sake, Bach has sometimes been criticized for ending the *St. Matthew Passion* this way, with Christ in the tomb, with no word of the coming resurrection. But surely that is a misguided criticism, for it fails to take into account that the *St. Matthew Passion* is a liturgical work and its liturgical function was to be the Gospel lesson for the Good Friday Vespers service. As such this work, great as it is in every sense of that term, is not a whole. It is part of a much bigger whole. Bach did not intend for this work to stand by itself. It was meant to be one part of something bigger — a Vespers service — which itself was part of something bigger — all the services of that liturgical day — which in turn were part of Holy Week, which was part of the Lenten season, which was part of the whole liturgical year in which in due time Easter would come and with it an Easter cantata or oratorio. But for this service, on this day, there was no harm — in fact there was, and is, great value — in pausing at the tomb, peering into its depth, and contemplating the depth of our sin and the greater depth of our Savior's love.

Resurrection of Jesus

Heidelberg Catechism Q. & A. 45

Q. How does Christ's resurrection benefit us?

A. By his resurrection he has overcome death, so that he might make us share in the righteousness he won for us by his death.

* * * * * * *

1 Corinthians 5:6-8

Your boasting is not good. Don't you know that a little yeast works through the whole batch of dough? Get rid of the old yeast that you may be a new batch without yeast — as you really are. For Christ, our Passover lamb, has been sacrificed. Therefore let us keep the Festival, not with the old yeast, the yeast of malice and wickedness, but with bread without yeast, the bread of sincerity and truth.

Mark 16:1-8

When the Sabbath was over, Mary Magdalene, Mary the mother of James, and Salome bought spices so that they might go to anoint Jesus' body. Very early on the first day of the week, just after sunrise, they were on their way to the tomb and they asked each other, "Who will roll the stone away from the entrance of the tomb?"

But when they looked up, they saw that the stone, which was very large, had been rolled away. As they entered the tomb, they saw a young man dressed in a white robe sitting on the right side, and they were alarmed.

"Don't be alarmed," he said. "You are looking for Jesus the Nazarene, who was crucified. He has risen! He is not here. See the place where they laid him. But go, tell his disciples and Peter, 'He is going ahead of you into Galilee. There you will see him, just as he told you.'"

Cantata 4: *Christ lag in Todes Banden*

Sinfonia

Verse 1. Chorus

Christ lag in Todes Banden	Christ lay in the bonds of death,
Für unsre Sünd gegeben,	for our sins given;
Er ist wieder erstanden	he is again arisen
Und hat uns bracht das Leben;	and has to us brought life.
Des wir sollen fröhlich sein,	For this we should joyful be,
Gott loben und ihm dankbar sein	praise God and to him thankful be
Und singen halleluja,	and sing hallelujah.
Halleluja!	Hallelujah!

Verse 2. Duet (soprano, alto)

Den Tod niemand zwingen kunnt	That death no one could conquer
Bei allen Menschenkindern,	among all mortal children.
Das macht' alles unser Sünd,	This was all caused by our sin,
Kein Unschuld war zu finden.	no innocence was to be found.
Davon kam der Tod so bald	Hence came death so suddenly
Und nahm über uns Gewalt,	and took over us the power,
Hielt uns in seinem Reich gefangen.	held us in its kingdom captured.
Halleluja!	Hallelujah!

Verse 3. Aria (tenor)

Jesus Christus, Gottes Sohn,	Jesus Christ, God's Son,
An unser Statt ist kommen	in our place has come
Und hat die Sünde weggetan,	and has sin done away with,
Damit dem Tod genommen	thereby from death has taken
All sein Recht und sein Gewalt;	all its right and its power;
Da bleibet nichts denn Tods Gestalt,	there remains nothing but death's image,
Den Stach'l hat er verloren,	the sting has it lost.
Halleluja!	Hallelujah!

Verse 4. Chorus

Es war ein wunderlicher Krieg,	It was a wondrous battle,
Da Tod und Leben rungen,	when death and life struggled;
Das Leben behielt den Sieg,	life retained the victory,

149

Es hat dem Tod verschlungen.
Der Schrift hat verkündigt das,
Wie ein Tod den andern frass,
Ein Spott aus dem Tod ist worden.
Halleluja!

it has death devoured.
Scripture has foretold it,
how one death the other devoured,
a joke of death has been made.
Hallelujah!

Verse 5. Aria (bass)

Hie ist das rechte Osterlamm,
Davon Gott hat geboten,
Das ist hoch an des Kreuzes Stamm
In heisser Lieb gebraten,
Das Blut zeichnet unsre Tür,
Das hält der Glaub dem Tode für,
Der Würger kann uns nicht mehr
    schaden.
Halleluja!

Here is the true Passover lamb,
whereof God has commanded,
which is high on the cross's branch
in ardent love roasted.
The blood marks our door,
that our faith displays to death,
the strangler can us no more
    harm.
Hallelujah!

Verse 6. Duet (soprano, tenor)

So feiern wir das hohe Fest
Mit Herzensfreud und Wonne,
Das uns der Herre scheinen lässt.
Er est selber die Sonne,
Der durch seiner Gnaden Glanz
Erleuchtet unsre Herzen ganz,
Der Sünden Nacht ist verschwunden.
Halleluja!

Thus celebrate we the high feast
with joy of heart and delight,
which for us the Lord lets shine.
He is himself the sun,
who through his grace's radiance
illumines our hearts entirely;
sin's night has vanished.
Hallelujah!

Verse 7. Chorus

Wir essen und leben wohl
In rechten Osterfladen,
Der alte Sauerteig nicht soll
Sein bei dem Wort der Gnaden,
Christus will die Koste sein
Und speisen die Seel allein,
Der Glaub will keins andern leben.
Halleluja!

We eat and live well
on the true Easter bread.
The ancient leaven shall not
be with the word of grace.
Christ will the food be
and nourish the soul alone,
for faith will on none other live.
Hallelujah!

There is more than one way to respond to the incredible miracle of Easter; there is more than one way to sing hallelujah. The most common way is with "all the stops pulled." A burst of rhythmic energy and the glory of trumpets seem to be essential for an Easter celebration. Our expectation for this particular kind of response is so common that it is liable to rule out all other possibilities. It would seem that this expectation was not much different in Bach's time. Certainly Bach fulfilled it in his Easter Cantata 31, *Der Himmel lacht! Die Erde jubilieret! [The heavens laugh! The earth rejoices!]* and his *Easter Oratorio,* both of which begin with flourishes of trumpets and tympani.

Of course, such an expectation is understandable and fitting. After the pain and sorrow of Good Friday the news of resurrection cannot but elicit an exuberant outburst of joy. The two days, Good Friday and Easter, appear side-by-side in the "Crucifixus" and "Et resurrexit" in the Credo of the Mass. Nowhere in music does the contrast between the sorrow of Good Friday and the unalloyed joy of Easter find more vivid expression than in the *Mass in B Minor.* After the "Crucifixus" with its incessant descending chromatic bass, its throbbing rhythm, its drooping melodic lines, its pungent dissonances, and finally its heart-rending modulation paving the way to the pregnant moment of silence between the movements, the sonic glory of trumpets, the upward surging lines, the "run and not be weary" rhythm of "Et resurrexit" are exactly right.

But there is more than one way to respond to Easter; there is more than one way to sing hallelujah. If there is nothing but loud, fast, brassy exuberance, awe and wonder can get lost. Easter also invites a more contemplative response in which the believer steps back and reflects in overwhelmed amazement on the incredible outcome of an incredible course of events. So quieter forms of expression are appropriate, even necessary, for balance and fullness. And they are not necessarily less joyful. It is interesting to note that Bach's *Easter Oratorio* contains both types of response right from the outset, for it begins uniquely with two instrumental numbers. The first one is the typical trumpet and drum celebration; the second is a quiet, contemplative movement, an adagio oboe solo of sublime beauty.

Cantata 4, one of Bach's earliest cantatas, has little of the typical Easter fanfare in it. There are no trumpets. It is in a rigid form in which every movement is based on the same melody, a chorale tune by Martin Luther. It is in a minor key. In fact all eight movements are in the same key — E minor. It begins with a somber sinfonia, its first phrase of text contains the grim word "Todes Banden" ["bonds of death"], and the entire second stanza is completely dark. Spitta characterized the whole cantata as "gloomy" and likened it to a "gnarled and yet majestic . . . primeval oak."

> If we listen to the cantata all through, as a whole, the effect is at first somewhat monotonous, in consequence of the persistency of the chorale melody and of the key of E minor, and from the uniformly low and gloomy pitch of feeling throughout. A dim and mournful light, as of the regions of the north, seems to shine upon it; it is gnarled and yet majestic, like the primeval oak of the forest. From the total absence of all Italian forms, it bears a German and exclusively national stamp. Such a product of art could never have matured under a southern sun — a work in which the Spring festival of the church, the joyful and hopeful Eastertide, is celebrated in tones at once so grandiose and so gloomy. (2:397)

But neither the charge of monotony nor the charge of gloominess can hold up. As we shall see, Bach had more than enough skill and imagination to deal with the threat of monotony brought on by sticking to one basic tune and one key throughout an eight-movement work. He also had more than enough compositional resources and sensitivity to the breadth of religious feeling to express Easter joy without recourse to trumpets and major keys. And he certainly needed those resources because, despite the darker shades that are present in the text, it is ultimately a text of overwhelming joy. It is a text that expands on the first benefit of the resurrection given in the Catechism: Jesus "has overcome death."

The chorale which furnishes all of the text of Cantata 4 was written by Martin Luther in the early years of the Reformation and appeared in the first published chorale books in 1524. Although it is ultimately a joyful text, it has its somber elements. That it is an Easter chorale and not a Passion chorale is apparent from the past tense used in the first line, "Christ lag in Todes Banden" ["Christ lay in the bonds of death"]. But that line also gives a clue that this chorale is not going to celebrate the resurrection without also taking a backward look so as to understand the full significance and marvel of it all. There is something of the nature of a ballad in this text as stanza by stanza it unfolds a marvelous story that begins with death and ends with joyous feasting.

The first verse gives an overview. The first two lines tell of the death of our Lord and the reason for it — "unsre Sünd" ["our sins"]. The next two lines report the resurrection and its happy consequence for us — it "hat uns bracht das Leben" ["has brought life to us"]. The second half of the verse tells what our response should be — "Des wir wollen fröhlich sein" ["for this we should be joyful"]. The remaining verses supply the details. Verse 2 starts at the beginning and tells of our lost and helpless estate as captives held by the power of death. Verse 3 tells that Christ conquered death. Verse 4 follows up with some reflection on the nature of the "wunderlicher Krieg" ["wondrous battle"] between death and life. It also mentions that this "wondrous battle" and its outcome were foretold in Scripture. Verse 5 then makes the connection between this event and the event in Scripture that foretold it, namely, the Passover. Verses 6 and 7 tell of the celebration following the victory.

In addition to the dramatic progression of the text, Luther also gave it a beautiful symmetry. Verse 4, in which the "wondrous battle" is described, stands in the middle. On either side of it is a stanza speaking of Jesus' work (verse 3) and a stanza identifying him as the true Easter Lamb (verse 5). The relationships between verses 2 and 6 and between 1 and 7 are not as complete as between 3 and 5 but they are there nonetheless. Verse 6 concludes by saying that "the night of sin," the topic of verse 2, has vanished, and verse 7, like verse 6, speaks of the celebration that verse 1 said should be our response. Bach caught this symmetry and reinforced it musically. Verses 1, 4, and 7 are choral, 2 and 6 are duets, and 3 and 5 are solos. (See figure 12 below.)

FIGURE 12: The Chiastic Structure of Cantata 4

Verse 1 — "for this we should joyful be"   chorus
Verse 2 — captivity to death due to our sin   duet
Verse 3 — Jesus Christ   solo
Verse 4 — "a wondrous battle"   chorus
Verse 5 — the true Easter Lamb   solo
Verse 6 — "the night of sin has disappeared"   duet
Verse 7 — "We eat . . . the true Easter bread"   chorus

Luther's text is not only exciting in its contents and beautiful in its structure, it is also rich in scriptural and liturgical allusions, particularly in the central verses (3, 4, and 5) about the victory of life over death and the Passover Lamb. The key passage for verses 3 and 4 is 1 Corinthians 15:54-55, which contains the image of death swallowing death (cf. verse 4) and the mockery of death which has lost its "Stach'l" ["sting"] (cf. verse 3):

> When the perishable has been clothed with the imperishable, and the mortal with immortality, then the saying that is written will come true: "Death has been swallowed up in victory." "Where, O death, is your victory? Where, O death is your sting?"

The key passages for verse 5 are not only the Old Testament passages dealing with the Passover Lamb, e.g., Exodus 12:3-29, but also the Epistle lesson for Easter, 1 Corinthians 5:6-8, which contains two important phrases from the Eucharist liturgy: "For Christ our Passover lamb, has been sacrificed. Therefore let us keep the Festival." (The second sentence is the opening line of verse 6.)

The three central verses also contain allusions to a medieval Easter chant, "Victimae paschali laudes immolent Christiani" ["Let Christians dedicate their praises to the Paschal victim"]. Its opening words contain the central imagery of verse 5 as well as the injunction to praise of verse 1; its second line contains the basic thought of verse 3; and its third line contains the idea of the "wondrous battle" in which life conquered death.

"Victimae paschali" is a type of chant known as a sequence. It dates back to the eleventh century when sequences proliferated in the liturgy. It was still well-known in Luther's day, as was a twelfth-century German song derived from it, "Christ ist erstanden" ["Christ is arisen"]. Luther was particularly fond of "Christ ist erstanden." He wrote: "Whoever wrote this hymn had the right conception of Easter. One ultimately tires of all songs, but 'Christ ist erstanden' must be sung every year. The Holy Spirit inspired the person who wrote this song" (quoted from Buszin, 90-91). Interestingly, in the earliest chorale books, "Christ lag in Todes Banden" is described as "'Christ ist erstanden' improved"! Luther's chorale tune for "Christ lag" shows the influence of both its Latin and German models. Its opening phrase is identical with the opening phrase of "Victimae paschali" and very similar to that of "Christ ist erstanden."

Cantata 4 uses Luther's chorale text in its entirety without any additions, something Bach did very rarely. In addition to using the entire chorale text, Bach, as we noted above, used the chorale tune as the basis for all the movements. So Luther's tune is never absent from the music. For a worshiper who knows the chorale's deep historical and liturgical roots, it provides a strong sense of the connection that exists among believers across time.

Bach was masterful in composing music which both provided a wealth of variety around the same tune and captured the essence of the words. In each movement he treated the chorale tune in a different way, and in each the music vivifies the words and impresses them on a worshiper's mind and heart.

The cantata begins with a brief sinfonia that sets a somber mood but ends with some rays of hope. The first four measures simply employ the opening two notes of the chorale melody, a falling half-step, a musical motive that evokes the feeling of a sigh. For two more measures these sighs are heard in various guises in the various parts and then, for two more measures, in antiphony as the lower four parts answer the first violin. Both the mournful character of the falling half-step and the slow, halting rhythmic movement contribute to the somber mood. In the fifth measure, the first violins finally get past the first two notes of the chorale melody and play the first phrase in its entirety with a modest cadential flourish at the end. If the listener has not realized it before, he now knows where those halting first notes came from and can remember the opening words of the familiar chorale which recall Christ's death. This opening is a look back at the cross and the grave.

The rest of the sinfonia abandons the chorale melody except for a rather hidden reference to its second phrase in the continuo. Instead it is given over to a simple ascending motive, first in quarter notes and then in eighth notes, which suggest something hopeful. It will turn out that these ascending notes have a relationship to the hallelujah at the end of the melody, but a listener is not likely to make that connection yet at this point. A cadential flourish brings the movement to a close before the hopeful sign can become anything more than a small hint.

Verse 1 is the most elaborate movement of the cantata. The chorale melody is sung in long notes (mostly half notes) by the sopranos. They begin alone on the word "Christ" and hold it for two measures before they settle into their basic half-note movement. While the sopranos hold their first note, the lower three voices enter in quick succession. Their opening notes bear some resemblance to the chorale melody, but they move mostly in eighth notes. The first and second violins enter in quick succession after the voices, and throughout most of the movement they will have their own independent parts, which will play an important role in defining the mood. In fact the violins are no sooner in than they start to play with a lively motive that will be prominent during the first half of the movement. Rhythmically it consists of three sixteenth notes followed by a quarter note. Melodically the three sixteenth notes turn out to be the opening three notes of the chorale tune but played eight times as fast as they are sung in the soprano part. This motive is playfully tossed back-and-forth between the first and second violins in such a way that one or the other is always playing sixteenth notes. So a three-tiered rhythmic texture results — sopranos singing the melody in half notes, below them the lower voices and strings in eighth notes, and above them the violins in sixteenth notes. There is nothing somber here. The music emphasizes the past tense of the verb of the first phrase — "Christ *lay* in the bonds of death," but not any more!

When Bach got to the third phrase of text — "er ist wieder erstanden" ["he is again arisen"] — he changed the procedure a little. Instead of the sopranos beginning the new phrase, the lower three voices present the chorale melody in a little fugal exposition before the sopranos come in with their half-note version. While the lower voices are preparing the way for the soprano entrance, the sixteenth-note movement subsides momentarily, allowing the new set of words to come through clearly. They are the key words of the whole piece, "er ist wieder erstanden" ["he is again arisen"]!

With the fifth phrase Bach again changed the procedure a little bit. This time there is a double lead-in to the sopranos' singing of the chorale. First the violins lead, and then the lower voices lead before the sopranos come in with the chorale. The lower voices are particularly significant here. As they have done since phrase 2, they introduce the chorale melody in faster note values in imitation. This time, however, instead of each voice taking its turn with the chorale-derived theme, they enter in close succession. In addition, when they get to the word "fröhlich" ["joyful"], they break away from the chorale melody into roulades of sixteenth notes which very quickly take over the whole texture and increase the level of joyful celebration. The instruments' joy even spills over beyond the conclusion of the singing of the words. So this section concludes as it began, with the instruments alone. It is the only phrase of text in the movement framed by instrumental interludes, Bach's way of highlighting "fröhlich."

Phrase 6 again begins in the normal way, with the lower three voices leading the way with imitative entries based on the chorale melody. But a new rhythm is introduced, triggered this time by the word "loben" ["praise"]. The rhythm is an eighth note followed by two sixteenth notes; it will dominate the whole section. Although this new rhythm slightly reduces the rhythmic animation, it in no way reduces the joyful affect. In fact, Bach so frequently used this rhythm in situations of joy that Schweitzer labeled it Bach's "joy motive."

For phrase 7 there is another lessening of the rhythmic animation. It drops to eighth notes. But again there is no lessening of the joy. The joyful affect remains particularly because of the way the instruments and voices perform pairs of eighth notes back-and-forth in playful antiphony. When the voices do it, they are singing "halleluja," breaking it apart in the middle and tossing the two-syllable motives back-and-forth like this:

```
alto:   hal-le - - - lu-ja
tenor:          hal-le - - - lu-ja.
```

But the fun has only begun. After several measures of this, Bach marked "Alla breve" in the music, indicating a speeding up of the tempo for the final section, which is entirely devoted to singing what phrase 7 enjoined, "Halleluja!" After the excitement of the previous phrases, Bach was faced with the danger that the final hallelujahs would be a letdown due to the meager material the chorale melody provided him — only a five-note descending minor scale from B down to E. Of course, the faster tempo would help. Still, the best thing to do would seem to be to abandon the chorale tune except for a brief obbligatory appearance in the soprano part and surround it with exciting music in the lower voices and violins. But Bach was never one to jump to the easy solution, and this case was no exception. Instead of making as little use of the meager tune as possible, he decided to use it *exclusively*. He even abandoned independent violin parts and simply had them double the soprano part. In other words, he decided to build the climax of Easter joy out of a simple five-note scale pattern using no independent instrumental parts.

What Bach did with the simple five-note scale is simple enough to describe, but very hard to do. Only a consummate craftsman could imagine and achieve so much from so little. First he gave it two lively new versions. The first one he gave a syncopated beginning; the second one he simply speeded up to straight eighth notes and turned upside-down so that it ascended a fourth instead of descending a fifth. And then in a contrapuntal *tour de force,* Bach combined these two motives in a seemingly infinite number of ways (and tossed in a little of the antiphony from the previous section for good measure). For twenty-seven measures these two motives run up and down through the texture in a kaleidoscope of combinations with unflagging exuberance. Toward the end, over a pedal point in the bass, the violins again become independent and add antiphonal octave leaps to the exuberance. It is hard to imagine how anyone could hear gloom in this. The light shining through is anything but "dim and mournful"!

But there is gloom in verse 2. Here the text takes us back to the beginning of the story and tells of our helpless captivity in the clutches of death. The music is scored as a soprano and alto duet with continuo accompaniment. There are no obbligato instruments. It begins with continuo alone, playing a two-measure melody that will serve as a quasi-ostinato throughout the movement. The most characteristic interval in this continuo melody is the falling second, derived again from the opening of the chorale melody.

When the voices come in, they, too, sing the falling second derived from the opening of the chorale melody. Sung to the words "den Tod" ["that death"] in slow quarter notes in the same halting antiphonal style used in the sinfonia, this opening is indeed dark. It does not lighten when the soprano finally gets past the opening two notes and words to sing the whole first phrase and, subsequently, the whole chorale tune. It is sung at a slow pace and with certain notes unnaturally lengthened or broken up with rests or in other ways distorted. Particularly noteworthy are the distortions of the fifth and seventh phrases. In the fifth phrase the voices get stuck on "der Tod" ["death"] and repeat it back-and-forth four times before finishing the phrase. Gerhard Herz describes the passage as follows:

> Bach . . . tries to hold off death as long as possible. The voices seem to come up against a wall at the words "der Tod" and the phrase "Hence came death/so suddenly" is torn apart (after "Tod"). Only two beats, set to the German syllables "so bald" (so soon), remain to complete the cantus firmus phrase. But by inserting two echoes . . . and by tone and word repetitions ("der Tod" five times!), Bach succeeds in delaying the final half-cadence for over two measures. (*Bach: Cantata No. 4*, 96)

In the seventh phrase the soprano abandons the chorale melody when the words speak of being held captive in death's kingdom, rising chromatically to a high E on "seinem Reich" ["its kingdom"] while the alto subtly picks up the remainder of the chorale melody. After the high E, the soprano drops an octave and gets stuck on the low E while the alto gets stuck on the F♯ of the chorale melody. Together they are stuck for five slow beats on the E/F♯ dissonance, an almost literal expression of being held captive.

Throughout the movement dissonances are rife and contribute to the sense of darkness and the feeling of pain. The dissonances become most painful on the final hallelujahs where they are the result of singing the descending scale of the chorale melody in or against slowly syncopated lines. The chains of dissonances that result are excruciating yet beautiful. But in spite of all the pain, these are still genuine hallelujahs. There is no irony involved. Over and over we hear the dissonance of pain resolve into the consonance of joy.

Verse 3 is about Jesus' conquest of sin and death. The tenor sings of it in the clearest, most direct way. He sings the sturdy chorale tune for the most part without any distortions or ornamental additions. The two exceptions are in the sixth phrase and in the final hallelujah. Underneath the chorale tune is a steadily and powerfully marching continuo "that struts in a vigorously contoured motif that cadences practically every measure" (Herz, *Bach: Cantata No. 4*, 98). Above the chorale tune and the marchlike bass "the violins exult in a militantly joyous [part]" whose unrelenting rush of sixteenth notes is interrupted only twice — in the same two places that Bach altered the chorale melody in the tenor.

Verse 3 begins with the violins and continuo playing a four-measure ritornello before the tenor comes in. The running sixteenth notes of the violin part are made up of two motives that derive from the chorale melody — the opening three notes (down a step and back up) and the final five notes (the descending scale of the hallelujah). These two motives pervade the perpetual motion sixteenth notes, which continue until phrase 5, the phrase that tells of the conclusion of Jesus' work — it took away "all sein Recht und sein Gewalt" ["all its (death's) right and its power"]. The violins come to a cadence and rest, allowing the tenor's first three words, "all its right," to be heard without interference. The sixteenth notes resume briefly as the tenor completes the phrase. But then a bigger change occurs between phrases 5 and 6. The violin changes from playing its running sixteenth notes to playing eighth-note chords in double, triple, and quadruple stops. Describing these chords, Gerhard Herz says, "Bach slashes away at the enemy [death] with telling results. . . . Their blows send the [continuo] reeling in fast-falling sixteenths, down to the bottom tone E" (*Bach: Cantata No. 4*, 98). The continuo reaches the low E, and the slashing ends as soon as the tenor has sung "da bleibet nichts" ["there remains nothing"]. Not only do the slashing violin double stops end; so does everything else. After "nichts" there is a moment of silence, a moment of "nothing." When the tenor resumes to finish the phrase, the tempo slows from allegro to adagio. The chorale melody is rhythmically distorted by a long-held note on "Tods" ["death's"] and by ornaments that produce the traditional four-note cross configuration and include many sharped notes (another cross symbol). The music is proclaiming the death of death! Nothing is left but "Tods Gestalt" [death's image"]. For those who claim the cross of Christ, the reality of death is no more.

After this dramatic moment, the music resumes its normal course — its marching bass, its sturdy, unadorned chorale, and its exultant sixteenth notes in the violin. "In the wake of the Adagio it acquires the ring of victory" (Herz, *Bach: Cantata No. 4,* 99).

The hallelujahs still remain to be sung, and here, for the second time, the tenor departs from the simple chorale tune. He does not abandon it, but he ornaments it and expands it. In doing so he joins the violins in their exultant sixteenth-note movement. This enables the violins to leave their sixteenth notes for a few beats to play, in eighth notes as at the end of stanza 1, the inverted (i.e., ascending) version of the chorale melody's hallelujah. For the last hallelujah, the tenor also takes up the inverted version. The melisma he sings on the first syllable — "ha-" — is broken up in the middle with a short rest, giving the music a laughing quality. Herz asks rhetorically, "Does Bach here deride the fallen Death?" Indeed he does, anticipating the words at the end of the next verse — "Ein Spott aus dem Tod ist worden" ["a joke has been made of death"].

On one level the story has now been told. But Luther went on in the next two verses to marvel at, and to look more deeply into, the battle that has been fought and won. Verse 4 being the central stanza, Bach returned to the full chorus and wrote a three-part imitative motet around the chorale tune. This time he placed the chorale tune in the alto and left it completely unaltered or adorned. He did, however, put it in the key of B minor, the only time he put the tune in a key other than E minor (though the music as a whole remains in E minor). The STB motet always precedes the entrance of the chorale tune. It has an elaborate contrapuntal texture in which themes derived from the chorale tune are joined by a variety of counterthemes. Coming after a solo number and with a text that reflects on the "wunderlicher" ["wondrous"] nature of the battle described there, this movement strikes me as conversation, at once animated and awestruck, about the battle.

Among the contrapuntal devices used by Bach in this movement are some canons. Especially noteworthy is the canon he wrote for the sixth phrase "wie ein Tod den andern frass" ["how one death (i.e., Christ's) the other devoured"]. This indeed is what is so wondrous about the battle, and Bach wrote for it a wondrous canon that has four successive entrances only two eighth notes apart. The close succession of entrances give the impression of one part swallowing the next. "What is left when all the voices have 'devoured one another'? Precisely nothing! Each voice comes to a dead end. What remains is scornful laughter" (Herz, *Bach: Cantata No. 4*, p. 104) as the voices playfully, and with more than a touch of derision, toss back-and-forth a two-note motive on "ein Spott" ["a joke"].

The final hallelujahs are sung in a long, descending sequence that may sound anticlimactic to some. But if we keep the conversation idea in mind, it sounds like a winding down after all, at least for the moment, has been said. The altos simply sing the five descending notes of the chorale melody; the basses have a confident figure which, nevertheless, grows quieter as it descends; the sopranos have a hint of sighing in their line; and the tenors maintain the prevailing eighth-note movement in something of the jocular vein. Each voice in the conversation has final reflections on a particular facet of the story, and each subsides into a peaceful ending.

That peaceful ending provides a fitting preparation for the beginning of verse 5. Here reflection on the story goes deeper; it goes back to Old Testament prophecy and to the story of the Passover lamb, a shadow and type of Christ. So the movement begins with a musical motive that unmistakably calls to mind the sacrifice of the true Passover Lamb, the Lamb of God. It begins with a descending chromatic line in the continuo, the Baroque "emblem of lament" that Bach, throughout his career, associated so powerfully with the crucifixion.

After this brief reminder from the continuo, the bass soloist enters with the chorale tune. For this movement Bach found yet another way to treat the chorale tune. The basic procedure is to have the bass soloist sing a phrase of the tune and then have the first violin repeat the phrase with rich harmonic support from the lower strings. While the violins have the chorale tune, the bass is free to interpret the words with a newly invented melody. As in previous movements, Bach established a basic "mode of operation" only to depart from it to bring rhetorical force to certain words and phrases.

The first break in the pattern is small but telling. It occurs near the end of the third phrase on the word "Kreuzes" ["cross's"] as the violins are

161

playing the chorale melody. When the violins get to the note for "Kreuzes," they first hold that note for a whole measure and then ornament it in the next measure with the traditional four-note cross symbol. At the same time the bass soloist sings the word "Kreuzes" in parallel motion with the violins. To further emphasize "Kreuzes," Bach arrested the harmonic movement for a measure so the bass and violins could sing and play the cross symbol without interference from other parts. And the chord on which he held up the harmonic movement is made up entirely of sharped notes (another symbol of the cross).

The fourth phrase resumes the normal procedure, but the fifth and sixth phrases depart from it radically. These phrases relate the blood sprinkled over the doorpost at Passover to Jesus' blood, the blood that "der Glaube" ["our faith"] displays to death. The continuo leads in with the first three notes of the chorale melody. The bass soloist then starts the phrase, but when he gets to the third note the first violins enter, again with the first three notes of the phrase. These three "false starts" give a sense of wonder to the music as the singer ponders this incredible mystery.

After the three false starts, the bass finally sings the entire phrase but not without some substantial and significant changes. The verb "zeichnet" ["marks"] is repeated, and the melody line, though kept intact, is ornamented with wide-ranging leaps. These leaps form a series of vivid cross symbols. Then the first violins take up the leaping ornamental line with its cross-shapes while the lower strings all play a four-note accompanimental motive that duplicates the cross motive the first violins and bass soloist had on "Kreuzes" ["cross"] back in the third phrase.

After a cadence the first violins pick up the melody of phrase 5 again and present it without change or ornamentation. The bass also returns to phrase 5, entering two beats after the violins and singing it with even more ornamental leaps which form even more vivid cross symbols. From there the bass continues right into phrase 6, which he sings without ornamentation but with strangely elongated notes. Again there is a sense of great mystery. The first violins follow the normal pattern by repeating the melody, and they seemingly have the rhythm back in order until they get to the note for the word "Tode" ["death"], on which they get stuck for three measures. The harmony in the lower parts also gets stuck at that point, and the bass soloist makes an enormous leap down to a low E♯. Whittaker likens this to the moment at the close of the "Crucifixus" of the *Mass in B Minor* when "one listens breathlessly, gripped by some mysterious power" (1:212).

His observation is fitting because what follows (phrase 7) is a startling burst of energy and exuberance not unlike the "Resurrexit" in the *Mass*. The key changes abruptly from B minor to G major; the bass leaps up to a high D (almost two octaves above the low E♯ he had recently been stuck on) and holds it for nearly four measures; and the first violins play sixteenth notes reminiscent of the triumphant exuberance of verse 3 accompanied by strong cadential chords in the lower strings. In every way the music affirms that "der Würger kann uns nicht mehr schaden" ["the strangler can us no more harm"]. And when Bach reached the word "nicht" he again interjected a note of derision, a reminder of the words at the end of verse 4: death has been made "ein Spott" ["a joke"]. The bass sings "nicht" four times with "nothing" following it but empty rests.

The first violins continue with their statement of phrase 7, but the bass soloist cannot wait for them to finish before singing "halleluja!" So while they play their phrase, he sings "halleluja" in a jocular vein (in cross-shapes!) reminiscent of the tenors at the end of verse 4. Then both the first violins and the bass sing and play motives derived from the leaping ornamentation heard earlier in the stanza. The bass concludes with one more hallelujah that spans two octaves (!), and with large leaps he outlines the most vivid cross symbol yet. This and all the cross symbols in this triumphant conclusion to the verse seem to me to take up Emperor Constantine's battle cry of many centuries earlier (but without his political meaning), "In hoc signo vinces" ["In this sign conquer"].

When the bass has finished his final hallelujah, the violins add a cadential flourish in sixteenth notes that again recall the note of victory sounded in verse 3.

After the victory, the celebration! Stanza 6 celebrates the victory with a dance. If I am not mistaken in thinking that the tempo must be lively and the dotted rhythms in the continuo are to be blended into the prevailing triplets of the voices, it is a gigue. The soprano/tenor duet starts simply enough with the chorale tune in quarter notes, but at the end of the phrase, on the words "mit Herzensfreud und Wonne" ["with joy of heart and delight"], both voices break into a melisma of continuous triplets. The melodic shape of the triplets, like so much else in this cantata, is derived from the opening three notes of the chorale. Once introduced, the triplet figures soon dominate the verse. Their lively but gently rolling movement gives this movement a springlike freshness, and spring, of course, is the season in which Easter occurs. Is it simply coincidence that Bach began the triplet movement on the word "Wonne" and that the month of May, the month traditionally associated with spring, is known in German as "der Wonnemonat" ["month of delight"]?

The last stanza brings the celebration to its climax, the celebration of the Eucharist. Bach, as would later be his custom in Leipzig, chose to set this in a four-part chordal harmonization and thus bring the work to conclusion with the chorale as the congregation was accustomed to sing it. As is always the case with Bach's four-part harmonizations, this one is incomparable and in some mysterious way is, as he instructed his organ students, "according to the sense [*Affect*] of the words" (*The New Bach Reader,* 336). Although Bach gave us six wonderful and widely different ways to sing hallelujah at the end of the previous verses, he was still able in this simple harmonization of the five-note descending scale at the end of this final verse to give us yet another way, a way that, for all its simplicity, touches still deeper and richer veins of joy.

Part III: Discipleship

"By his resurrection he has overcome death." This, according to the Heidelberg Catechism, is the first benefit of Christ's resurrection. It is the theme at the heart of Cantata 4. But the Catechism lists two other benefits: "Second, by his power we too are already now resurrected to a new life. Third, Christ's resurrection is a guarantee of our glorious resurrection." Although neither of these benefits received attention in the previous chapter, they will not be ignored since they are related to the topics of the first and fourth chapters of this third section.

Our topic in this third section, discipleship, is not exactly the topic of Part III of the Catechism, but is closely related to it. Part III of the Catechism deals with our response to our deliverance from sin and death. Gratitude is the proper, indeed the inevitable, response of those who truly know from what they have been delivered. But that gratitude cannot be expressed by words only; it must also be expressed in deeds, "so that," as the Catechism puts it, "in all our living we may show that we are thankful to God for all he has done for us, and so that he may be praised through us." The Catechism also says that "we do good because Christ by his Spirit is also renewing us to be like himself" (Answer 86), and in that way links following and being like Jesus — that is, discipleship — with our response of gratitude.

Part III of the Catechism has two sections. The first deals with the Ten Commandments and the second with the Lord's Prayer. This puts the Heidelberg Catechism squarely in line with a long-standing tradition. Catechisms traditionally had four sections, one for each of four topics — the Ten Commandments, the Creed, the Lord's Prayer, and the sacraments. Martin

165

Luther's Large and Small Catechisms both have that structure. So does the Heidelberg Catechism, but it is less immediately apparent because it is embedded in the larger threefold structure of misery, deliverance, and gratitude (or, in the terms of this book, death, deliverance, and discipleship).

> The first section, on *misery,* uses the summary of the law as the teacher of sin and the pointer to Christ. The second section, on *deliverance,* follows the sequence of the Apostles' Creed and concludes with a section on the sacraments as God's gracious guarantees of our only comfort. The third part explains the thanks, the *gratitude,* that a believer shows to God for Christ's complete deliverance. That section includes the Ten Commandments as the norm to follow in thankful living. Since prayer is "the most important part of the thankfulness God requires of us" (Q & A 116), the catechism concludes with a discussion of the Lord's Prayer. (Klooster, 823)

Of the two sections in Part III, I will focus on the section on the Ten Commandments because it is more directly connected to the theme of discipleship. It is introduced by questions having to do with "the dying-away of the old self, and the coming-to-life of the new." The connection between the Law and the coming-to-life of the new self will be the main focus of the first chapter in this section. Then I will depart from the Catechism's order but not from its teachings on discipleship. Instead of going on to the section on the Lord's Prayer, I will go back to an earlier question that has important implications for discipleship — "Why are you called a Christian?" The threefold answer provides the focus for the remaining three chapters — to confess his name, to be a living sacrifice, and to reign with him eternally.

Coming-to-Life of the New Self

Heidelberg Catechism Q. & A. 45, 90, and 91

Q. How does Christ's resurrection benefit us?

A. By his power we too are already now resurrected to a new life.

Q. What is the coming-to-life of the new self?

A. It is wholehearted joy in God through Christ and a delight to do every kind of good as God wants us to.

Q. What do we do that is good?

A. Only that which arises out of true faith, conforms to God's law, and is done for his glory. . . .

Martin Luther thought it important for Christians to sing the Lord's Prayer, the Creed, and the Ten Commandments. To make this possible, he made versifications of those texts. They are: "Vater unser im Himmelreich" ["Our Father in heaven"], "Wir glauben all an einen Gott" ["We all believe in one God"], and "Dies sind die heil'gen zehn Gebot" ["These are the holy ten commandments"].

Most of us probably do not have much trouble conceiving of the Lord's Prayer as a hymn, but to sing the Creed and, even more, the Ten Commandments probably seems odd to many of us. Concerning the Nicene Creed, Albert Schweitzer wrote, "If ever there was a text put together without any idea of its being set to music it is this . . ." (2:317). I expect many of us would think that his words are even more applicable to the Ten Commandments. Nevertheless, as Ulrich Leupold says in his edition of Luther's chorales, Luther "considered it very important for the church to have hymns on the Ten Commandments." Leupold goes on to explain that if the "idea of writing a hymn on the Ten Commandments seems preposterous" to us, it is because we

> have become so accustomed to think of poetry as an expression of the personal feelings and emotions of the writer that we cannot conceive of a merely "utilitarian" use of poetry. Hymnody in our own age has been defined as "lyrical religion." We find it difficult to think of a merely didactic hymn without sentimental overtones.
>
> But Luther proceeded from different premises. Very soberly he thought of the hymn as a means of instilling the Word of God in the people. While some of his hymns were born out of his most personal ex-

periences and reflected the struggles and victories of his own faith, others were mere versifications of the Catechism. (*Luther's Works*, 53:277)

Bach, as we have seen, set the Nicene Creed to music when he completed the *Mass in B Minor*, but he never set its entire chorale version to music, nor did he set the entire chorale versions of the Ten Commandments or the Lord's Prayer. Although he often included settings of individual chorale stanzas in his cantatas and Passions, only very rarely did he write cantatas that included all the stanzas of a chorale. (Cantata 4 is a notable exception.) So, for example, although certain stanzas from the Lord's Prayer chorale ("Vater unser") were set to music by Bach for use in larger works, he never set all the stanzas as a single work.

Bach did, however, set the melodies of these three chorales as chorale preludes for organ and in that sense can be said to have set the Lord's Prayer ("Vater unser"), the Creed ("Wir glauben"), and the Ten Commandments ("Dies sind") to music. He set "Vater unser" four times, "Wir glauben" twice, and "Dies sind" three times. He also incorporated the melody of "Dies sind" into the complex first movement of Cantata 77. The four settings of "Dies sind" shed some interesting and instructive light on Bach's attitude toward the law. In particular they point up two things that many fail to understand — first, that living by the law is not a drudgery but a joy; and, second, that law and freedom are not antithetical but closely related.

People love freedom and they love to sing about it. That is no surprise. Slavery and tyranny of all sorts have been a constant blot on human history. So enslaved and tyrannized people have sung songs longing for freedom (think, e.g., of a Negro spiritual like "When Israel Was in Egypt Land") or songs celebrating it (think, e.g., of "America"). But people do not typically sing songs longing for or celebrating law. They might recognize it as necessary for the functioning of society and, if they are of a religious bent, as a teacher of sin, but neither of these are functions people typically yearn for or celebrate.

Luther's view of the law included those two functions.

It could be used, first, as a *civil* protection against chaos. The law is a dike against sin. Through the "order" of government, and the government's laws against stealing, killing, bearing false witness, and the like, God providentially prevents a fallen creation from sliding completely into chaos and ruin.

The second use of the law, in Luther's view, is its chief use. This is a *theological* or religious use. The law is a mirror in which the sinner sees his shabbiness, his misery, his desperate need of the Savior. The law strikes terror in him, and drives him to despair. Only in despair does he see his need of justification by grace. (Plantinga, 30)

Of Bach's four settings of "Dies sind," the large one from *Clavier Übung* III (BWV 678), if listened to casually, is the one least likely to be puzzling to those who view the law only as "a dike against sin" and "a mirror in which the sinner sees his shabbiness." If the piece is performed slowly, as it often is, it seems to have an overall somber cast. But to hear it as simply a somber reflection upon the law is to oversimplify a very complex piece. Peter Williams points out that many commentators "have been uncertain of the purpose or character of the movement" (2:202).

But at least the character of its opening measures is clear enough. It starts as a pastorale. There is a drone in the bass while the two upper parts play a quiet melody in imitation in a gently moving 6/4 meter. This melody begins with three stepwise descending quarter notes, which are followed by a leap up to a sustained note, and then concludes with arpeggiated eighth notes. That whole sequence comes back only once, but the arpeggiated eighth notes are quite prominent throughout the piece. Their presence keeps the opening pastorale affect in mind. Following the pastoral theme is a "sighing" motive — two pairs of eighth notes falling by step. This, too, is heard throughout the piece. Its plaintive character is intensified the several times it is accompanied by a slowly descending chromatic line (the Baroque "emblem of lament"). The sighing and lamentation express sorrow for the sin that the law reveals, a sorrow that is all the more poignant against the backdrop of the innocence suggested by the pastorale.

But that is not all there is. The piece is also filled with running sixteenth-note figures, mostly stepwise in movement. If the tempo is not too slow, these figures give a lively sense of movement throughout the piece that counterbalances the more halting movement of the sighs. And (again if the tempo is not too slow) the bass part in the pedals has a bit of lilt in its step as it moves along in steady quarter notes in 6/4 meter. So it seems to me that this piece contains at least as much expression of a joyful response to the law as of sorrow for the sin that the law convicts us of. But be that as it may, the other pieces based on "Dies sind," especially the other two chorale preludes, leave little room for doubt that Bach thought

169

of the law as more than a teacher of sin and a provider of some civic stability.

The chorale prelude on "Dies sind" in the *Orgel-Büchlein* (BWV 635) has the chorale melody in half notes in the top part. This expressively neutral statement of the chorale melody serves simply to call its text to mind and to serve as the structural basis for the piece. Underneath the chorale melody, the lower three parts play two different kinds of themes, both of which impart a decidedly joyful affect to the piece. One of the themes is an eighth-note version of the first phrase of the chorale melody. In other words, it is the first phrase of the chorale melody played four times faster than it is played in the soprano part. This lively version of the first phrase is tossed around from part to part, sometimes in alternation, sometimes in imitation, and sometimes simultaneously in two parts. When it is played simultaneously in two parts, one of the parts plays the theme upside down. It is all very playful. What adds to the playfulness is the shape of the theme itself. It begins, unusually, with five repeated notes and then ascends by step up a fourth. The repeated notes, when played on an organ, will naturally be detached. At a lively pace, these detached eighth notes lend a playful character to the chorale theme. They also make for a clarity of texture that brings out Bach's playful treatment of that theme.

The final thematic ingredient in BWV 635 is running sixteenth-note figures, not unlike those that appear in BWV 678. After the first two beats of the piece, there is no moment when these sixteenth notes are not running through the texture in one part or another, or, toward the end, even in two parts at a time. Again, it is all very playful, especially if one recognizes that the sixteenth-note figures are generally grouped in the shape of a stepwise ascent or descent of a fourth. In other words, they are the last four notes of the first phrase of the chorale melody played eight times as fast as they are in the soprano.

Bach's response to the law in the small chorale prelude for "Dies sind" from *Clavier Übung* III (BWV 679) is, if anything, even more playfully and exuberantly joyful than in BWV 635. I will discuss it in more detail later. Here it will suffice to note that it is a lively, bouncing gigue.

Why these joyful responses to the law? Bach certainly would have known Luther's teaching about the law. As a boy he undoubtedly memorized the answer to the final question on the Ten Commandments in Luther's Small Catechism: "God warns that he will punish all who break these commandments. Therefore we are to fear his wrath and not disobey him." But he also would have memorized the rest of the answer with its more positive slant: "But he promises grace and every blessing to all who keep these commandments. Therefore we are to love and trust him, and gladly do what he commands." Of course, Bach knew that he did not, indeed could not, "keep these commandments" and "do what [God] commands." So the positive note at the end of the answer could not by itself have prompted his joyful response to the law. Bach must have learned somewhere in his Lutheran training something akin to the Heidelberg Catechism's view of the law. To be sure, in Part I the Heidelberg Catechism uses the law (in the form of Jesus' summary) as a teacher of sin. But in the much bigger portion that it allocates to the law in Part III, the law has the more joyful function of teaching us how to live a life of gratitude.

Luther's view of the law was not limited to the two functions already mentioned. The last part of the answer in his Shorter Catechism hints at a third aspect in his teaching about the law which Paul Althaus summarizes as follows:

> [The] will of God no longer confronts the justified as the demand of the law, that is, in the form of the law. For Christ and his Spirit live in them through faith. Therefore they do what the law wants of themselves. Christ does it in them. The Spirit has produced new drives within them in the form of loving God and his laws and hating evil. They now rejoice in God's law. . . .
>
> The law thus "begins to be a joyous thing," and the Christian becomes willing to fulfill it and is at least able to make a beginning in fulfilling it. He no longer stands under a demand but is joyfully moved toward God's law by the power of the Holy Spirit. Christ leads man out of his condition under the law back to that of joyous obedience of the law, which men knew before the fall into sin. (267)

This is exactly in line with the Heidelberg Catechism's teaching about the law in Part III, where it is seen as an important aspect of our response of gratitude. Actually it is more accurate to say that the Heidelberg Catechism is in line with Lutheran teaching, for, as Althaus points out, the placing of the law after redemption and under gratitude "occurs in Lutheran catechisms as early as 1547" (273). Like the authors of the catechisms, Lutheran and Reformed alike, Bach knew that the new self has a "wholehearted joy in God through Christ and a delight to do every kind of good . . . which conforms to God's law." His chorale preludes on "Dies sind" express that joy, even to the point of dancing a jig.

171

An aspect of law that is often misunderstood is its relationship to freedom. If it is hard for our old selves to fathom a joyful response to the law, it is at least as hard for them to understand the connection between law and freedom because on the surface they appear to be opposites. Where there is one, the other, it seems, needs to be absent. But Bach understood that there is a relationship between law and freedom, and his entire musical output seems to me to demonstrate the relationship.

Two opposite and seemingly incompatible aspects of the reception of Bach's music suggest that there is a relationship between law and freedom. On the one hand Bach has become the composer most readily associated with "classical" music. More specifically he is associated with all that is learned, difficult, intellectual, and contrived in music. He is first on the list of composers of "masses and fugues and ops" that Gilbert and Sullivan's Mikado threatens to inflict on music-hall singers in his attempt to make "the punishment fit the crime." This aspect of Bach's reputation is not new. The famous criticism by his contemporary, Johann Adolph Scheibe, voiced the opinion of many (cf. p. 47). In calling Bach's music "turgid and confused," "artificial," in "conflict with Nature," and the result of "onerous labor," Scheibe was saying the same thing as those today who view his music as learned, intellectual, and contrived. No doubt there is some truth in that view of Bach. In no other composer's works do fugues and canons and other complex sorts of counterpoint loom so large. And it is no accident that Bach's music, more than any other, has been the basis for the academic training of music students in harmony and counterpoint.

But that is only one side of Bach. Malcolm Boyd points out that

> To-day a performance of the B minor Mass or of the Brandenburg Concertos can be relied on to fill a cathedral or concert hall, and festivals devoted largely or exclusively to Bach are commonplace in the musical calendar. Every generation of music lovers seems to find in the works of this incomparable artist that *Gemütsvergötzung*, that "refreshment of spirit," which his title-pages promised, and which his music so richly provides. (221)

That "refreshment of spirit" which Bach's music provides explains why popular recordings of his music bear titles like "The Music of Jubilee" or "The Joy of Bach" — certainly not titles suggestive of stuffy academicism. It also partly explains why no other "classical" composer has been "jazzed up" more successfully than Bach and why the Swingle Singers' best hits were arrangements of his music. These are symptoms of what all Bach lovers know: there is no more exuberantly festive music, no more intensely expressive music, no more sublimely beautiful music, and no music so full of life as that of J. S. Bach.

To the modern mind, with its high premium on freedom and rights and with its facile equation of unfettered spontaneity with joy, these two sides of Bach present an anomaly. If both views of Bach are correct, then it would seem that Bach must have been some kind of artistic split personality; sometimes he was a stuffy academician writing canons and fugues while at other times he took off his powdered wig, unbuttoned his waistcoat, and "let it all hang out." But that is not true. There are not some stuffy academic pieces that no one listens to and some "unbuttoned" pieces that people enjoy. The Brandenburg Concertos, the *Well-tempered Clavier*, the Goldberg Variations, and the *Mass in B Minor*, for example, are among Bach's more popular works. Yet these are works filled with the utmost in compositional complexity and sophistication. One is bound to be astonished, as Boyd puts it, "that music which makes so few concessions to the listener should enjoy an immense popular following" (221).

In this 250th anniversary of Bach's death, amidst all the hubbub of special concerts, festivals, conventions, recordings, and what-have-you, we would do well to take some time to consider why Bach's music can be at once learned and popular, technical and exuberant, disciplined and expressive, strict and free. It seems to me that one of the most beneficial functions Bach's music can perform for our harried, confused generation is to stand as a monumental testimony to the intimate relationship between freedom and law.

Christianity has always taught the paradoxical truth that true freedom can be achieved only within the context of law.

> The implication, for instance, of the Adam and Eve story is that if they *had* bowed to the interdict placed on the forbidden fruit, life and not death would have been the guerdon. That is, paradoxically, if they had knuckled under to what looked emphatically like a *denial* of their freedom ("Thou shalt not" is not a very convincing corollary to the "Have dominion" charge), they would have discovered something unimaginable to them — something that, according to the story, was at that very point lost to them and us for the duration of human time. (Howard, 113)

Throughout Scripture one runs into startling juxtapositions of law and freedom. The God who gave the law to his people is the one who delivered them "out of the land of slavery" (Exodus 20:2). Psalm 119:44-45 says without flinching:

I will always obey your law,
    forever and ever.
I will walk about in freedom,
    for I have sought out your precepts.

Paul could say, in two consecutive breaths, "you were called to be free" and "serve one another" (Galatians 5:13), and James wrote about the "law that gives freedom" (1:25). Christians know, therefore, that there is a sense in which Sam Levenson's phrase, "the statutes of liberty," is not tongue-in-cheek and we sing without a touch of irony, "Make me a captive, Lord, and then I shall be free."

Although this fundamental paradox was submerged during this past century's clamor for rights and freedoms, it was not lost. Rudolf Bultmann, for example, understood that "Genuine freedom is not subjective arbitrariness, but freedom from the motivation of the moment. It is possible only when conduct is determined by a motive which transcends the present moment, that is, by law" (quoted in Mellers, p. 75). Charles Williams, in one of his Arthurian poems, wrote perceptively about the moment a young slave of Taliessin recognized that "servitude and freedom were one and interchangeable" (149). And Igor Stravinsky, perhaps the finest composer of our century, stated the paradox very bluntly in his *Poetics of Music:* "The more art is controlled, limited, worked over, the more it is free." He went on to say,

> my freedom will be so much the greater and more meaningful the more narrowly I limit my field of action and the more I surround myself with obstacles. Whatever diminishes constraint diminishes strength. The more constraints one imposes, the more one frees oneself of the chains that shackle the spirit. (pp. 66 and 68)

As in everything else, true freedom in music is found on the far side of rules and discipline; it is not a matter of unfettered spontaneity. When Luther praised Josquin des Prez, the greatest composer of his day, as a composer who made the notes do what he wanted them to do while other composers had to do what the notes wanted, he was not saying that Josquin was a sixteenth-century John Cage. Cage had no meaningful freedom. As Thomas Howard points out in connection with Andy Warhol, absolute openness of option is slavery and the taskmaster is ennui. Instead, Luther realized that Josquin's freedom, like the freedom attained by the athlete, the ballet dancer, or the saint was a freedom that was the result of rigorous discipline. Had Luther lived two centuries later he would have made the same statement about Bach. No other composer was more rigorously disciplined, and no other composer has ever been more free to make the notes do what he wants. No other repertory of music stands as a more eloquent testimony to the interdependency of freedom and law. I mention just two examples. The D♯-minor Fugue from the first book of the *Well-Tempered Clavier* overflows with complex, sophisticated contrapuntal techniques, and yet there is no more sublimely beautiful piece of music. The chorus "Cum Sancto Spiritu" from the *Mass in B Minor* contains two strict fugal expositions within a very precise ritornello form, but there is no more exuberant, even ecstatic, music. Wilfrid Mellers hears "Bacchic [pun intended?] abandonment" in the movement. After hearing it one might be tempted to remark as Susan did after the Bacchic romp in *Prince Caspian,* "I wouldn't have felt very safe with Bacchus and all his wild girls if we'd met them without Aslan." "I should think not," said Lucy (133).

One could go on citing examples of the inseparability of Bach's disciplined technique from his freedom and power of expression. Those who dismiss the paradox by saying his music is expressive in spite of all the technical complexities have it wrong. Bach's music is expressive not in spite of them but through them.

That Bach understood and rejoiced in the relationship of law to freedom can be inferred from Cantata 77, which begins with a chorus based on Jesus' summary of the law:

Du sollst Gott, deinen Herren, <u>lieben</u>   You shall <u>love</u> God, your Lord,
von ganzem Herzen, von ganzer Seele,   with all your heart, with all your soul,
von allen Kräften und von ganzem   with all your strength and all your
   Gemüte   mind
und deinen Nächsten als dich selbst.   and your neighbor as yourself.
  (Luke 10:27)

On this text Bach wrote a fugue, the most "learned" of musical forms, consisting of ten choral expositions (ten, of course, being a number

175

symbol for the law). For the main theme of the fugue Bach turned to the first phrase of the Ten Commandments chorale, "Dies sind die Heilgen zehn Gebot," and turned it upside down and backwards. Not content with that ingenious way of uniting Christ's summary of the law (the words being sung) with the Ten Commandments (the theme to which they are sung), Bach devised another way to introduce the Ten Commandments chorale and to bring in some more symbolism with it. He framed the fugue with the entire "Dies sind" tune in canon between the trumpet (symbolizing the voice of God) and the instrumental basses (the foundation). Canons traditionally symbolized law not only because the word itself means law or rule, but also because canons are the strictest kind of counterpoint consisting of one part imitating another exactly. But it is no ordinary canon that Bach wrote in this movement; it is a canon in which the trumpet plays the chorale melody at normal speed while the basses play it with the note-lengths doubled. Bach could have let it go at that, but since the basses take twice as long as the trumpet to play each phrase, he had room for the trumpet to play more. So he had the trumpet play the first phrase again after each of the other phrases. In addition he decided to turn the four-phrase chorale melody into five phrases so as to give him another way of introducing the symbolically significant number ten. With five phrases to work with, and with the repetitions of the first phrase, the trumpet makes ten statements. (See figure 13 on p. 177.) Note that in its tenth statement, the trumpet plays the entire chorale melody. The reason the trumpet has time to play the whole melody is that the basses hold their last note for ten measures.

To write a fugue on what might be called an artificially derived theme and involving the amount of contrapuntal intricacy that this one does is no small feat. To write a canon in augmentation using a pre-existing chorale melody and then to complicate it with periodic returns of the first phrase is not easy. To be able to combine that fugue and that canon in a single piece all the while filling it with meaningful number symbols is something possible only by someone who has disciplined his craft to the highest level. But the first movement of Cantata 77 is not merely a technical *tour de force*. The result of all the technical strictures is not artificial and constricted but a freely flowing piece that beautifully expresses something of Bach's love for God's law. Like so many of Bach's works, this one stands as a demonstration of the relationship between law and freedom. And I cannot help but think that Bach made this demonstration especially emphatic here because of the text he was setting.

FIGURE 13: **The Statements of Chorale Phrases in Cantata 77,
First Movement**

Statement no.	Phrase(s) of chorale played
1	1
2	1
3	2
4	1
5	3
6	1 & 3
7	4
8	1
9	5
10	1-5

I would say the same for the small chorale prelude on "Dies sind" in *Clavier Übung* III, BWV 679. In this setting, as in Cantata 77, Bach first "bound" himself to that most learned of musical forms, the fugue. But he could not freely invent a theme for that fugue because it had to bear some resemblance to the chorale tune or its point would be lost. As if those restrictions were not enough, he seems to have set himself the additional task of filling the piece with the number ten as the symbol of the law (again as in Cantata 77). There are ten statements of the fugue theme, which is ten beats long and ten half-steps in range; and the piece concludes over a pedal point ten beats long. And remember, this chorale prelude is a wonderfully exuberant gigue. In two minutes Bach's piece expresses almost as much delight in the law as do the 176 verses of Psalm 119. Moreover, with all its restrictions, this gigue dances along so freely that it provides yet one more small demonstration in sound, among so many bigger ones in Bach's music, of the inseparability of law and freedom. Bach, I have no doubt, would have agreed with G. K. Chesterton:

> I could never conceive or tolerate any Utopia which did not leave to me the liberty for which I chiefly care, the liberty to bind myself. Complete anarchy would not merely make it impossible to have any discipline or fidelity; it would also make it impossible to have any fun. (121)

Anointed to Confess His Name

Heidelberg Catechism Q. & A. 32

Q. Why are you called a Christian?

A. Because by faith I am a member of Christ and so I share in his anointing. I am anointed to confess his name. . . .

* * * * * * *

Isaiah 11:1-5

A shoot will come up from the stump of Jesse; from his roots a Branch will bear fruit. The Spirit of the LORD will rest on him — the Spirit of wisdom and of understanding, the Spirit of counsel and of power, the Spirit of knowledge and of the fear of the LORD — and he will delight in the fear of the LORD.

He will not judge by what he sees with his eyes, or decide by what he hears with his ears; but with righteousness he will judge the needy, with justice he will give decisions for the poor of the earth. He will strike the earth with the rod of his mouth; with the breath of his lips he will slay the wicked. Righteousness will be his belt and faithfulness the sash around his waist.

Luke 1:39-56

At that time Mary got ready and hurried to a town in the hill country of Judea, where she entered Zechariah's home and greeted Elizabeth. When Elizabeth heard Mary's greeting, the baby leaped in her womb, and Elizabeth was filled with the Holy Spirit. In a loud voice she exclaimed: "Blessed are you among women, and blessed is the child you will bear! But why am I so favored, that the mother of my Lord should come to me? As soon as the sound of your greeting reached my ears, the baby in my womb leaped for joy. Blessed is she who has believed that what the Lord has said to her will be accomplished!"

And Mary said:

"My soul glorifies the Lord
    and my spirit rejoices in God my Savior,

for he has been mindful
of the humble state of his servant.
From now on all generations will call me blessed,
for the Mighty One has done great things for me —
holy is his name.
His mercy extends to those who fear him,
from generation to generation.
He has performed mighty deeds with his arm;
he has scattered those who are proud in their inmost thoughts.
He has brought down rulers from their thrones
but has lifted up the humble.
He has filled the hungry with good things
but has sent the rich away empty.
He has helped his servant Israel,
remembering to be merciful
to Abraham and his descendants forever,
even as he said to our fathers."

Mary stayed with Elizabeth for about three months and then returned home.

Cantata 147: *Herz und Mund und Tat und Leben*

Part I

1. *Chorus*

Herz und Mund und Tat und Leben	Heart and mouth and deed and life
Muß von Christo Zeugnis geben	must of Christ witness give
Ohne Furcht und Heuchelei,	without fear and hypocrisy,
Daß er Gott und Heiland <u>sei</u>.	that he <u>is</u> God and Savior.

2. *Recitative* (tenor)

Gebenedeiter Mund!	Blessed mouth!
Maria macht ihr Innerstes der Seelen	Mary makes her innermost soul <u>known</u>
Durch Dank und Rühmen <u>kund</u>;	through thanks and praise.
Sie fänget bei sich an,	She begins by herself
Des Heilands Wunder zu erzählen,	of the Savior's wonders to relate,
Was er an ihr als seiner Magd	what he through her, as his maid,
getan.	has done.
O menschliches Geschlecht,	O human race,

179

Des Satans und der Sünden Knecht,	of Satan and of sin the slave,
Du bist befreit	you are set free
Durch Christi tröstendes Erscheinen	through Christ's comforting appearance,
Von dieser Last und Dienstbarkeit!	from this burden and slavery!
Jedoch dein Mund und dein verstockt Gemüte	Yet your mouth and your stubborn spirit
Verschweigt, verleugnet solche Güte;	are silent, denying such goodness.
Doch wisse, daß <u>dich</u> nach der Schrift	Yet know that, according to Scripture,
Ein allzuscharfes Urteil trifft!	an all too sharp judgment will strike <u>you</u>!

3. Aria (alto)

Schäme dich, o Seele, <u>nicht</u>,	Be <u>not</u> ashamed, O soul,
Deinen Heiland zu bekennen,	your Savior to confess,
Soll er dich die seine <u>nennen</u>	if he <u>is to name</u> you as his own
Vor des Vaters Angesicht!	before his Father's face!
Doch wer ihn auf dieser Erden	For whoever him on this earth
Zu verleugnen sich nicht scheut,	from denying does not hesitate,
Soll von ihm verleugnet werden,	shall by him be denied
Wenn er kommt zur Herrlichkeit.	when he comes in majesty.

4. Recitative (bass)

Verstockung kann Gewaltige verblenden,	Stubbornness can the mighty blind
Bis sie des Höchsten Arm vom Stuhle stößt;	until them the Highest's arm from their throne thrusts.
Doch dieser Arm erhebt,	Yet this arm exalts —
Obschon vor ihm der Erde Kreis erbebt,	although before it the earth's sphere quakes —
Hingegen die Elenden,	in turn the wretched
So er erlöst.	whom he redeems.
O hochbeglückte Christen,	O highly favored Christians,
Auf, machet euch bereit,	up, make yourselves ready,
Itzt ist die angenehme Zeit,	now is the welcome time,
Itzt ist der Tag des Heils:	now is the day of salvation.
der Heiland heißt	The Savior calls
Euch Leib und Geist	you, body and soul,
Mit Glaubensgaben rüsten,	with gifts of faith to arm yourselves.
Auf, ruft zu ihm in brünstigem Verlangen,	Up, call to him in burning longing
Um ihn im Glauben zu empfangen!	so as him in faith to receive.

180

5. *Aria* (soprano)

Bereite <u>dir</u>, Jesu, noch itzo die Bahn,
Mein Heiland, erwähle
Die gläubende Seele,
Und siehe mit Augen der Gnade
    mich an!

Make ready, Jesus, yet now the way <u>to you</u>;
my Savior, elect
this believing soul
and look with eyes of grace
    upon me.

6. *Chorale*

Wohl mir, daß ich Jesum habe,
O wie feste halt ich ihn,
Daß er mir mein Herze labe,
Wenn ich krank und traurig <u>bin</u>.
Jesum hab ich, der mich liebet
Und sich mir zu eigen gibet;
Ach drum laß ich Jesum nicht,
Wenn mir gleich mein Herze
    bricht.

Blest am I that I have Jesus.
O how firmly hold I him,
so that he my heart refreshes
when I <u>am</u> sick and sorrowful.
Jesus have I, who me loves
and himself to me entrusts.
Ah, therefore leave I Jesus not,
even though in me my heart
    should break.

Part II

7. *Aria* (tenor)

Hilf, Jesu, hilf, daß ich auch
    dich bekenne
In Wohl und Weh, in Freud und Leid,
Daß ich dich meinen Heiland nenne
In Glauben und Gelassenheit,
Daß stets mein Herz von deiner
    Liebe brenne.

Help, Jesus, help, so that I also
    you confess
in well-being and woe, in joy and sorrow,
that I you my Savior name
in faith and composure,
that ever my heart with your
    love would burn.

8. *Recitative* (alto)

Der höchsten Allmacht Wunderhand
Wirkt im Verborgenen der Erden.
Johannes muß mit Geist erfüllet werden,
Ihn zieht der Liebe Band
Bereits in seiner Mutter Leibe,
Daß er den Heiland kennt,
Ob er ihn gleich noch nicht
Mit seinem Munde nennt,
Er wird bewegt, er hüpft und springet,

The Highest's almighty hand of wonder
works in the hidden places of the earth.
John must with the Spirit be filled,
him draws the bond of love
already in his mother's womb,
that he the Savior knows,
although he him still not yet
with his mouth names.
He becomes stirred; he leaps and springs

181

Indem Elisabeth das Wunderwerk
   ausspricht,
Indem Mariae Mund der Lippen
   Opfer bringet.
Wenn ihr, o Gläubige,
Des Fleisches Schwachheit merkt,
Wenn euer Herz in Liebe brennet,
Und doch der Mund den Heiland
   nicht bekennet,
Gott ist es, der euch kräftig stärkt,
Er will in euch des Geistes Kraft erregen,
Ja Dank und Preis auf eure
   Zunge legen.

so that Elizabeth the miracle
   proclaims,
so that Mary's mouth the offering
   of lips brings.
If you, O believers,
the weakness of the flesh mark,
if your heart with love burns,
and still your mouth the Savior
   does not confess,
God it is who powerfully strengthens you;
he will in you the Spirit's power inspire,
yes, thanks and praise upon your
   tongue shall lay.

9. Aria (bass)

Ich will von Jesu Wundern singen
Und ihm der Lippen Opfer bringen,
Er wird nach seiner Liebe Bund
Das schwache Fleisch, den irdschen Mund
Durch heilges Feuer kräftig zwingen.

I will of Jesus' wonders sing
and to him the offering of lips bring.
He will by his love's bond
my weak flesh, my earthly mouth
through holy fire powerfully compel.

10. Chorale

Jesus bleibet meine Freude,
Meines Herzens Trost und Saft,
Jesus wehret allem Leide,
Er ist meines Lebens Kraft,
Meiner Augen Lust und Sonne,
Meiner Seele Schatz und Wonne;
Darum laß ich Jesum nicht
Aus dem Herzen und Gesicht.

Jesus remains my joy,
my heart's comfort and sap.
Jesus prevents all sorrow,
he is my life's strength,
my eye's desire and sun,
my soul's treasure and bliss.
Therefore let I Jesus not
out of my heart and sight.

Cantata 147 had its origins in Weimar as a cantata for the fourth Sunday of Advent. The Gospel lesson for that day was John 1:19-28. The librettist, Salomon Franck, took as his starting point verses 20 and 27: "He [John the Baptist] did not fail to confess, but confessed freely, 'I am not the Christ. . . . He is the one who comes after me, the thongs of whose sandals I am not worthy to untie.'"

After Bach moved to Leipzig, he had no opportunity to reuse this cantata because in Leipzig, during Advent, cantatas were sung only on the first Sunday, and Franck's text did not fit the lessons for that day. However, Luther had not abolished all the Marian feasts from the liturgical calendar, so in eighteenth-century Leipzig they still celebrated The Visitation of the Blessed Virgin Mary on July 2. This feast celebrates the visit of the pregnant Mary to the pregnant Elizabeth, the story told in the Gospel lesson for the day. Here was a story that Bach found to be as connected to the theme of confessing Jesus as Christ as was the story of John's witness in the wilderness. He joined the opening chorus and the arias with new recitatives and turned the Weimar Advent cantata into a Visitation cantata for Leipzig. In the new version, Part I takes Mary's Magnificat and Part II takes John's leaping in the womb as models of confessing Jesus. Bach completed the adaptation by adding a new chorale at the end of Parts I and II. That chorale is perhaps the best known of all of Bach's works, for it is widely performed in all kinds of arrangements that are generally known in English as "Jesu, Joy of Man's Desiring."

Although the incidents of Mary's song and John's leaping make for good connections with the theme of confessing, the overall coherence of this cantata might not be immediately apparent. The end of Part I (nos. 4 and 5) might seem to wander away from the main theme, and the chorale at the end of both parts, beautiful and beloved though it be, might seem a bit disconnected, perhaps even just "tacked on."

Of all the movements, nos. 4 and 5 might seem most closely related to the cantata's original Advent function (though no. 4 was not a part of the original). The second half of no. 4 sounds like an Advent call to prepare for the Savior's coming.

O hochbeglückte Christen,	O highly favored Christians,
Auf, machet euch bereit,	up, make yourselves ready,
Itzt ist die angenehme Zeit,	now is the welcome time,
Itzt ist der Tag des Heils:	now is the day of salvation.
der Heiland heißt	The Savior calls
Euch Leib und Geist	you, body and soul,
Mit Glaubensgaben rüsten,	with gifts of faith to arm yourselves.
Auf, ruft zu ihm in brünstigem	Up, call to him in burning
Verlangen,	longing
Um ihn im Glauben zu empfangen!	so as him in faith to receive.

The believer responds in the aria that follows (no. 5) by asking Jesus to prepare to "elect this believing soul" ["erwähle die gläubende Seele"]. But even though there is a strong Advent flavor to these movements, they also have a connection to the theme of confessing that I hope will become apparent as we follow the course of movements.

The first movement states the theme of Cantata 147: In everything you say and do, confess that Christ is God and Savior. It is at one and the same time an exhortation to confess Christ and an example of how that confession should be made. The words are cast in the form of an exhortation: You, the disciple — you, who are called Christian — with all your "heart and mouth and deeds and life must give witness of Christ." The music shows how that confession should be made; or rather, as I shall point out later, it shows one of two essential characteristics of how that confession should be made.

This movement is splendid as only Bach can be splendid. It is in C major and is scored for solo trumpet along with oboes, bassoon, and strings. Structurally it has elements of concerto, fugue, and da capo form all forged into a large-scale chiasm. (See figure 14 on p. 185.)

This movement says much about both the nature and the content of a Christian's confession. The words, though they are relatively few, say much; with the music they say even more. They start with a progression. The confession begins with the heart ["Herz"] and proceeds to the mouth ["Mund"], it spills over into deeds ["Tat"] and pervades all of life ["Leben"]. Salomon Franck must have had in mind Scripture passages like the following:

"For out of the overflow of the heart the mouth speaks." (Matthew 12:34)

But someone will say, "You have faith; I have deeds." Show me your faith without deeds and I will show you my faith by what I do. (James 2:18)

So whether you eat or drink or whatever you do, do it all for the glory of God. (1 Corinthians 10:31)

Bach set the opening line, "Herz und Mund und Tat und Leben," to a fugue subject (theme b) that underscores the progression in the text. It rises with each of the first three nouns — "Mund" is higher than "Herz" and "Tat" is higher than "Herz." Then, so as to bring the line to a climax

FIGURE 14: The Chiastic Form of Cantata 147, First Movement

Form

(chiasm)	theme	description	text
X	a	orch. ritornello	
Y	b	fugal exposition	"Herz . . . geben"
	a/c	orch. rit. with new theme [c] in choir	"Herz . . . geben"
	d + e	coda	"ohne Furcht. . . ." [d] "daß er Gott. . . ." [e]
Z	a/c	orch. rit. with new theme [c] in choir	"Herz . . . geben"
	d+e	coda	"ohne Furcht. . . ." [d] "daß er Gott. . . ." [e]
Y	b	fugal exposition	"Herz . . . geben"
	a/c	orch. rit. with new theme [c] in choir	"Herz . . . geben"
	d + e	coda	"ohne Furcht. . . ." [d] "daß er Gott. . . ." [e]
X	a	orch. ritornello	

and graphically make the point that this confession runs through all of life, Bach ended the subject with a long, sixteenth-note melisma (up to thirty beats in length!) on "Leben."

After the fugal exposition on the opening lines of text, Bach returned to the ritornello in the orchestra but superimposed a new theme (c) in the choir, still to the words of the opening lines, "Heart and mouth and deed and life must give witness of Christ." The new theme is very striking, consisting of a steady eighth-note sequence that alternates between upward and downward leaps — in other words, it makes a series of cross symbols. If the fugue subject (theme b) emphasizes the nature of the Christian's confession (it is all-pervasive), theme c emphasizes its content. The words say it is witness of Christ; the music reminds us that this means witness to what Christ has done. Theme c, with its cross symbols, reminds us of his crucifixion, while the festive trumpet music reminds us most immediately of his incarnation since the Gospel lesson for the day includes the Magnificat. And beyond the incarnation it calls to mind the other events associated with the trumpet — the resurrection, ascension, second coming, and eternal reign.

Then the words go back to telling about the nature of our confession. It must be "ohne Furcht und Heuchelei" ["without fear and hypocrisy"]. Bach made these words stand out in several ways: the instruments drop out, the rush of sixteenth notes ceases, there is a deflection to a minor key, and the harmonies are dissonant and a bit slippery. (Notice all this especially the second time the words occur.) But his music not only makes these words stand out, it also shows us what our confession should *not* be like. Rather, it should be like the music of the rest of the movement, which is dominated by the character of the trumpet — strong and courageous, bright and clear.

The clear, unequivocal nature of our confession is also illustrated by the music Bach wrote for the final phrase of text. In a strong and clear chordal texture and with straightforward harmonies moving with certainty toward the cadence, the choir sings "daß er Gott und Heiland sei" ["that he is God and Savior"]. So in this phrase the music tells us something about the nature of our confession while the words tell us its content.

After the splendid opening chorus sets out the main theme of the cantata, the solo movements that follow develop it. The recitatives present the voice of the preacher, the arias the response of the disciple. In the first recitative (no. 2) the preacher first holds up Mary's song as an ideal confession and then admonishes his audience for not following Mary's example.

O menschliches Geschlecht,	O human race,
Des Satans und der Sünden Knecht,	of Satan and of sin the slave,
Du bist befreit	you are set free
Durch Christi tröstendes	through Christ's comforting
Erscheinen	appearance,
Von dieser Last und Dienstbarkeit!	from this burden and slavery!
Jedoch dein Mund und dein	Yet your mouth and your
verstockt Gemüte	stubborn spirit
Verschweigt, verleugnet solche Güte;	are silent, denying such goodness.

He ends with a warning of judgment.

Doch wisse, daß <u>dich</u> nach der Schrift	Yet know that, according to Scripture,
Ein allzuscharfes Urteil trifft!	an all too sharp judgment will strike <u>you</u>!

The disciple responds in the following alto aria (no. 3), admonishing herself not to be ashamed to confess her Savior. The text is based on passages like Luke 9:26 and 2 Timothy 2:12.

> If anyone is ashamed of me and my words, the Son of Man will be ashamed of him when he comes in his glory and in the glory of the Father and of the holy angels.

> If we disown him, he will also disown us.

All this is clearly related to the theme of confession, but the relationship becomes less transparent when we get to the next two movements. As mentioned above, nos. 4 and 5 have a clear relationship to the season of Advent. That is understandable because the aria, no. 5, comes from the Weimar version and as such it was originally intended for Advent. But a closer look reveals that the text is not quite as normal an Advent text as first appears. To be sure, it contains one of the key words of Advent, "bereite" ["prepare"]. In Advent it is usually the believer who is told to prepare for the coming of Christ. But here it is Jesus who is being asked to do the preparing —

Bereite <u>dir</u>, Jesu, noch itzo die Bahn	Make ready, Jesus, yet now the way <u>to you</u>;
Mein heiland, erwähle	my Savior, elect
Die gläubende Seele,	this believing soul
Und siehe mit Augen	and look down with eyes
der Gnade mich an!	of grace on me.

This movement is a "prayer of [the] Soul offering itself to Christ" (Unger, 506). Importantly, however, the Soul does so in recognition of the words Jesus spoke to his disciples, "You did not choose me, but I chose you to go and bear fruit" (John 15:16).

This aria, it seems to me, makes sense in relation to confession if we recognize that a regression is taking place, a regression that is necessary before progression can take place. The regression here is the regression John was speaking of when he said, "He [Jesus] must become greater, and I must become less" (John 3:30). Although in the first aria (no. 3) the disciple admonished herself not to be ashamed of Christ, there was something self-serving behind it — if she denies him on earth she will be denied by him when he comes in glory. In the second aria (no. 5) she is responding to

187

the preacher's bidding in no. 4 to "call to him [Jesus] with ardent desire" ["ruft zu ihm in brünstigem Verlangen"]. Emptying the self to the point of recognizing that all starts with grace — "look with eyes of grace upon me" ["siehe mit Augen der Gnade mich an"] — is the necessary downward step a disciple must take before her confession can become genuine. Helmut Thielicke, commenting on the verse, "You show that you are a letter from Christ" (2 Corinthians 3:3), puts it this way:

> . . . when an individual is designated as the letter of Christ it is not because the individual is a member or pillar of the church but rather because he or she is the bearer of what Luther called the "strange dignity." By that Luther meant the opposite of everything we call our own, for example, our ability to function in our own profession or in some social endeavor. Our dignity is strange or alien because it is grounded in what God (one who is other, i.e., alien) has done for us, what he has applied to us, and that by which he has bought us with a great price. (21-22)

Two things are significant to note about the music. First, the downward movement of the disciple in these two arias (nos. 3 and 5) is underscored by the downward movement of the tonality. After the C major beginning (no flats or sharps), the first aria drops to A minor (still no flats or sharps but minor). The second aria drops further to D minor (one flat). Second, the soloist is an alto in the first aria and a soprano in the second, a movement in the direction of greater childlikeness. (Bach's soprano, remember, would have been a boy.)

Passing by for the moment the chorale that ends Part I, we see a change of direction in the tenor aria that begins Part II (no. 7). The key is F major (still one flat, but now major) and the voice is tenor. The upward direction of the tonality and the deepening of the voice correspond to the prayer of no. 7, which recognizes the need for Jesus' help and asks him to instill yet deeper love so that the heart "with your love would burn" ["von deiner Liebe brenne"]. (Note the emphasis given "brenne" by two very long melismas.)

The final recitative (no. 8) does two things. First, like the first recitative it draws on the Gospel lesson for an example of confessing Christ. This time it is the example of the baby John in Elizabeth's womb. Although he could not yet utter a word, he leaped in the womb when Elizabeth heard Mary's greeting.

Der höchsten Allmacht Wunderhand	The Highest's almighty hand of wonder
Würkt im Verborgenen der Erden.	works in the hidden places of the earth.
Johannes muß mit Geist	John must with the Spirit
erfüllet werden,	be filled,
Ihn zieht der Liebe Band	him draws the bond of love
Bereits in seiner Mutter Leibe,	already in his mother's womb,
Daß er den Heiland kennt,	that he the Savior knows,
Ob er ihn gleich noch nicht	although he him still not yet
Mit seinem Munde nennt,	with his mouth names.
Er wird bewegt, er hüpft	He becomes stirred; he leaps
und springet. . . .	and springs. . . .

Second, it continues the emphasis begun in the second aria (no. 5) that God is the initiator. It was "the Highest's almighty hand of wonder" ["der höchsten Allmacht Wunderhand"] that worked in John even "in the hidden places of the earth" ["im Verborgenen der Erden"]. So

Wenn euer Herz in Liebe brennet,	if your heart with love burns,
Und doch der Mund den Heiland	and still your mouth the Savior
nicht bekennet,	does not confess,
Gott ist es, der <u>euch</u> kräftig stärkt,	God it is who powerfully strengthens <u>you</u>;
Er will in euch des Geistes Kraft erregen,	he will in you the Spirit's power inspire,
Ja Dank und Preis auf eure	yes, thanks and praise upon your
Zunge legen.	tongue shall lay.

The disciple responds again to the words of the preacher with an aria (no. 9). The key has risen back to the starting point of C major and the voice has "matured" to bass. Furthermore the trumpet has returned for the first time since the opening chorus. The disciple has reached the level where he will confess his Lord:

Ich will von Jesu Wundern singen	I will of Jesus' wonders sing
Und ihm der Lippen Opfer bringen.	and to him the offering of lips bring.

And he recognizes it is the "holy fire" ["heilges Feuer"] that has overcome "the weak flesh, the earthly mouth" ["das schwache Fleisch, den irdschen Mund"].

It would seem that the cantata is complete after the bass aria. The "story" of the disciple's regression/progression is complete. So is the parallel regression/ progression of the music; we are back at the home key of C major and the trumpet has returned. Only the absence of the choir in no. 9 might leave a bit of a feeling of incompleteness. (See figure 15 below.)

FIGURE 15: **The Regression/Progression of the Disciple in Cantata 147**

Introduction

1. Choir	Nature and content of a disciple's witness	C major (0; major)

Regression

2. Recitative (preacher)	Mary's example; human stubbornness	
3. Aria (disciple — alto)	Warning self that denial of Christ now means denial by him later	A minor (0; minor)
4. Recitative (preacher)	Continued warning against stubbornness; call to receive Christ	
5. Aria (disciple — soprano)	Recognition that Christ first calls us; need of grace	D minor (1♭; minor)

Progression

7. Aria (disciple — tenor)	Prayer for help to confess; prayer that the heart would burn with Jesus' love	F major (1♭; major)
8. Recitative (preacher)	John's example; Spirit's power	
9. Aria (disciple — bass)	"I will sing of the wonders of Jesus"; Spirit's power	C major (0; major)

But there remains the chorale (nos. 6 and 10), a movement that on its own has achieved far greater popularity than the cantata as a whole. Is it just a nice piece of music that provides a choral ending to each of the two parts of the cantata but which otherwise does not fit in the overall scheme? In both places it is in the key of G major, a key outside the tonal boundaries of the rest of the cantata. Its being a tonal "outsider" is most apparent at the end of Part I. It follows directly after the D minor of no. 5, getting to its own key of G major by skipping all the intervening keys in the sharp direction (F major, A minor, C major, and E minor) and jumping two notches beyond the C major of the opening chorus. At the end of Part II, its G major key is more logical. It is a fifth above C major (no. 9) just as C major is a fifth above F major (no. 7). But even though it is part of a logical sequence of keys, it "trangresses" the C major boundary set up by the opening chorus and the final aria with trumpet (no. 9).

The words are the key to understanding the role the chorale plays in the whole cantata. That they were not just tacked on but carefully selected is suggested by the fact that they are the sixth and sixteenth (!) stanzas of a chorale by Martin Jahn (publ. 1661), "Jesu, meiner Seelen Wonne" ["Jesus, my soul's delight"]. Both stanzas are about "having" Jesus; they are, in a word, the disciple's confession. They are not preparatory for confession or about confession. They *are* the confession.

Fittingly, there is a progression from the stanza used at the end of Part I to the one at the end of Part II. Although both stanzas make genuine confessions about the relationship of the disciple to Jesus, the one at the end of Part II runs deeper. At the end of Part I, the disciple holds Jesus firmly *so that* Jesus refreshes him when he is sick and sorrowful ["O wie feste halt ich ihn,/Daß er mir mein Herze labe,/Wenn ich krank und traurig bin"]. At the end of Part II, the chorale begins with a line that resonates with one of the most beloved chorales, one that speaks of love for Jesus above all else. To most of the people in Bach's congregation I expect the opening line, "Jesu bleibet meine Freude," would have called to mind "Jesu, meine Freude," best known in English as "Jesus, Priceless Treasure." Other lines add that Jesus is, among other things, our comfort, strength, and treasure. It is particularly significant that he is our "Augen Lust" ["eye's desire"]. According to 1 John 2:16, "Augen Lust" "comes not from the Father but from the world." But here the confession is that Jesus is our "Augen Lust"; for his disciples, Jesus has taken the place of the false desires and fleeting pleasures of the world.

The words of these chorale stanzas provide the content of the disci-

191

ple's confession; the music, I think, illustrates its manner and tone. Earlier I said that the music of the first movement exemplifies the manner of the disciple's confession. It should be courageous and clear (like a trumpet sound), "without fear and hypocrisy." But there is another characteristic a disciple's confession should have. It should be gracious and winsome, reflecting Jesus. The music of the instruments, with its beautifully flowing triplets surrounding the simple chorale in the voices, exemplifies that graciousness and winsomeness.

Anointed to Be a Living Sacrifice

Heidelberg Catechism Q. & A. 32

Q. Why are you called a Christian?

A. Because by faith I am a member of Christ and so I share in his anointing. I am anointed . . . to present myself to him as a living sacrifice of thanks. . . .

* * * * * * *

Ephesians 4:22-28

You were taught, with regard to your former way of life, to put off your old self, which is being corrupted by its deceitful desires; to be made new in the attitude of your minds; and to put on the new self, created to be like God in true righteousness and holiness.

Therefore each of you must put off falsehood and speak truthfully to his neighbor, for we are all members of one body. "In your anger do not sin": Do not let the sun go down while you are still angry, and do not give the devil a foothold. He who has been stealing must steal no longer, but must work, doing something useful with his own hands, that he may have something to share with those in need.

Matthew 9:1-8

Jesus stepped into a boat, crossed over and came to his own town. Some men brought to him a paralytic, lying on a mat. When Jesus saw their faith, he said to the paralytic, "Take heart, son; your sins are forgiven."

At this, some of the teachers of the law said to themselves, "This fellow is blaspheming!"

Knowing their thoughts, Jesus said, "Why do you entertain evil thoughts in your hearts? Which is easier: to say, 'Your sins are forgiven,' or to say, 'Get up and walk'? But so that you may know that the Son of Man has authority on earth to forgive sins. . . ." Then he said to the paralytic, "Get up, take your mat and go home." And the man got up and went home. When the crowd saw this, they were filled with awe; and they praised God, who had given such authority to men.

Cantata 56: *Ich will den Kreuzstab gerne tragen*

1. Aria

Ich will den Kreuzstab gerne tragen,	I will the cross-staff gladly carry;
Er kömmt von Gottes lieber Hand,	it comes from God's loving hand.
Der führet mich nach meinen Plagen	It leads me after my torments
Zu Gott, in das gelobte Land.	to God, into the promised land.
Da leg ich den Kummer auf einmal ins Grab,	There lay I my suffering once-for-all in the grave,
Da Wischt mir die Tränen mein Heiland selbst ab.	there my Savior himself wipes from me my tears.

2. Recitative

Mein Wandel auf der Welt	My sojourn in the world
Ist einer Schiffahrt gleich:	is like a ship journey:
Betrübnis, Kreuz und Not	affliction, cross and distress
Sind Wellen, welche mich bedecken	are waves which submerge me
Und auf den Tod	and of death
Mich täglich schrecken;	daily frighten me.
Mein Anker aber, der mich hält,	My anchor, though, which holds me,
Ist die Barmherzigkeit,	is the mercy
Womit mein Gott mich oft erfreut.	with which my God often gladdens me.
Der rufet so zu mir:	He calls thus to me:
Ich bin bei dir,	I am with you;
Ich will dich nicht verlassen noch versäumen!	I will neither leave nor neglect you!
Und wenn das wütenvolle Schäumen	And when the raging foam
Sein Ende hat,	its end has,
So tret ich aus dem Schiff in meine Stadt,	then will I step out of my boat into my city

193

Die ist das Himmelreich,	which is the kingdom of Heaven,
Wohin ich mit den Frommen	where I, with the faithful,
Aus vieler Trübsal werde kommen.	out of many tribulations will come.

3. Aria

Endlich, endlich wird mein Joch	Finally, finally must my yoke
Wieder von mir weichen müssen.	again from me be lifted.
Da krieg ich in dem Herren <u>Kraft</u>,	Then obtain I <u>strength</u> in the Lord;
Da hab ich Adlers Eigenschaft,	there have I the eagle's quality;
Da fahr ich auf von dieser Erden	there soar I from this earth
Und laufe sonder <u>matt</u> zu werden.	and run without becoming <u>weary</u>.
O gescheh es <u>heute</u> noch!	O that it would happen yet <u>today</u>!

4. Recitative and arioso

Ich stehe fertig und bereit,	I stand ready and prepared
Das Erbe meiner Seligkeit	the inheritance of my blessedness
Mit Sehnen und Verlangen	with yearning and longing
Von Jesu Händen zu empfangen.	from Jesus' hands to receive.
Wie wohl wird mir geschehn,	How blessed to me will it be
Wenn ich den Port der Ruhe	when I the port of rest
werde sehn.	will see.

Da leg ich den Kummer auf einmal	There lay I my suffering once
ins Grab,	in the grave,
Da wischt mir die Tränen <u>mein</u>	there <u>my Savior himself</u> wipes
<u>Heiland selbst</u> ab.	from me my tears.

5. Chorale

Komm, o Tod, du Schlafes	**Come, O death, you of sleep**
Bruder,	**the brother;**
Komm und führe mich <u>nur</u> fort;	**come and <u>simply</u> lead me away.**
Löse meines Schiffleins Ruder,	**Loosen my little ship's rudder;**
Bringe mich an sichern Port!	**bring me to secure port!**
Es mag, wer da will, dich scheuen,	**Let him, whoever wills it, shun you,**
Du kannst mich vielmehr erfreuen;	**you can me much more gladden,**
Denn durch dich komm ich herein	**for through you come I in**
Zu dem schönsten Jesulein.	**to the most beautiful little Jesus.**

Two things are likely to strike many of us as odd or even problematic about Cantata 56, a solo cantata for bass. First, it seems to have little, if anything, to do with the Scripture lessons for the day. Second, there seems to be too much in it about the promised land and too much yearning for death, especially in a cantata that is ostensibly about cross-bearing, about self-sacrifice. I will address the first problem now and save comment on the second until the end.

Regarding the first problem, the first thing to be said is that even if the cantata text is not a commentary on the Scripture lessons for the day, it is not necessarily a bad "sermon." It might be poor liturgical form for a preacher to ignore the Scripture lessons, but he still might preach a good, scriptural sermon. Second, the text of Cantata 56 is not entirely without connection to the lessons but its connection is of a type that most of us are not accustomed to. It is related allegorically to the beginning of the Gospel lesson: "Jesus stepped into a boat, crossed over and came to his own town." The unknown author, like many before and after him, made the sea voyage a metaphor for life. There is a second, less obvious, allegorical feature of the text. The man Jesus healed was a paralytic who, as we can readily imagine, walked with the aid of a crutch. The crutch ("Kreuzstab" ["cross-staff"] in the text) is the cross that supports the pilgrim on his journey.

We have grown unaccustomed to allegory, particularly in preaching, but it was common in Bach's time. Some of us might not like allegory, and some might even look on it with disapproval, at least in preaching. But we would do well to remember that there is plenty of authority behind the allegorical use of Scripture. In treating Scripture allegorically, the preachers and poets of Bach's time were following a tradition that was, as C. S. Lewis says somewhere, "scholastic, patristic, apostolic, and dominical." It is a method that is easily abused, as its best practitioners (e.g., St. Augustine) have admitted. But the charge of abuse can hardly be leveled against the unknown librettist of Cantata 56. The text he wrote is thoroughly biblical; indeed, as we shall see, it is shot through with biblical allusions. His libretto might not literally be about what the Gospel lesson is about, but it is about something that is central to the Gospel — the relationship of cross-bearing to discipleship.

In the Heidelberg Catechism, we confess that Christ "is our only high priest who has set us free by the one sacrifice of his body [on the cross]." In our turn, we are urged by Paul to offer ourselves as "living sacrifices, holy and pleasing to God" (Romans 12:1). The most powerful and all-encompassing image Scripture has for describing our sacrifice is the

195

image of cross-bearing, and the most direct uses of the image are in the words of Christ himself. Early in his ministry, when sending out the twelve disciples, he said: "anyone who does not take his cross and follow me is not worthy of me" (Matthew 10:38). Later, immediately after we have read that "Jesus began to explain to his disciples that he must go to Jerusalem and suffer many things . . . and that he must be killed," we hear him say it again: "If anyone would come after me, he must deny himself and take up his cross and follow me" (16:21 and 24).

Bach knew that cross-bearing was central to discipleship. As we have seen (cf. pp. 128-32 and 141-47), he brought it out prominently in both of his Passions. Where could one more tellingly make the point that discipleship is cross-bearing? The inseparable relationship of discipleship to cross-bearing also looms large in the cantatas. Nowhere is the relationship more movingly and profoundly expressed than in the first movement of Cantata 56.

Whittaker calls Cantata 56 "a description of a Pilgrim's Progress" (1:373). He describes the first movement as showing the Pilgrim walking "heavily laden" through life. But although the cross he bears is heavy, he travels in hope because it comes from his Father's loving hand. What is more, his cross is not only a burden, it is also a "Kreuzstab" ["cross-staff"], a walking stick or crutch that brings him to the "gelobte Land" ["promised land"].

The reference to the promised land, of course, is rich with scriptural allusions. It brings to mind Joshua, an Old Testament type of Jesus, who led Israel into the promised land flowing with milk and honey. Furthermore, the hope of a promised land carries the implication that this world is not our home and so it also brings to mind passages like Hebrews 11:13-16:

> All these people were still living by faith when they died. They did not receive the things promised; they only saw them and welcomed them from a distance. And they admitted that they were aliens and strangers on earth. People who say such things show that they are looking for a country of their own. If they had been thinking of the country they had left, they would have had opportunity to return. Instead, they were longing for a better country — a heavenly one. Therefore God is not ashamed to be called their God, for he has prepared a city for them.

Because the Pilgrim travels in the hope of this promise, at the end of the movement he can lay all his cares in the grave where the Savior himself will wipe away his tears as promised in Isaiah — "The Sovereign Lord will wipe away the tears from all faces" (25:8) — and twice repeated in Revelation (7:17 and 21:4).

The text of the first movement has six lines grouped into three pairs. The first two pairs (A A') belong together structurally; the third pair (B) stands apart. (See figure 16 below.)

FIGURE 16: **The Structure of the Text of Cantata 56,**
First Movement

	Line	Syllables	Rhyme	
A	1	9	a	"tragen"
	2	8	b	"Hand"
A'	3	9	a	"Plagen"
	4	8	b	"Land"
B	5	11	c	"Grab"
	6	11	c	"ab"

The structural contrast between the A sections and the B section corresponds with a contrast in content. In the two A sections the first line has something grim about it whereas the second line explains why the grim aspects of life can be born "gladly" ["gerne"]. The "cross-staff" ["Kreuzstab"] of the first line is carried gladly because "it comes from God's loving hand" ["er kommt von Gottes lieber Hand"], and the "torments" ["Plagen"] of the third line can be born because they lead "into the promised land" ["in das gelobte Land"]. That is why in the contrasting B section, the Pilgrim can lay his cares in the grave.

Bach's music reflects the poetic structure and content perfectly. The A sections are permeated by, and their character determined by, a single theme. It is a theme that Bach shaped precisely to the words of the opening line, "Ich will den Kreuzstab gerne tragen" ["I will the cross-staff gladly carry"]. He set the affirmative opening words, "Ich will," to an ascending fourth, an interval of strong and affirmative character — it is ascending, it is a perfect consonance, and it moves from the dominant of the scale to the tonic. The theme continues up the tonic triad which, because it is minor, gives a darker coloring to the affirmation. There is no lessening of the resolve, but there is a hint of recognition that the way will be hard. How hard is revealed by the fourth word, "Kreuzstab." But to make sure the significance of that word would not be lost, Bach emphasized it by introducing a foreign note into the ascending triad of the theme. The note is a C♯. The ♯ sign (called "Kreuz" in German) is a familiar visual symbol of the cross in German Baroque music, but here it points to the cross aurally as well, first by being an unexpected foreign note in an otherwise normal tonic triad, and second, by producing strong dissonances, both melodic and harmonic. For the next word, "gerne" ["gladly"], Bach introduced one fleeting statement of Schweitzer's "joy" motive. The final word, "tragen" ["carry"], he set to a melisma made primarily out of the "sigh" motive. The melisma is long (taking up eight of the theme's eleven measures!), suggesting that the disciple is in this cross-bearing for the long haul; it is a lifelong commitment.

This wonderfully illustrative and expressive theme dominates both A sections although its opening changes for the new text at the beginning of A′ (line 3). It is heard in the opening instrumental ritornello in turn in violin II, violin I, and continuo, and even after the solo bass enters with it, it continues to make its appearance in the instruments as well as the voice. Although the opening of the theme is recurrent, the part of the theme that is most prominent is the sighing melisma. This imparts a heaviness to the music that is underscored by heavy scoring in which all three upper string parts are doubled by oboes. Whittaker comments that "Bach does not interpret the words as meaning that trials are over; he legitimately pictures the Pilgrim as being more heavily laden than the text would suggest" (1:374).

The Pilgrim may be heavy-laden, but he knows that there is sure hope because the "Kreuzstab" comes from God's loving hand ["er kommt von Gottes lieber Hand"]. So in the midst of the trials and tribulations the hopeful words of the second and fourth lines are underscored by the music. For the words "er kommt von Gottes lieber Hand" ["it comes from God's loving hand"] and "in das gelobte Land" ["to the promised land"] — after the sighing melismas on "tragen" and "Plagen" — the music becomes strongly and clearly declamatory and cadences for the only times in the A sections in major keys. In the music for lines 2 and 4, Bach expressed what the Heidelberg Catechism says in Answer 26: "I trust him so much that I do not doubt he will provide whatever I need for body and soul, and will turn to my good whatever adversity he sends me in this sad world."

Although Bach probably did not know these words, he certainly knew those of the chorale "Was Gott tut das ist wohlgetan" ["Whatever God does, that is well done"], a chorale he used frequently in his cantatas, including at the end of Cantata 12, another great cross-bearing cantata.

Was Gott tut, das ist wohlgetan,	Whatever God does, that is well done,
Dabei will ich verbleiben,	in that would I remain.
Es mag mich auf die rauhe Bahn	Although he may <u>drive</u> me on a harsh road
Not, Tod und Elend <u>treiben</u>,	of need, death and misery,
So <u>wird Gott</u> mich ganz väterlich	<u>God will hold</u> me right fatherly
In seinem Armen <u>halten</u>:	in his arms.
Drum laß ich ihn nur walten.	Therefore allow I him only to rule.

Because of the Pilgrim's faith in the loving Father hand of God, he need no longer fear death. Death, in fact, becomes the way to eternal bliss, the grave the place to throw the cares of life, the place where the Savior wipes away all tears. The music Bach wrote to accompany these thoughts in the B section contrasts strongly with the music of the A sections. Although the sighing motives are still present in the orchestra, the lyrical triplets in the voice put them in a different context and give to the whole section a feeling of comfort. Also contributing to the comforting affect of the B section are the keys. Major keys become more prominent and the music sinks into the lowest tonal region of the whole movement — A♭ major (4 flats). This symbolizes the grave, but even more it releases the tension created by all the sharped notes on "Kreuzstab" in the A section and conveys a sense of peace.

The B section, with its notes of comfort and peace, beautifully sets up the second movement. This movement is one of those recitatives, like "Siehet, siehet" of Cantata 61 (cf. pp. 83-85), in which Bach painted a picture with the simplest of musical devices. Although such movements are seemingly naive in their simplicity, somehow, like medieval miniatures, they convey something of great depth. The picture here is of the sea, and it is depicted simply by the cello playing arpeggios that suggest the rolling of the waves. The Pilgrim sings that "sadness, cross, and trouble are billows which cover me" ["Betrübnis, Kreuz und Not sind Wellen, welche mich bedecken"], words that call to mind Psalm 69.

> Save me, O God, for the waters have come up to my neck. I sink in the miry depths, where there is no foothold. I have come into the deep waters; the floods engulf me. . . . Rescue me from the mire, do not let me sink; deliver me from those who hate me, from the deep waters. Do not let the floodwaters engulf me or the depths swallow me up or the pit close its mouth over me. (1-3, 14-15)

But the "waves" in the cello are hardly frightening and the key of the movement is major. Is the music an ironic commentary on the text? In a sense, yes, but not in the sense that it belittles the Pilgrim's trials and tribulations. Rather, it portrays those trials and tribulations from a broader perspective. The words of the first movement have already suggested that perspective. First, the trials and tribulations are from the Father's loving hand, the same Father whose "Barmherzigkeit" ["compassion"] is the "Anker" ["anchor"]. He comforts the Pilgrim with his presence. He says: "Ich bin bei dir, ich will dich nicht verlassen noch versäumen" ["I am with you, I will not leave nor forsake you"] — a combination of Isaiah 43:5 and Hebrews 13:5. Second, the trials and tribulations lead to the promised land. So when the voyage is over (and here the arpeggios in the cello stop), the Pilgrim will arrive in his own city ("in meine Stadt"), which is the Kingdom of Heaven ("Himmelreich"), where he will join the righteous who have come out of great tribulation ("aus vieler Trübsal" [Revelation 7:14]). From that perspective the Pilgrim can say with Paul: "I consider that our present sufferings are not worth comparing with the glory that will be revealed in us" (Romans 8:18). From that perspective the "billows" experienced in this world are, in reality, no more than gently undulating arpeggios.

With an eye on the time when the voyage will be over, the Pilgrim sings the next aria (no. 3). With great joy and vigor he anticipates the time when the prophecies of Isaiah will be fulfilled, when his yoke will be lifted:

> In that day their burden will be lifted from your shoulders, their yoke from your neck; the yoke will be broken because you have grown so fat [i.e., like a sturdy animal] (Isaiah 10:27) —

and his energy will be like that of an eagle —

They will soar on wings like eagles; they will run and not grow weary, they will walk and not be faint. (Isaiah 40:31)

Even though the specific references to "yoke" and "eagles" do not appear until the B part, the music of the whole movement, with its energetic eighth notes in the continuo, its ascending scales and sequences, and its running sixteenth notes, soars like an eagle and runs without getting weary. It is a typically Bachian allegro that literally goes on and on with unflagging energy.

But this cantata is about the Pilgrim's journey; the final destination is not yet attained. In the B part of this aria, the Pilgrim yearns for the arrival. The yearning is reflected by the change to a minor key and by the rhetorical isolation of the exclamations "O!" and "heute." "O gescheh es heute noch" ["O let it happen today"]!

The following recitative (no. 4) continues the yearning for the "Port der Ruhe" ["port of rest"] and introduces another scriptural image, "Erbe" ["inheritance"], another object of the Pilgrim's yearning.

Whatever you do, work at it with all your heart, as working for the Lord, not for men, since you know that you will receive an inheritance from the Lord as a reward. (Colossians 3:23-24)

Praise be to the God and Father of our Lord Jesus Christ! In his great mercy he has given us new birth into a living hope through the resurrection of Jesus Christ from the dead, and into an inheritance that can never perish, spoil or fade — kept in heaven for you. (1 Peter 1:3-5)

For this reason Christ is the mediator of a new covenant, that those who are called may receive the promised eternal inheritance. . . . (Hebrews 9:15)

It ends with a surprising and moving return to the words and music of the B section of the opening movement:

| Da leg ich den Kummer auf einmal ins Grab, | There lay I my suffering once in the grave, |
| Da wischt mir die Tränen <u>mein Heiland selbst</u> ab. | there <u>my Savior himself</u> wipes from me my tears. |

201

The yearning reaches its climax in the closing chorale (no. 5). The Pilgrim asks for death to come because it is through death that he comes to Jesus. Being in the key of C minor, one step in the flat direction from the other movements of the cantata, the affect is tilted in the soft or mild direction; the key conveys peace even though the minor mode is a reminder of death's darkness. The first two phrases have a syncopated half note on the opening word, "Komm," which intensifies the poignant yearning of the Pilgrim. Then, in the middle phrases, the music moves to cadences in E♭ major and the affect of peace and comfort comes through unalloyed. Finally, in the last two lines, there is an upward thrust, first to a strong cadence on G major on "hinein" ["inside"] and then to a triumphant cadence in C major on "Jesulein" ["little Jesus"]!

I said at the outset that it might be wondered why this cantata, which begins with a clear enough statement about cross-bearing and discipleship, spends so much time looking forward to the consummation. Doesn't discipleship have to do with obedience, work, and service here and now? Wouldn't a cantata based on Ephesians 4:22-28, the Epistle lesson for the day, be more appropriate for the theme of discipleship? Does the consummation, important though it might be, have anything at all to do with discipleship? Didn't Bach, with his frequent yearning for death, lay himself open to charges that his Christianity was nothing but promises of "pie in the sky by-and-by"?

Two things can be said to these questions and charges. First, even though yearning for death and the promised land is strong not only in Cantata 56 but in many of Bach's works, it is not there to the neglect of other topics. Although the question of balance and proportion might be worth discussing, it should not be thought that the topics of obedience, work, and service are missing from Bach's cantatas. For example, Cantata 77, based on the summary of the law, and Cantata 39, "Brich dem Hungrigen dein Brot" ["Break with the hungry your bread"], issue clear calls to serve one's neighbor.

Second, the reward of heaven is not a matter of "pie in the sky," nor is it unrelated to discipleship. C. S. Lewis arrived at the relationship between reward and discipleship through a distinction between "proper" and "mercenary" rewards. He made the distinction by drawing an analogy between the reward of heaven and the enjoyment of Greek poetry.

An enjoyment of Greek poetry is certainly a proper, and not a mercenary, reward for learning Greek; but only those who have reached the stage of enjoying Greek poetry can tell from their own experience that this is so. The schoolboy beginning Greek grammar cannot look forward to his adult enjoyment of Sophocles as a lover looks forward to marriage or a general to victory. He has to begin by working for marks, or to escape punishment, or to please his parents, or, at best, in the hope of a future good which he cannot at present imagine or desire. His position, therefore, bears a certain resemblance to that of the mercenary; the reward he is going to get will, in actual fact, be a natural or proper reward, but he will not know that till he has got it. Of course, he gets it gradually; enjoyment creeps in upon the mere drudgery, and nobody could point to a day or an hour when the one ceased and the other began. But it is just in so far as he approaches the reward that he becomes able to desire it for its own sake; indeed, the power of so desiring it is itself a preliminary reward.

The Christian, in relation to heaven, is in much the same position as this schoolboy. Those who have attained everlasting life in the vision of God doubtless know very well that it is no mere bribe, but *the very consummation of their earthly discipleship;* but we who have not yet attained it cannot know this in the same way, and cannot even begin to know it at all except by continuing to obey and finding the first reward of our obedience in our increasing power to desire the ultimate reward. Just in proportion as the desire grows, our fear lest it should be a mercenary desire will die away and finally be recognized as an absurdity. (C. S. Lewis, "The Weight of Glory," 2-3; emphasis mine)

Given this line of thinking, there is a connection between cross-bearing discipleship and longing for heaven. As an aria from Cantata 12 has it, "Kreuz und Krone sind verbunden" ["Cross and crown are bound together"]. To divorce the two would be unscriptural. Cross-bearing for its own sake is not what the Bible teaches.

The New Testament has lots to say about self-denial, but not about self-denial as an end in itself. We are told to deny ourselves and to take up our crosses in order that we may follow Christ; and nearly every description of what we shall ultimately find if we do so contains an appeal to desire. If there lurks in modern minds the notion that to desire our own good and earnestly to hope for the enjoyment of it is a bad thing, I submit that this notion has crept in from Kant and the Stoics and is no part of the Christian faith. Indeed, if we consider the unblushing promises of reward and the staggering nature of the rewards promised in the Gospels, it would seem that our Lord finds our desires, not too strong, but too weak. We are half-hearted creatures, fooling about with drink and sex and ambition when infinite joy is offered us, like an ignorant child who wants to go on making mud pies in a slum because he cannot imagine what is meant by the offer of a holiday at the sea. ("The Weight of Glory," 1-2)

In *Mere Christianity,* Lewis discusses longing for heaven in connection with hope. Since hope is one of the theological virtues,

a continual looking forward to the eternal world is not (as some modern people think) a form of escapism or wishful thinking, but one of the things a Christian is meant to do. It does not mean that we are to leave the present world as it is. If you read history you will find that the Christians who did the most for the present world were just those who thought most of the next. The Apostles themselves, who set on foot the conversion of the Roman Empire, the great men who built up the Middle Ages, the English Evangelicals who abolished the Slave Trade, all left their mark on Earth, precisely because their minds were occupied with Heaven. It is since Christians have largely ceased to think of the other world that they have become so ineffective in this. (104)

I suggest that Bach can be counted as one of those "who did most for this present world" precisely because his mind was "occupied with Heaven." Works like Cantata 56 can serve as a powerful corrective for Christians who "have largely ceased to think of the other world." It puts all our goals as disciples in the perspective of our final goal.

Anointed to Reign with Him Eternally

Heidelberg Catechism Q. & A. 45 and 32

Q. How does Christ's resurrection benefit us?

A. Christ's resurrection is a guarantee of our glorious resurrection.

Q. Why are you called a Christian?

A. Because by faith I am a member of Christ and so I share in his anointing. I am anointed . . . to reign with him eternally.

* * * * * * *

1 Thessalonians 5:1-11

Now, brothers, about times and dates we do not need to write to you, for you know very well that the day of the Lord will come like a thief in the night. While people are saying, "Peace and safety," destruction will come on them suddenly, as labor pains on a pregnant woman, and they will not escape.

But you, brothers, are not in darkness so that this day should surprise you like a thief. You are all sons of the light and sons of the day. We do not belong to the night or to the darkness. So then, let us not be like others, who are asleep, but let us be alert and self-controlled. For those who sleep, sleep at night, and those who get drunk, get drunk at night. But since we belong to the day, let us be self-controlled, putting on faith and love as a breastplate, and the hope of salvation as a helmet. For God did not appoint us to suffer wrath but to receive salvation through our Lord Jesus Christ. He died for us so that, whether we are awake or asleep, we may live together with him. Therefore encourage one another and build each other up, just as in fact you are doing.

Matthew 25:1-13

"At that time the kingdom of heaven will be like ten virgins who took their lamps and went out to meet the bridegroom. Five of them were foolish and five were wise. The foolish ones took their lamps but did not take any oil with them. The wise, however, took oil in jars along with their lamps. The bridegroom was a long time in coming, and they all became drowsy and fell asleep.

"At midnight the cry rang out: 'Here's the bridegroom! Come out to meet him!'

"Then all the virgins woke up and trimmed their lamps. The foolish ones said to the wise, 'Give us some of your oil; our lamps are going out.'

"'No,' they replied, 'there may not be enough for both us and you. Instead, go to those who sell oil and buy some for yourselves.'

"But while they were on their way to buy the oil, the bridegroom arrived. The virgins who were ready went in with him to the wedding banquet. And the door was shut.

"Later the others also came. 'Sir! Sir!' they said. 'Open the door for us!'

"But he replied, 'I tell you the truth, I don't know you.'
"Therefore keep watch, because you do not know the day or the hour."

Cantata 140: *Wachet auf, ruft uns die Stimme*

1. Chorus

Wachet auf, ruft uns die Stimme	**Wake up, calls to us the voice**
Der Wächter sehr hoch auf der Zinne,	**of the watchmen very high on the tower.**
Wach auf, du Stadt Jerusalem!	**Wake up, you city of Jerusalem!**
Mitternacht heißt diese Stunde;	**Midnight is this very hour;**
Sie rufen uns mit hellem Munde:	**they call to us with bright voices:**
Wo seid ihr klugen Jungfrauen?	**Where are you wise virgins?**
Wohl auf, der Bräutgam kömmt;	**Take cheer, the bridegroom comes.**
Steht auf, die Lampen nehmt!	**Rise up, your lamps take!**
Alleluja!	**Alleluia!**
Macht euch bereit	**Make yourselves ready**
Zu der Hochzeit,	**for the wedding.**
Ihr müsset ihm entgegengehn!	**You must to him go out!**

2. Recitative (tenor)

Er kommt, er kommt,	He comes, he comes,
Der Bräutgam kommt!	the bridegroom comes!
Ihr Töchter Zions, kommt heraus,	You daughters of Zion, come out,
Sein Ausgang eilet aus der Höhe	his journey hastens from the heights
In euer Mutter Haus.	to your mother's house.
Der Bräutgam kommt, der einem Rehe	The bridegroom comes, who <u>like</u> a roe
Und jungen Hirsche <u>gleich</u>	and young stag
Auf denen Hügeln springt	on the hills springs
Und euch das Mahl der Hochzeit bringt.	and to you the meal of the wedding brings.
Wacht auf, ermuntert euch!	Wake up, bestir yourselves,
Den Bräutgam zu empfangen!	the bridegroom to receive!
Dort, sehet, kommt er hergegangen.	There, look, he comes along.

3. Duet (soprano, bass)

SOUL: Wann kömmst du, mein Heil?	When will you come, my salvation?
JESUS: Ich komme, dein Teil.	I am coming, your own.

Ich warte mit brennendem Öle.
Eröffne den Saal
   Ich öffne den Saal
Zum himlischen Mahl!
   Zum himlischen Mahl!
Komm, Jesu!
   Ich komme; komm, liebliche Seele!

I am waiting with burning oil.
Throw open the hall
   I open the hall
for the heavenly meal!
   for the heavenly meal!
Come, Jesus!
   I am coming; come, lovely soul!

4. Chorale

Zion hört die Wächter singen,
Das Herz tut ihr vor Freuden
   springen,
Sie wachet und steht eilend auf.
Ihr Freund kommt vom Himmel
   prächtig,
Von Gnaden stark, von Wahrheit
   mächtig,
Ihr Licht wird hell, ihr Stern
   geht auf.
Nun komm, du werte Kron,
Herr Jesu, Gottes Sohn!
Hosianna!
Wir folgen all
Zum Freudensaal
Und halten mit das Abendmahl.

Zion hears the watchmen singing,
her heart with joy is
   springing,
she wakes and stands quickly up.
Her friend comes from heaven
   glorious,
in grace strong, in truth
   mighty,
her light is bright, her star
   rises.
Now come, you worthy crown,
Lord Jesus, God's Son!
Hosanna!
We follow all
to the joyful hall
and join the evening meal.

5. Recitative (bass)

So geh herein zu mir,
Du mir erwählte Braut!
Ich habe mich mit dir
Von Ewigkeit <u>vertaut</u>.
Dich will ich auf mein Herz,
Auf meinen Arm gleich wie ein
   Siegel <u>setzen</u>
Und dein betrübtes Aug <u>ergötzen</u>.
Vergiß, o Seele, nun
Die Angst, den Schmerz,
Den du erdulden müssen;

So come within to me,
you, my chosen bride!
I have <u>betrothed</u> myself to you
from eternity.
You will I <u>set</u> on my heart,
on my arm, like a
   seal
and <u>delight</u> your troubled eye.
Forget, O soul, now
the anxiety, the pain,
which you had to suffer.

207

Auf meiner Linken sollst du ruhn,	Upon my left hand shall you rest
Und meine Rechte soll dich <u>küssen</u>.	and my right hand shall <u>kiss</u> you.

6. Duet (soprano, bass)

SOUL: Mein Freund ist mein,	My friend is mine,
JESUS: Und ich bin sein,	and I am his,
Die Liebe soll nichts scheiden.	our love shall nothing sever.
Die Liebe soll nichts scheiden.	our love shall nothing sever.
Ich will mit dir in Himmels	I will with you on heaven's
Rosen weiden,	roses feed,
Du sollst mit mir in Himmels	You shall with me on Heaven's
Rosen weiden,	roses feed,
Da Freude die Fülle, da Wonne	there joy to the full, there rapture
wird sein.	will be.
Da Freude die Fülle, da Wonne	there joy to the full, there rapture
wird sein.	will be.

7. Chorale

Gloria sei dir gesungen	**Glory be sung to you**
Mit Menschen- und englischen	**with mortal and angelic**
Zungen,	**tongues,**
Mit Harfen und mit Zimbeln schon.	**with harps and with cymbals too.**
Von zwölf Perlen sind die Pforten,	**Of twelve pearls are the portals.**
An deiner Stadt sind wir Konsorten	**In your city are we consorts**
Der Engel hoch um deinen Thron.	**of angels high around your throne.**
Kein Aug hat je gespürt,	**No eye has ever sensed,**
Kein Ohr hat je gehört	**no ear has ever heard**
Solche Freude.	**such joy.**
Des sind wir froh,	**Of this are we joyous,**
Io, io!	**io, io!**
Ewig in dulci jubilo.	**Eternally in dulci jubilo.**

In Cantata 56, the disciple rejoiced in the vision and anticipation of the promised land, but did not reach it. In Cantata 140 the goal is reached. But before the goal is reached there is a word of warning lest it slip away. Cantata 140 begins with a warning to watch and be ready, for, as the Epistle lesson says, "the day of the Lord will come like a thief in the night." The disciple must live as a child of the light and always be prepared for the coming of the Bridegroom like the five wise virgins in Jesus' parable, a parable that ends with the same warning as the Epistle lesson, "Therefore keep watch, because you do not know the day or the hour." Such a warning might be heard with fear or with joy. Cantata 140 presents it entirely from the perspective of the wise virgins who hear it with joy. There is no element of "Dies irae" ["Day of wrath"] in Cantata 140.

The relationship of Cantata 140 to both lessons, but especially to the Gospel, is so obvious as to need no further comment. But what about its relationship to the Catechism (which, of course, was not Bach's concern)? The Catechism says nothing about the wedding feast, the image in the cantata, and the cantata says nothing about reigning, the image used in the Catechism. But although the imagery is different the topic is the same. As C. S. Lewis explained:

> The promises of Scripture [regarding the world to come] may very roughly be reduced to five heads. It is promised, firstly, that we shall be with Christ; secondly, that we shall be like Him; thirdly, with an enormous wealth of imagery, that we shall have "glory"; fourthly, that we shall, in some sense, be fed or feasted or entertained; and, finally, that we shall have some sort of official position in the universe — ruling cities, judging angels, being pillars of God's temple. ("The Weight of Glory," 7)

Without having counted, I think that in the cantatas Bach probably used Lewis's first category the most. Think, for example, of the last line of Cantata 56 — "Zu dem schönsten Jesulein" ["to the most beautiful little Jesus"]. In Cantata 140 he used the fourth category because that is the imagery used in the parable on which it is based. The authors of the Catechism used the fifth category because it fit their particular approach to the question, "Why are you called a Christian?" Since Christ means "anointed" and Christ was anointed to be prophet, priest, and king, so, too, his followers share in that threefold anointing, including being anointed to be kings. But whatever the imagery, it all points to the same thing, something that can only be pointed to by imagery because, as Paul said in 1 Corinthians 2:9 and as Philipp Nicolai echoed in the chorale verse in the last movement of Cantata 140, "No eye has seen, no ear has heard, no mind has conceived what God has prepared for those who love him."

Cantata 140 is both symmetrical and dynamic in its overall structure. The pattern of movements is both a chiasm and a series of "scenes" that present successive stages in an unfolding drama. It also blends communal and individual imagery. Bach placed settings of Nicolai's chorale, with its congregational associations and communal words, at the beginning, in the middle, and at the end. In between are recitatives and duets that are filled with imagery drawn mainly from the Song of Solomon. The duets are cast in the form of dialogues in which the soprano represents the Soul of the believer and the bass represents Jesus. (See figure 17 below.)

FIGURE 17: The Chiastic Form and Dramatic Progression of Cantata 140

Movement	Form	Keys	"Scenes"
1.	Chorale fantasy	E♭ major	The watchmen awaken the faithful
2.	Recit. (Evangelist)	C minor	The Bridegroom is sighted
3.	Duet (Soul/Jesus)	C minor	The Soul's yearning and Christ's assuring words
4.	Chorale trio	E♭ major	The arrival
5.	Recit. (Jesus)	to B♭ major	Christ accepts the Bride
6.	Duet (Soul/Jesus)	B♭ major	Bliss of union
7.	4-part chorale	E♭ major	Eternal hymn of praise

As is typical with Bach, the first movement of Cantata 140 is the most complex and presents the topic on a grand scale. Its basic structure is simple enough, but its wealth of detail can be overwhelming. There are three basic ingredients — the chorale, the instrumental ritornello, and what I will call vocal "commentary."

The first ingredient, the chorale, is sung in long notes by the sopranos. Significantly, they are doubled by a "corno" [horn], i.e., an instrument the people of Bach's day would have recognized as akin to the signalling instruments used by town watchmen. In addition to this symbolic use of an instrument there are symbolic features in the chorale itself. First, the opening notes are an ascending triad, i.e., the notes played by a natural horn, particularly fitting for the watchmen's cry, "Wachet auf" ["Wake up"]. Second, the form of the chorale is a bar form — A A B. The music of the first three phrases (A) is repeated exactly for the second three phrases (so A again). New music is used for the remaining phrases (B). Bar forms were frequently used in the secular love songs of the medieval Minne-singers and Meistersingers and were common in "dawn songs." In a dawn song two lovers lament the coming of dawn because it means they must part. "Wachet auf" is a dawn song but with a difference. In it dawn is not lamented, for to children of the light (cf. the Epistle lesson) it means the coming of the "morning star," or, in the imagery of the chorale, the Bride-groom. Third, the text, as it was laid out in some of the early collections, is in the shape of a goblet or chalice, symbolizing the "Abendmahl" ["eve-ning meal" = the eucharist] (cf. the reference in the text at the end of movement 4).

> Wachet auf, ruft uns die Stimme
> Der Wächter sehr hoch auf der Zinne,
> Wach auf, du Stadt Jerusalem!
> Mitternacht heißt diese Stunde;
> Sie rufen uns mit hellem Munde:
> Wo seid ihr klugen Jungfrauen?
> Wohl auf, der Bräutgam kömmt;
> Steht auf, die Lampen nehmt!
> Alleluja!
> Macht euch bereit
> Zu der Hochzeit,
> Ihr müsset ihm entgegengehn!

The second main ingredient in this movement, the ritornello, is played in its entirety by the instruments at the beginning, between the two A sections, and at the end. It is played in part between every phrase of the chorale. Motives from it are also played while the choir is singing.

In its entirety the ritornello contains three distinct sections. Each section is more rhythmically animated than the previous one, reflecting the growing eagerness of those awaiting the Bridegroom. It begins with four measures of dotted rhythms characteristic of the French overture. The French overture, as will be remembered, was associated with royal pomp and splendor and, by extension, all stately ceremonial occasions — in this case the wedding of Christ and his bride, the church. In the next four measures the upper instruments increase their rhythmic activity to sixteenth notes interrupted by ties while the dotted rhythms move down to the continuo. Both parts hint at the opening notes of the chorale melody. Finally, in the third section, the first violins break into uninterrupted sixteenth notes and the continuo into uninterrupted eighth notes bringing the rhythmic animation and the sense of eager anticipation to its peak.

After the opening ritornello comes to its final cadence, the sopranos come in with the chorale melody. After two measures the lower three voices enter with the third main ingredient of the movement, their musical "commentary" on words of the chorale. As they move along in more rapid rhythms under the long notes of the chorale, they present motives that illustrate or emphasize key words of the phrase being sung. (See figure 18 on p. 213.)

The figure describes how the "commentary" in the lower voices illustrates or gives rhetorical emphasis to the words. But two further points need to be made. First, notice that the lower voices keep getting closer to the entrance of the chorale in the two A sections (phrases 1-6). In phrases 1 and 4 they start out respectfully behind the chorale by two measures. Then in phrases 2 and 5 they wait only one measure. And at phrases 3 and 6 they don't wait at all; they come in simultaneously with the chorale. Like the ritornello, the lower voices express a growing eagerness; they literally "can't wait."

That process continues into the B section. In phrases 7 and 8 the lower voices precede the chorale by one measure. Then in phrase 9 they jump ahead of the chorale entrance by fourteen measures! The reason for this unusually early entry is not hard to find. Phrase 9 is the climax, the shout of "Alleluja!" The chorale melody, however, supplies only four notes for this climactic word, hardly enough for the climax of a grand movement like this one. So Bach wrote a joyful, fugal exposition based on a highly melismatic subject to highlight "Alleluja!"

Another sort of climax occurs in the final three phrases, where Bach wanted to make sure the point of the parable would not be missed. The point is, "Make yourselves ready!" Although that point is made as the lower voices urgently and busily "discuss" it under phrase 10, Bach was not satisfied that this would be enough. So in phrase 11 he did something he had not done before in this movement. He made the lower voices continue to sing the words of phrase 10, "Macht euch bereit" ["Make yourselves ready"], while the sopranos went ahead with phrase 11, "zu der Hochzeit" ["for the wedding"]. Not until the sopranos have sung their last

FIGURE 18: Key Words and Musical Commentary in Cantata 140, First Movement

Phrase	Key word(s)	Description of "commentary" in the lower parts
1.	"Wachet auf" ["Wake up"]	Begin two measures after the chorale in imitation with a decorated version of the opening three notes of the chorale, i.e., the rising triad imitating the natural horn of the watchman.
2.	"hoch" ["high"]	Begin one measure after the chorale in imitation with an ascending scale to "hoch." Note also that in addition to the ascending scales, the continuo drops out for two measures, leaving no true bass, only higher parts.
3.	"wach auf" ["Wake up"]	Begin simultaneously with the chorale. All three lower voices sing declamatory quarter-note chords with large upward leaps to "auf." After they break into imitation, each point-of-imitation begins with an upward leap.
4.	"Mitternacht" ["Midnight"]	Same as 1.
5.	"hellem" ["bright"]	Same as 2. The word the ascending scales go up to is now "hellem."
6.	"Wo?" ["Where?"]	Same as 3. This time the chordal declamation and the upward leaps give rhetorical emphasis to the urgent question, "where?"
7.	"Wohl auf" ["Take cheer"]	Begin one measure ahead of the chorale with ascending leaps in close imitation from the lower to the higher parts.
8.	"Steht auf" ["Rise up"]	Same as 7.
9.	"Alleluja"	Begin fourteen measures ahead of the chorale with a fugal exposition whose subject, mostly in sixteenth notes, makes clear reference to the second section of the ritornello.
10.	"Macht euch bereit" ["Make yourselves ready"]	Begin simultaneously with the chorale with a four-note motive tossed about among the parts in a way suggestive of urgency and busyness.
11.	None	Continue to sing the words of phrase 10.
12.	"Ihr" ["you"]	Same as 3 and 6 except that a single declamatory chord on "ihr" replaces the the two chords on "Wach auf" and "Wo, wo."

note do the lower voices complete the sentence and sing "zu der Hochzeit." And then, just to be triply sure the point gets made, Bach, again for the only time in this movement, had the lower voices continue to sing after the chorale melody had finished. Bach extended the lower voices three measures beyond the end of the chorale in the soprano so that the whole sentence, "Make yourselves ready for the wedding," gets sung in clear, chordal declamation. And then, to really bring the point home, in phrase 12 he had the lower voices rhetorically repeat the word "ihr" ["you"] on quarter-note chords on the first beat of the first two measures before finishing the sentence — "You . . . , you . . . , you must go out to meet him!"

In the second movement the tenor soloist, the voice of the Evangelist in the Passions, announces the coming of the Bridegroom and calls the daughters of Zion to come out to meet him. This leads to the first of the two love duets between the Soul and Jesus. In this duet (no. 3) the two voices are joined by a piccolo violin which is tuned a third higher than the normal violin. Gerhard Herz suggests that Bach was "influenced by the instrument's association with night music, which Leopold Mozart noted in 1756" (p. 130). (Remember, the parable on which the cantata is based takes place at midnight.) Whatever associations the instrument might have had, it contributes a highly florid obbligato which André Pirro called "a whirlwind host of unutterable feelings" (Herz, *Bach: Cantata No. 140*, 162). Against the background of the violin's arabesques, the two voices go back and forth in short phrases, the questions and pleas of the Soul always answered with assurance and comfort by Jesus. But only on the phrase, "zum himmlischen Mahl" ["to the heavenly meal"] do they sing together. The promise of union is not yet fulfilled, but the time is drawing near.

In the next movement (no. 4), the central chorale movement, the Bridegroom arrives. If "Jesu, Joy of Man's Desiring" is the most widely known of Bach's works, this movement is probably not far behind. Bach himself must have been particularly fond of it because he arranged it for organ and placed it first in the collection of chorale preludes he published in 1748 or 1749, called the *Schübler Chorales*. It is as an organ piece that it has become well known.

In the cantata the tenor soloist (or tenor section of the choir) sings the chorale unadorned except for some modest cadential ornamentation. Below the chorale the basso continuo moves in steady quarter notes that increase in speed to eighth notes as the music approaches cadences. Its steady, unhurried movement gives the music a processional character fitting for the next to the last line of text — "Wir folgen all zum Freudensaal" ["We follow all to the joyful hall"]. But it is the obbligato instrumental part above the chorale that dominates the piece and is mainly responsible for its overall affect. It adds something of the sway of a dance to the processional march of the continuo. Its movement is graceful, at once light and grave. It expresses great joy but in a measured way fitting for the dignity of the occasion. Bach's scoring adds to the dignity. He scored the obbligato for all the violins (except the piccolo violin) and violas to play in unison. The sound of unison strings playing in a relatively low range is deep and rich.

The Bridegroom has arrived (no. 4) and accepts his chosen Bride in the next recitative (no. 5). In words that recall God's promise to unfaithful Israel in Hosea 2:19, he says, "Ich habe mich mit dir von Ewigkeit vertraut" ["I have myself to you, from eternity, betrothed"]. And later: "Vergiß, o Seele, nun die Angst, den Schmerz, den du erdulden müssen" ["Forget, O soul, now the anxiety, the pain, which you had to suffer"]. Sung by a bass voice, the voice traditionally associated with Jesus, and accompanied by strings, this recitative is reminiscent of Jesus' recitatives in the *St. Matthew Passion*. Tonally it begins in the cantata's central key of E♭ major, moves further in the flat direction, threatens to go all the way to A♭ minor (seven flats!) on the phrase "dein betrübtes Aug" ["your troubled eye"], but cadences comfortingly in A♭ major for the word "vergiß" ["forget"]. From there it moves upward to the end, where it arrives in B♭ major to set up the following duet.

The duet (no. 6) is another Soul/Jesus duet with one obbligato instrument. But beyond the similarity in texture, this duet is a complete contrast to the first. That one expressed the Soul's yearning for Jesus; this one expresses the joy of their union. C minor has given way to B♭ major, the highest key of any movement in the whole cantata. The slow 12/8 meter has been replaced by a lively 4/4 meter. The piccolo violin has yielded to the oboe, the instrument Bach so often associated with love of Jesus. And the back-and-forth dialogue of the voices is now delightfully playful and includes several canonic passages whose strictness does not detract from but contributes to the playfulness. Appropriately the singing voices come together in two places. In the first part they come together on the words "die Liebe soll nichts scheiden" ["our love shall nothing separate"], words that recall some of the most comforting words in Scripture:

> For I am convinced that neither death nor life, neither angels nor demons, neither the present nor the future, nor any powers, neither height

nor depth, nor anything else in all creation, will be able to separate us from the love of God that is in Christ Jesus our Lord. (Romans 8:38-39)

In the second part they sing together the words "da Freude die Fülle" ["there joy to the full"], words that come from Luther's translation of Psalm 16:11: "You have made known to me the path of life; you will fill me with joy in your presence, [Luther: Vor Dir ist Freude der Fülle] with eternal pleasures at your right hand."

The final chorale is the climax. In language redolent with Scripture, it sings of the heavenly song that believers will sing with the angels in the new Jerusalem. As was his custom, Bach simply wrote a four-part harmonization of the chorale tune for the last movement. In addition to a harmonization that even by Bach's own standards is superb, there are a couple subtle things that enhance the glory of this movement. First, Bach instructed that the piccolo violin play the melody an octave higher. Second, it is in E♭, a key that forces the melody all the way up to a high G. This high range is reminiscent of the high range of the chorale at the end of Part II of the *Christmas Oratorio*, where, like here (only now it is forever), the music is sung by "Menschen- und englischen Zungen" ["human and angelic tongues"] — and note that what is sung here, "Gloria," is also what the angels sang to the shepherds.

Although no one would question the high artistic value of Bach's four-part harmonizations, there is still a lingering question about their appropriateness as the last, climactic movement of a cantata. Can they bear the weight of the climax? Aren't they, in their brevity and relative simplicity, rather anti-climactic? As C. Hubert H. Parry realized long ago, such questions arise from those for whom the chorales do not have long and deep liturgical and devotional roots. His response is worth repeating at length.

> It was the deep-seated veneration for the chorale and its devotional associations which gave it significance enough to serve such a purpose [as the last movement of a cantata]. In later times, when the works can hardly be heard at all except in the secular surroundings of a concert room, it is natural for those who undertake performances to look for such cantatas as have the chorales expanded by free instrumental accompaniments, or such exceptional cantatas as have free choruses at the end. . . . But on the other hand it may be said that Bach's unique manner of harmonising the final chorales gives them special fascination; and it

may be further added that in such a case the advantages of musical culture are yet again manifested; for while those who are ignorant of the
conditions for which these cantatas were composed would be puzzled at
the inadequacy of the finale, those who are more happily placed can,
with the help of a little experience, so transfer themselves in imagination to the situation which Bach had in his mind, as to feel through the
exercise of developed artistic perception almost the full meaning of the
concluding chorale and its adequacy as an element of design. (386-387)

It is important to underscore what Parry said about Bach's "unique
manner of harmonising the final chorales," for it is not hyperbole to say
that Bach could say as much and reach the same depths of meaning with
the limited resources of a four-part harmonization as he could with the
full-scale resources of choir and orchestra that he typically used for first
movements. But I would add that the "full meaning of the concluding
chorale" is not only available to those who possess a sufficient "musical
culture" to "transfer themselves in imagination to the situation which
Bach had in his mind." It is even more available to those, regardless of
their musical culture, who still know the chorales through their use of
them in worship. I doubt that anyone who still sings "Wachet auf" in worship would find Bach's harmonization at the end of Cantata 140 to be in-
adequate to its task of representing the eternal "Gloria" coming from the
tongues of angels and the redeemed.

*   *   *

But of course no music can really be adequate to the task of representing
what "ear has not heard." Still, without denying that fact, I cannot entirely
discredit the long-lived and widespread tradition that links music to the
joy and glory of heaven. I cannot dismiss as pure fancy George Herbert's
lines addressed to church music:

> But if I travel in your company,
>   You know the way to heaven's door. ("Church-Music," ll. 11-12)

Here is not the place for an extended discussion of that tradition. I can
only say that I believe, as Peter Kreeft puts it, that we live on an "earth
haunted by heaven." And like him (and many others), I have found music to
be "perhaps the most mysteriously moving of all earthly hauntings" (68). So

when he goes on to say that he knows "three intelligent, sensitive souls who were saved from atheism and despair only by the music of Bach," I don't find that incredible, for of all the music I've heard, it is some of the music of Bach that more than any other makes me think I'm listening in at "heaven's door." The heaven-haunted music I hear in Bach can be found in any of his instrumental genres — suites, sonatas, concertos, fugues — as well as in his church music. But, of course, in his church music, words can lead us to places where there is likely to have been a special intention to try to capture something of what "ear has not heard" and make it audible. I conclude with some remarks about three such choruses in the *Mass in B Minor*.

The first is the opening chorus of the *Gloria,* which consists of the words of the angels to the shepherds:

Gloria in excelsis Deo,   Glory to God in the highest,
et in terra pax hominibus   And on earth peace to men
    bonae voluntatis.   of good will.

This is music meant to represent the music sung by the angels who dwell in the presence of God. There are two parts to it corresponding to the two phrases of text. The key word of the first part is "gloria" ["glory"] and of the second part is "pax" ["peace"]. The "glory" music is bright — no, brilliant — with its three trumpets, D major key, and infectious 3/8 dance rhythms. The "peace" music is slower and quieter. The trumpets drop out and the principal thematic material features gently caress pairs of eighth notes. After the "pax" theme has been stated homophonically and then developed in a quasi-antiphonal way, it becomes the subject for a fugal exposition. As the subject is heard in all the voices in turn, the instruments (still without trumpets) play a light, transparent, chordal accompaniment. Then there is a return to homophonic writing, and the trumpets return but only to play sustained notes. Out of this emerges a second fugal exposition in which the instruments double the voices. The trumpets, which dropped out at the beginning of the fugal exposition, return with the entrance of the final voice part, the second sopranos, doubling it an octave higher, thus uniting their sonic glory with the peace theme. Following the second exposition there is another homophonic section featuring a rising sequence punctuated by chords in the trumpets and then two more statements of the subject, the second of which brings the movement to a close, again with the first trumpet doubling the second sopranos an octave higher. Glory and peace are brought together. Two of the most frequently used ideas to give us an inkling of that which "has not entered into the imagination of man" are presented together here.

· It strikes me, however, that the glory in this movement, especially in the first section, has a decidedly earthy cast. Splendid and exciting though it be, it is not music that surpasses what might be written to celebrate the glory of an earthly king (except to the extent that Bach's excellence makes it surpassing). But I don't think Bach erred here. Although "Gloria" is music meant to echo the music of the angels, that angelic music was sung to shepherds and needed to be "translated" for them to understand. Hence its somewhat down-to-earth cast.

To hear Bach's conception of heavenly glory directly, without "translation," we can turn to the "Sanctus."

Sanctus, sanctus, sanctus,	Holy, holy, holy,
pleni sunt caeli et terra gloria ejus.	full are heaven and earth of your glory.

The text comes out of Isaiah 6.

> In the year that King Uzziah died, I saw the LORD seated on a throne, high and exalted, and the train of his robe filled the temple. Above him were seraphs, each with six wings: With two wings they covered their faces, with two they covered their feet, and with two they were flying. And they were calling to one another:
>
> "Holy, holy, holy is the LORD Almighty;
> the whole earth is full of his glory."
>
> At the sound of their voices the doorposts and thresholds shook and the temple was filled with smoke.

The "Sanctus," then, is sung by the angels in the very heart of heaven — around the throne of God — and as such it presents the composer with a greater challenge than the song of the angels to the shepherds. In the "Sanctus" from the *Mass in B Minor,* Bach kept some of the same features found in the "Gloria" — notably trumpets and the bright D major key — but otherwise it is a strikingly different piece. Probably the most immediately noticed difference is in the rhythm. Instead of the lively dance of the "Gloria," the "Sanctus" moves more slowly in sustained chords that are animated by constantly rolling triplets. Underneath, the basses, when they are not simply punctuating stationary chords, move in a strong sequence

219

of octave leaps ascending or descending by step. The trumpets do not play much of a role in the thematic material; they generally serve to punctuate the chords on the shouts of "Sanctus."

Spitta heard some definable connections between this music and the Isaiah passage from which the text came.

> [T]he words of Isaiah have determined even the details of the composition — "I saw the Lord sitting upon a throne high and lifted up and His train filled the temple. Above it stood the Seraphim; each one had six wings," &c. The majestic soaring passages in which the upper and lower voices seem to respond to each other are certainly suggested by the last words "and they cried one to another." In the bars where the five upper parts hold out in reverberating harmony against the broad pinion strokes of the violins and wooden wind instruments, the blare of trumpets and thunder of drums, while the bass marches solemnly downwards [or upwards] in grand octaves, we feel with the prophet that "the posts of the door moved at the voice of him that cried, and the house was filled with smoke." (3:60-61)

Although Spitta's connections are fitting, the music is finally ineffable. Somehow, to use Parry's words, it is suggestive "of the rolling of tumultuous harmonies through the infinite spaces of heaven" (322). Somehow Bach managed, through purely sonic means, to give us some sense of what it is to come into the presence of the holy God. And what makes his achievement in this piece all the more astonishing is that he was able to add a pervasive symbolic component that in no way interferes with its goal of letting us listen in at the very door of heaven. The symbol that pervades the piece is the number three, a symbol, of course, of the Trinity. From the continuously rolling triplets to the overall structure, there is little in the piece that doesn't come in threes. There are three trumpets, three oboes, three upper string parts, and a six-part choir that is divided into three upper and three lower voices. There are three threefold shouts of "sanctus." Indeed, the whole piece consists of three large three-part sections. (See figure 19 on p. 221.) There can be no doubt that "the multitudinous hosts singing in adoration" are singing to the triune God.

What I have been discussing so far is only the first part of the "Sanctus," a prelude, if you will, to a mighty fugue to follow. The fugue completes the text with the words "Pleni sunt caeli et terra gloria ejus" ["full are the heavens and earth with your glory"]. The subject of the fugue is a

FIGURE 19: **The Trinitarian Structure of the "Sanctus" from the**
Mass in B Minor

I. A.   1. "Sanctus" + triplet connection
          2. "Sanctus" + triplet connection
          3. "Sanctus" + triplet connection extended (3 + 3 groups of triplets)
      bridge octave theme in basses
   B.   1. "Sanctus" + triplet connection
          2. "Sanctus" + triplet connection
          3. "Sanctus" + triplet connection extended (3 + 3 groups of triplets)
      bridge octave theme in basses
   C.   1. "Sanctus" + triplet connection
          2. "Sanctus" + triplet connection
          3. "Sanctus" + triplet connection extended (3 + 3 groups of triplets)

II. A.   1. octave theme in basses; sustained chords in upper voices
          2. octave theme in basses; sustained chords in upper voices
          3. octave theme in basses; sustained chords in upper voices
      bridge octave theme in basses
   B.   1. "Sanctus" & triplets antiphonally between upper 3 and lower 3 voices
          2. "Sanctus" & triplets antiphonally between upper 3 and lower 3 voices
          3. "Sanctus" & triplets antiphonally between upper 3 and lower 3 voices
      bridge octave theme in basses
   C.   1. "Sanctus" in 3-part canon
        2-3. "Sanctus" in 2 × 3-part canon (each entry is by a pair of voices singing in thirds)
      bridge octave theme in basses

III. A.   1. octave theme in basses; sustained chords in upper voices
          2. octave theme in basses; sustained chords in upper parts
          3. octave theme in basses; sustained chords in upper parts
   B.   1. "Sanctus" & triplets antiphonally between upper 3 and lower 3 voices
          2. "Sanctus" & triplets antiphonally between upper 3 and lower 3 voices
          3. "Sanctus" & triplets antiphonally between upper 3 and lower 3 voices
   C.   Coda "Dominus" sung 9 (3 × 3) times

dance-like melody in 3/8 meter shaped by the contents of the text — a leap up to a high note for "caeli," a leap back down for "terra," and a melisma for "gloria." Needless to say, Bach, the supreme fugue writer, discovered all kinds of thrilling things to do with that subject, including one statement in which the trumpet doubles the basses two octaves and a third higher. Suffice it to say with Spitta, that this fugue

> so far exceeds any similar movement in the mass in ecstatic jubilation that we cannot help feeling that till this moment Bach has only given us the hymns of praise and joy of mortal Christians, but that here "the morning stars are singing together and the sons of God shouting for joy" (Job 38:7). (3:61)

Earlier I quoted C. S. Lewis on the ways the Bible talks about heaven. Of his five ways, the third one, that we shall have "glory," is the one most readily portrayed in music. I have suggested that "Gloria" sounds the glory of heaven "translated" for human ears and that "Sanctus" sounds the glory unmediated (insofar as that is humanly possible).

The third chorus under consideration here, "Dona nobis pacem," shows a different approach to the task of writing heavenly music. In Lewis's list of types of scriptural promise regarding the world to come, there is one important omission — peace and rest. I think that the yearning for peace is the deepest of all human yearnings. As St. Augustine put it in a well-known sentence at the beginning of his *Confessions,* "our heart is restless until it rests in you." Nicholas Wolterstorff calls peace our end and has assembled a wonderful list of scriptural references that is worth quoting at length.

> Isaiah hears God speaking thus:

> > Then justice shall make its home in the wilderness,
> > and righteousness dwell in the grassland;
> > when righteousness shall yield peace
> > and its fruit be quietness and confidence for ever.
> > Then my people shall live in a tranquil country,
> > dwelling in peace, in houses full of ease. (32:16-20)

> And later:

> > For behold I create new heavens and a new earth.
> > Former things shall no more be remembered,

nor shall they be called to mind.
Rejoice and be filled with delight,
you boundless realms which I create;
for I create Jerusalem to be a delight
for her people a joy;
I will take delight in Jerusalem and rejoice in my people;
weeping and cries for help
shall never again be heard in her. (65:17-25)

And in the best-known passage of all, Isaiah describes the anticipated shalom with a multiplicity of images of harmony — among the animals, between the animals and man:

Then a shoot shall grow from the stock of Jesse,
and a branch shall spring from his roots.
The spirit of the Lord shall rest upon him,
a spirit of counsel and power,
a spirit of knowledge and the fear of the Lord.
Then the wolf shall live with the sheep,
and the leopard lie down with the kid;
the calf and the young lion shall grow up together,
and a little child shall lead them;
and their young shall lie down together.
The lion shall eat straw like cattle;
the infant shall play over the hole of the cobra,
and the young child shall dance over the viper's nest. (11:1-8)

That shoot of which Isaiah spoke is He of whom the angels sang in celebration of His birth: "Glory to God in the highest heaven, and on earth *peace* for men on whom his favor rests" (Luke 2:24). He is the one of whom the priest Zechariah said that He "will guide our feet into the way of *peace* "(Luke 1:79). He is the one of whom Simeon said, "This day, Master, thou givest thy servant his discharge in *peace;* now thy promise is fulfilled" (Luke 2:29). He is the one of whom Peter said that it was by him that God preached "good news of *peace* to Israel" (Acts 10:36). He is the one of whom Paul, speaking as a Jew to the Gentiles, said that "he came and preached *peace* to you who were far off and *peace* to those who were near" (Ephesians 2:17). He is in fact Jesus Christ, whom Isaiah called the "prince of *peace*" (Isaiah 9:6). (79-80)

The Prince of Peace has come and has gained the victory. But although the war is over and Christ is victor, the fulfillment of the promises of peace is not yet complete and will not be until Christ comes again and ushers in the New Jerusalem, the city of peace. Therefore throughout the centuries the church, at the end of the Mass, has prayed, "Dona nobis pacem" ["grant us peace"]. That, then, is also the prayer of the final chorus of Bach's *Mass in B Minor*.

"Dona nobis pacem" is a *stile antico* fugue built on two subjects. The first is of the utmost simplicity, covering only the range of a fourth, mostly in stepwise motion, and moving in a placid rhythm. The second starts in long notes, continues with an eighth-note melisma, and broadens out again at the end. Although it is more rhythmically active than the first, the second theme in no way conveys any sense of agitation. Both themes are peaceful and serene. So although this is a prayer for peace, the music conveys the sense that peace is already attained. It conveys a certainty that the prayer will be, and in a sense already is, answered.

The movement starts simply enough with overlapping fugal expositions of the two subjects. The instruments, as is customary in *stile antico* movements, simply double the voices. Then follows a long stretch in which Bach explored various ways of combining the subjects both with themselves and with each other. At the end of this, after having presented five overlapping statements of the second subject, he turned again to the first subject and embarked on an incredible buildup of overlapping points-of-imitation. After seven of these, the trumpets become independent of the voices and play an eighth and a ninth statement of the subject. But the buildup continues. The voices add a tenth, an eleventh, a twelfth, and finally a thirteenth overlapping statement of the first subject! At the thirteenth statement the tympani enter for the first time and we expect that the climax has been reached. But before the thirteenth statement has cadenced, two statements of the second subject have commenced in close succession and their flowing eighth-notes sustain the energy until two more statements of the first theme are presented in close succession. In the first of these statements the altos are doubled by the second trumpet an octave higher; then, two beats later, the tenors sing the subject with the first trumpet doubling them two octaves higher! The trumpets soon break away from the voices, and the tympani joins once again to bring the music to a most glorious D major cadence. If properly executed, the buildup that Bach wrote with such incredible contrapuntal skill leads imperceptibly from peace to glory. Or, rather, glory imperceptibly *joins* with peace. There is no distinction. In "Dona nobis pacem" two of the main images of heaven — peace and glory — become one.

I add one final note about this movement. It is a parody. It was earlier used in 1731 as the opening chorus for Cantata 29, a cantata written for the inauguration of the new Leipzig town council. Its text was "Wir danken dir, Gott" ["We thank you, God"]. In 1733, when Bach wrote the Kyrie and Gloria of what is now the *Mass in B Minor* (cf. pp. 43-44), he took the music of that chorus and used it for part of the Gloria text, "Gratias agimus tibi propter magnam gloriam tuam" ["We give thanks to you for your great glory"]. This required little more than substituting a nearly equivalent Latin text for the original German text. Then, in his last years, as he was compiling the *Mass in B Minor,* when he needed to decide what to do for the final prayer, "Dona nobis pacem," he turned again to the music he had used twice before. As a result there are two movements in the *Mass in B Minor* — a prayer of thanks and a prayer for peace — that share the same music. By setting the prayer for peace to music that had earlier been used to say thanks, Bach was again expressing his confidence that the prayer was answered. Setting a prayer for peace to the music of a prayer of thanks was a way of saying "Amen," which means, as the last answer in the Heidelberg Catechism explains, "This is sure to be! It is even more sure that God listens to my prayer than that I really desire what I pray for."

*   *   *

According to the obituary notice, "On July 28, 1750, a little after quarter past eight in the evening, in the sixty-sixth year of his life, [J. S. Bach] quietly and peacefully, by the merit of his Redeemer, departed this life."

Glossary

Antiphony (adj. **antiphonal**): Music performed alternately by two or more groups of performers.

Aria: A piece for solo voice(s), usually within a larger composition such as opera, oratorio, or cantata, typically in a lyrical or virtuosic style. In Baroque operas the role of the arias is to portray the affect, or emotion, generated by the dialogue and action that took place in the preceding recitative. (See also **Recitative**.)

Basso continuo: The type of accompaniment that is the foundation for most of the music of the Baroque period. It consists of a single bass line with figures that indicate the harmony. It is typically performed by two types of instruments — bass melody instruments (e.g., cello, bassoon) to play the bass line and chordal instruments (e.g., harpsichord, organ, lute) to improvise the harmonies above the bass line.

BWV: The abbreviation for the *Thematisch-systematisches Verzeichnis des musikalischen Werke von Johann Sebastian Bach* [Thematic-Systematic List of the Musical Works of J. S. Bach], ed. Wolfgang Schmieder (Leipzig, 1950). It is also sometimes referred to as the Schmieder catalogue.

Cadence (adj. **cadential**): The moment of resolution at the end of a musical phrase, usually achieved by standard melodic and/or harmonic formulas. Cadences are analogous to punctuation marks and, like them, are points of articulation that have varying degrees of finality.

Canon (adj. **canonic**): Strict imitation throughout a musical passage. If the imitation continues throughout the whole piece, the piece is called a canon. Rounds are a type of canon that can continue *ad infinitum* because the ending of the melody fits with its beginning. (See also **Imitation** and **Point-of-Imitation**.)

Chiastic form: A form that is symmetrically organized around a central axis, e.g., ABCBA, ABACABA, etc. The name comes from the Greek letter *chi*, which is X-shaped. Because *chi* is the first letter in Christ and because its X-shape is similar to the cross, chiastic form is often symbolic of the crucifixion of Christ.

Chorale: Congregational hymns of the Lutheran church. Their melodies were the basis upon which composers wrote chorale preludes for organ. Bach often incorporated chorale melodies and texts into movements of his cantatas and Passions. Pieces that are commonly known as "Bach chorales" are four-part harmonizations that Bach made of chorale melodies for his cantatas and Passions. The melodies are generally not by Bach.

Concerto: An instrumental genre featuring contrast between a solo instrument or a small group of instruments and a larger instrumental ensemble.

Consonance (adj. **consonant**): A stable, blending, relaxed, sweet-sounding, etc., relationship between pitches. (See also **Dissonance**.)

Continuo (see **Basso continuo**)

Counterpoint (adj. **contrapuntal**): A musical texture comprised of simultaneous melodies of more or less equal importance as opposed to a texture made up of one principal melody with accompaniment. (See also **Homophony**.)

Countersubject: A recurring theme in a fugue that is stated at the same time as the subject. (See also **Fugue**.)

Da capo: An instruction in a musical score that tells a performer to go back to the beginning. Baroque arias are often in "da capo form" because after two contrasting sections (AB) there is the instruction to go back to the beginning to perform the first section again. The result is an ABA or "da capo" form.

Dissonance (adj. **dissonant**): An unstable, clashing, tense, harsh, etc., relationship between pitches. (See also **Consonance**.)

Dotted rhythm: A "jerky" rhythm consisting of a long note followed by a short note (or group of notes). The long one is at least three times the length of the short one. At a slow to moderate tempo, dotted rhythms give the music a stately, ceremonial kind of movement associated in the Baroque period with the pomp and circumstance of royal processions. (See also **French overture**.)

Exposition (see **Fugue**)

French Overture: A type of overture that originated in French opera during the seventeenth century. It has two sections. The first is in a slow to moderate tempo featuring dotted rhythms that give it a stately, ceremonial character. The second is fast and often fugal. Sometimes there is a third section that returns to the tempo and rhythm of the first.

Fugue (adj. **fugal**): A type of music in a prevailingly contrapuntal texture based on a theme (called the subject) that is stated in one part alone at the beginning and then enters in imitation in all the other parts. Throughout the rest of the piece the subject will make its appearance from time to time in different parts. The opening section in which the subject appears successively in all the parts is called the exposition.

Gamba (see **Viola da gamba**)

Homophony (adj. **homophonic**): A musical texture consisting of a melody and accompaniment. (See also **Counterpoint** and **Polyphony**.)

Imitation: The immediate repetition of a melody in a different part. (See also **Canon**, **Fugue**, and **Point-of-Imitation**.)

Melisma (adj. **melismatic**): A melodic passage in which there are many notes for a single syllable of text.

Modulation: A change of key.

Obbligato: An essential, independent instrumental part, as opposed to an instrumental part that merely doubles a voice part.

Oboe da caccia: A now obsolete oboe pitched a fifth lower than the modern oboe. Bach scored for it in about thirty works.

Oboe d'amore: An alto oboe pitched a minor third lower than the normal orchestral oboe.

Ostinato: A musical motive or melody that is persistently repeated throughout a piece. Baroque composers were fond of writing variations over an ostinato bass.

Parody: A composition in which new words have been fitted to a pre-existing piece. Changes made in the music for the new words can range from minor adjustments to quite extensive reworking of the musical materials.

Pedal Point: A long-held note in one part, usually the bass, while the other parts are moving.

229

Period: A group of two or more musical phrases that makes a complete statement.

Phrase: A relatively independent musical idea terminated by a cadence.

Point-of-Imitation: A type of imitation in which the successively entering parts imitate only the first few notes before proceeding freely. (See also **Canon**.)

Polyphony (adj. **polyphonic**): Music written for two or more independent parts. Often used as a synonym of counterpoint. (See also **Counterpoint** and **Homophony**.)

Recitative: A vocal solo in an opera, oratorio, or cantata in which the rhythms and melodic shapes are closely related to the rhythms and inflections of dramatic speech or oratory. Recitatives serve to carry the dialogue or narration of the story. (See also **Aria**.)

Ritornello: A section of a piece or movement that is stated in its entirety at the beginning and end and periodically returns, though usually not in its entirety, throughout the piece. Ritornellos are common in Baroque concerto movements and arias.

Staccato: A manner of playing or singing a succession of notes so that they are clearly separated from each other.

Stile antico: "Ancient style." A style of Baroque music resulting from a conscious imitation of the polyphonic choral music of the Renaissance.

Subject (see **Fugue**)

Tonic: The principal tone or chord in a key; the tone or chord toward which all others are drawn. It is the most stable tone or chord in a piece and therefore the one on which a piece tends to end.

Viola da gamba: The principal bowed stringed instrument of the Renaissance. It was still in use in the Baroque period but was increasingly being replaced by the instruments of the violin family. Gambas (as they are often called) are held on the lap or between the knees (like a cello) and have a fretted fingerboard and six or seven strings.

Works Cited

Althaus, Paul. *The Theology of Martin Luther*. Translated by Robert C. Schultz. Philadelphia: Fortress Press, 1966.

Ambrose, Z. Philip. *The Texts to Johann Sebastian Bach's Church Cantatas*. Neuhausen and Stuttgart: Hänssler Verlag, 1984.

Augustine, St. *Confessions*. Translated by Henry Chadwick. New York: Oxford University Press, 1991.

Bernstein, Leonard. "The Music of Johann Sebastian Bach." In *The Joy of Music*. New York: Simon and Schuster, 1959.

Blume, Friedrich. "Outline of a New Picture of Bach." *Music and Letters* 44 (1963): 214-27.

Bonhoeffer, Dietrich. *The Cost of Discipleship*. New York: Macmillan, 1963.

Boyd, Malcolm. *Bach*. New York: Schirmer Books, 1997.

Brown, Raymond E. *The Gospel According to John: A New Translation with Introduction and Commentary*. The Anchor Bible. Garden City, NY: Doubleday, 1970.

Buszin, Walter E. *Luther on Music*. St. Paul: North Central Publishing Co., 1958.

Butt, John. *Bach: Mass in B Minor*. Cambridge: Cambridge University Press, 1991.

Calvin, John. *The Gospel According to St. John*, Part II. Translated by T. H. L. Parker. Grand Rapids: Eerdmans, 1961.

—————. *A Harmony of the Gospels: Matthew, Mark and Luke*, volume 3. Translated by A. W. Morrison. Grand Rapids: Eerdmans, 1972.

Chafe, Eric. "Key Structure and Tonal Allegory in the Passions of J. S. Bach: An Introduction." *Current Musicology* 31 (1981): 39-54.

————. *Tonal Allegory in the Vocal Music of J. S. Bach.* Berkeley: University of California Press, 1991.

Chesterton, G. K. *Orthodoxy.* Glasgow: William Collins, 1961.

Dürr, Alfred. "New Light on Bach." *The Musical Times* 107 (1966): 484-88.

Geiringer, Karl. *Johann Sebastian Bach: The Culmination of an Era.* New York: Oxford University Press, 1966.

Herz, Gerhard. *Bach: Cantata No. 4.* Norton Critical Scores. New York: W. W. Norton, 1967.

————. *Bach: Cantata No. 140.* Norton Critical Scores. New York: W. W. Norton, 1972.

————. "Bach's Religion." *Journal of Renaissance and Baroque Music* (1946): 124-38.

Howard, Thomas. *An Antique Drum.* Philadelphia: J. B. Lippincott Co., 1969.

Jeske, Richard L. "Bach as Biblical Interpreter." In *The Universal Bach.* Philadelphia: American Philosophical Society, 1985.

Klooster, Fred H. "The Heidelberg Catechism." In *Psalter Hymnal Handbook,* edited by Emily R. Brink and Bert Polman, 822-24. Grand Rapids: CRC Publications, 1998.

Knapp, Raymond. "The Finale of Brahms' Fourth Symphony." *19th-Century Music* 13 (1989): 3-17.

Kreeft, Peter. *Heaven: The Heart's Deepest Longing.* San Francisco: Harper & Row, 1980.

Leaver, Robin A. *J. S. Bach and Scripture: Glosses from the Calov Bible Commentary.* St. Louis: Concordia Publishing House, 1985.

————. *J. S. Bach as Preacher: His Passions and Music in Worship.* St. Louis: Concordia Publishing House, 1982.

————. "The Mature Vocal Works and Their Theological and Liturgical Context." In *The Cambridge Companion to Bach,* edited by John Butt, 86-122. Cambridge: Cambridge University Press, 1997.

Lewis, C. S. *Mere Christianity.* New York: Macmillan, 1960.

————. *Prince Caspian.* New York: Macmillan, 1965.

————. "The Weight of Glory." In *The Weight of Glory.* Grand Rapids: Eerdmans, 1965.

Loewenich, Walter von. *Luther's Theology of the Cross.* Translated by Herbert J. A. Bouman. Minneapolis: Augsburg Publishing House, 1976.

Luther, Martin. *Luther's Works,* volume 53: *Liturgy and Hymns.* Edited by Ulrich S. Leupold. Philadelphia: Fortress Press, 1965.

————. "A Meditation on Christ's Passion." In *Luther's Works,* volume 42, translated by Martin H. Bertram, 7-14. Philadelphia: Fortress Press, 1969.

————. "Preface to the New Testament." In *Luther's Works,* volume 35, translated by Charles M. Jacobs, revised by E. Theodore Bachmann, 357-62. Philadelphia: Fortress Press, 1960.

Marissen, Michael. *Lutheranism, Anti-Judaism, and Bach's St. John Passion.* New York: Oxford University Press, 1998.

Mattheson, Johann. *Der vollkommene Capellmeister.* Translated by Ernest C. Harriss. Ann Arbor: UMI Research Press, 1981.

Melamed, Daniel R. *J. S. Bach and the German Motet.* Cambridge: Cambridge University Press, 1995.

Mellers, Wilfrid. *Bach and the Dance of God.* New York: Oxford University Press, 1981.

Meyer, Ulrich. *Biblical Quotation and Allusion in the Cantata Libretti of Johann Sebastian Bach.* Lanham, MD: The Scarecrow Press, 1997.

Minear, Paul. *Death Set to Music.* Atlanta: John Knox Press, 1987.

Music in the Western World: A History in Documents. Selected and annotated by Piero Weiss and Richard Taruskin. New York: Schirmer Books, 1983.

The New Bach Reader. Edited by Hans T. David and Arthur Mendel, revised and enlarged by Christoph Wolff. New York: W. W. Norton and Co., 1998.

Palisca, Claude V. *Baroque Music.* Third edition. Englewood Cliffs, NJ: Prentice Hall, 1991.

Parry, C. Hubert H. *Johann Sebastian Bach: The Story of the Development of a Great Personality.* New York: G. P. Putnam's Sons, 1909.

Pelikan, Jaroslav. *Bach Among the Theologians.* Philadelphia: Fortress Press, 1986.

Plantinga, Cornelius, Jr. *A Place to Stand.* Grand Rapids: CRC Publications, 1979.

Rilling, Helmuth. *Johann Sebastian Bach's B-minor Mass.* Translated by Gordon Paine. Princeton: Prestige Publications, 1984.

————. *Johann Sebastian Bach's St. Matthew Passion: Introduction and Instructions for Study.* Translated by Kenneth Nafziger. Frankfurt: C. F. Peters, 1976.

Robertson, Alec. *The Church Cantatas of J. S. Bach.* New York: Praeger Publishers, 1972.

Schmitz, Arnold. *Die Bildlichkeit der wortgebundenen Musik J. S. Bachs.* Mainz, 1950.

Schulze, Hans-Joachim. "Poetry and Poets." In *The World of the Bach Cantatas.* Edited by Christoph Wolff. New York: W. W. Norton and Co., 1995.

Schweitzer, Albert. *J. S. Bach.* Two volumes. Translated by Ernest Newman. Boston: Bruce Humphries Publishers, 1962.

————. *J. S. Bach, le musicien-poéte.* Leipzig: Breitkopf and Härtel, 1905.

Spitta, Philipp. *Johann Sebastian Bach.* Three volumes. Translated by Clara Bell and J. A. Fuller-Maitland. New York: Dover Publications, 1951.

Stauffer, George B. *Bach: The Mass in B Minor.* New York: Schirmer Books, 1997.

Steinitz, Paul. *Bach's Passions.* New York: Charles Scribner's Sons, 1978.

Stiller, Günther. *Johann Sebastian Bach and Liturgical Life in Leipzig.* Translated by Herbert J. A. Bouman, Daniel F. Poellot, and Hilton C. Oswald. St. Louis: Concordia Publishing House, 1984.

Stravinsky, Igor. *Poetics of Music.* New York: Vintage Books, 1960.

Taruskin, Richard. "Facing Up, Finally, to Bach's Dark Vision." In *Text and Act,* 307-15. Oxford: Oxford University Press, 1995.

Terry, Charles Sanford. *Bach: A Biography.* Second edition. London: Oxford University Press, 1933.

————. *Bach: The Mass in B Minor.* London: Oxford University Press, 1924.

Thielicke, Helmut. *Faith the Great Adventure.* Translated by David L. Scheidt. Philadelphia: Fortress Press, 1985.

Tovey, Donald Francis. *Essays in Musical Analysis,* volume 5. London: Oxford University Press, 1937.

Unger, Melvin P. *Handbook to Bach's Sacred Cantata Texts.* Lanham, MD: Scarecrow Press, 1996.

Van Wyck, Helen Hoekema. *The Use and Significance of Dance Rhythms in Johann Sebastian Bach's St. Matthew Passion.* Unpublished DMA document, Michigan State University, 1994.

Whittaker, W. Gillies. *The Cantatas of Johann Sebastian Bach: Sacred and Secular.* Two volumes. London: Oxford University Press, 1959.

Williams, Charles. *Taliessin through Logres.* . . . Grand Rapids: Eerdmans, 1974.

Williams, Peter. *The Organ Music of J. S. Bach,* volume 2. Cambridge: Cambridge University Press, 1980.

Wollny, Peter. "Genres and Styles of Sacred Music Around and After 1700." In *The World of the Bach Cantatas,* edited by E. Christoph Wolff, 19-33. New York: W. W. Norton and Co., 1995.

Wolterstorff, Nicholas. *Art in Action.* Grand Rapids: Eerdmans, 1980.

Index